Advance Praise

"It is gratifying to see, at last, a work propitiously aimed at bringing psychology back to what it must be, namely, a 'science of the soul'—in light of the teachings of sacred traditions, which for millennia have offered humanity not only the way for attaining spiritual well-being but also the means of nurturing and maintaining mental health. In *Psyche and the Sacred*, highly accomplished scholar and psychotherapist Dr. Bendeck Sotillos offers a must-read for anyone interested in understanding what has gone wrong with modern psychology and how it may be rectified to an authentic science worthy of the name."

—**Mahmoud Bina**, Former Professor Emeritus of Mathematics and Philosophy, Isfahan University of Technology, co-author of *Philosophy of Science in the Light of the Perennial Wisdom*

"The project encompassed in Samuel Bendeck Sotillos' *Psyche and the Sacred* is as ambitious as it is noble. Western psychology, the ideology of an ever-expanding global mental health industry, governed by an academy steeped in scientism and reductionism, has not so much abandoned the human spirit as rejected it entirely. It is this profession's hegemonic and secularizing disregard of the ancient human quest for the Transcendent and Absolute, its dismissal and even thwarting of spiritual traditions of all sorts in its theories and practices, that Dr. Bendeck Sotillos effectively indicts as pathologically complicit in 'treating' what it helps create. Through careful citation, engaging and powerful quotations, and erudite analysis, the essays comprising *Psyche and the Sacred* so deepen the reader's understanding of the spiritual and philosophical disconnections of psychology—and so-called 'mental health practice'—as to leave one longing for all that's been missing on the road to human wellbeing."

—**David Edward Walker**, PhD, Licensed Psychologist and author of *Coyote's Swing: A Memoir and Critique of Mental Hygiene in Native America*

"This groundbreaking work is a timely and essential contribution to the current discourse on mental health. It challenges the hegemony of Western, Eurocentric psychology, and reclaims the wisdom of traditional healing sciences. It masterfully diagnoses the epistemological crisis in modern therapy, and offers compelling arguments for a metaphysical outlook that honors the sacred. The book does not merely call for decolonization—it provides a way forward, rooted in authentic cross-cultural perspectives that recognize the true nature of human well-being. This is a must-read for scholars, clinicians, and others who seek a holistic approach to psychological healing."

—**G. Hussein Rassool**, Professor of Islamic Psychology, Centre for Islamic Studies and Civilizations, Charles Sturt University (Australia); author of *Islamic Psychology: Human Behaviour and Experience from an Islamic Perspective*

"In *Psyche and the Sacred*, Samuel Bendeck Sotillos presents a thorough account of traditional civilizations' understanding of the soul. Eastern philosophies and religions, in particular, have maintained a sacred view of humanity to this day, whereas Western scholarship has rejected it altogether. He analyses a range of approaches that can help us restore the Divine to our psychology. This is an excellent resource for understanding how we might be able to, spiritually, stitch ourselves back together again."

—**Darcia Narvaez**, Professor of Psychology Emerita, University of Notre Dame; co-author of *Restoring the Kinship Worldview: Indigenous Voices Introduce 28 Precepts for Rebalancing Life on Planet Earth*

"*Psyche and the Sacred* is a very important and timely addition to the field of healing. In order to meaningfully heal, Man needs to console his heart, tend to his aching soul, and nurse his invisible wounds. I believe that becomes possible through an intimate connection with the 'Divine.' I highly recommend this book by Samuel Bendeck Sotillos to anyone looking beyond the medical model for solutions to human suffering."

—**Omar Reda**, MD, board-certified psychiatrist, author of *The Wounded Healer: The Pain and Joy of Caregiving*

"Finally a book from a psychotherapist willing to explore the indispensable link between mental health and spirituality. Bendeck Sotillos reminds us that the essence of our well-being depends, ultimately, on being grounded in holiness, or at least in our best personal effort to cultivate spiritual virtues. Modern psychology, in its complicated quest for sanity, has tried to reinvent the wheel, when all we need to do is restore the healing sap of the heavenly circle girding human life. The author offers profound insights about traditional ways in which we can be reconciled to the timeless essence of who we really are, without which no lasting cure is possible. In doing so, he exposes the nature of modern man's alienation from his immortal being—the root cause of all our anxiety, depression, and neuroses. To delve into this enlightening book is to rediscover the providential thread of Ariadne that leads us out of the labyrinth of ego estrangement towards the immortal source of human joy."

—**Mark Perry**, professional translator, author of *The Mystery of Individuality: Grandeur and Delusion of the Human Condition*

"In this remarkably insightful book, Samuel Bendeck Sotillos once again displays his expertise as a leading bridge-builder between psychology, spirituality, and world religions. He demonstrates how today's global mental health pandemic is due, in large part, to our loss of connection to the sacred and the failure of modern secular psychologies to remedy a problem that needs to be treated by incorporating spiritual principles and practices. Today's psychologies tend to be reductionist, unable or unwilling to acknowledge the transcendent nature of our personality, which is rooted in the divine. Fortunately, humanity's great spiritual traditions continue to offer us a sacred psychology—a 'science of the soul'—that has proved effective for thousands of years in leading to true self-awareness and healing. This is a prophetic and timely book that deserves to be read by all."

—**Bradley Malkovsky**, Professor Emeritus of Comparative Theology, University of Notre Dame; former editor of the *Journal of Hindu-Christian Studies*

"An interdisciplinary and scholarly gift for the intellect, a wise guide for the effective clinician, and a rich source of nourishment for the human spirit."

—**William A. Richards**, PhD, Research psychologist at Johns Hopkins School of Medicine (1999–2023) and senior advisor at Sunstone Therapies; author of *Sacred Knowledge: Psychedelics and Religious Experiences*

"This book is both timely and timeless. It speaks with rare clarity about what is missing in our secular approach to well-being, and offers a courageous call to return to what is sacred, integrated, and enduring. With great reverence for Indigenous wisdom, traditional cosmologies, and sacred psychology, the author bridges worlds that are too often kept apart: science and Spirit, therapy and tradition, trauma and transcendence. I wholeheartedly recommend this book to fellow clinicians, seekers, and anyone hungry for a path to wholeness that honors both ancient wisdom and contemporary insights."

—**Jacqueline Vorpahl,** PhD, Clinical Psychologist, Educator, and Citizen of the Choctaw Nation of Oklahoma

"Samuel Bendeck Sotillos is the only psychotherapist that I know of that works from a universal and timeless ontological orientation."

—**Wolfgang Smith**, Physicist and Mathematician, author of *Physics: A Science in Quest of an Ontology*

Psyche and the Sacred

Integrating Mental Health and Spiritual Well-Being

Psyche and the Sacred

Integrating Mental Health and Spiritual Well-Being

Samuel Bendeck Sotillos

SENTIENT PUBLICATIONS

First Sentient Publications edition 2025

A paperback original

Book design by Laura Johanna Waltje
Cover Design by Laura Johanna Waltje

Library of Congress Control Number: 2024953047
Publisher's Cataloging-in-Publication Data

Names: Bendeck Sotillos, Samuel, 1972-, author.

Title: Psyche and the sacred : integrating mental health and spiritual well-being / Samuel Bendeck Sotillos.

Description: Includes bibliographical references. | Boulder, CO: Sentient Publications, 2025.

Identifiers: LCCN: 2024953047 | ISBN: 978-1-59181-350-7 (paperback) | 978-1-59181-351-4 (epub)
Subjects: LCSH Psychotherapy--Religious aspects. | Psychology, Religious. | Mental health--Religious aspects. | Spirituality--Health aspects. | Counseling--Religious aspects. | Mental health counseling--Religious aspects. | BISAC PSYCHOLOGY / Psychotherapy / Spiritually Integrated | BODY, MIND & SPIRIT / Entheogens & Visionary Substances | PSYCHOLOGY / Mental Health
Classification: LCC RC489.S676 .B46 2025 | DDC 362.2--dc23

SENTIENT PUBLICATIONS
A Limited Liability Company
PO Box 1851
Boulder, CO 80306
www.sentientpublications.com

Contents

Acknowledgements

My profound gratitude goes to Mr. John Paraskevopoulos and Ms. Abigail Tardiff of the Radius Foundation for their detailed reading of the manuscript, as well as for their considerable editorial advice and other recommendations. Many thanks are also due to Dr. Harry Oldmeadow, Mr. Mark Perry, Professor Patrick Laude, and Dr. Alireza K. Ziarani for their insightful suggestions regarding several important passages in this book. My appreciation is also extended to Professor Huston Smith (1919–2016), Dr. William Stoddart (1925–2023), Dr. Wolfgang Smith (1930–2024), Dr. Laleh Bakhtiar (1938–2020), Mr. Marty Glass (1938–2022), Dr. Mahmood Bina (1938–2025), and Professor Seyyed Hossein Nasr for sharing their discerning insights during the course of many helpful conversations on the theme of psychology. I am very thankful to Ms. Sharon Hamrick and St. Patrick's Seminary & University, who helped me obtain hard-to-find journal articles and other literature that proved invaluable in my research. For their thoughtful comments, I am also indebted to the peer reviewers who scrutinized the manuscript prior to publication.

Furthermore, my sincere thanks go to the following for their kind permission to reproduce earlier versions of the articles that appear in this publication: Professor Martin Dojčár, editor of *Spirituality Studies* (chapters 3, 4, and 5); Vishvanatha Kaviraja Institute, which publishes the *Journal of Comparative Literature and Aesthetics* (chapter 1); Mr. Christopher Quilkey, former editor of *The Mountain Path*, and the Sri Ramanansramam (chapter

2); and Professor Halil Eksi, editor of *Spiritual Psychology and Counseling* (chapter 6). Their kind consent is greatly appreciated.

I am very grateful to Mr. Terry Moore of the Radius Foundation, who supported me with a grant to conduct research for chapter 5 of this work. This acknowledgment would not be complete without conveying my sincere gratitude to all those First Peoples throughout the world who welcomed me into their communities. Their gracious hospitality, and willingness to share their traditional knowledge of healing medicines, will not be forgotten. My additional gratitude goes to Dr. Alireza K. Ziarani, Dr. Ali Karbasizadeh, Dr. Alireza Farhang, and Dr. Mohammadreza Raoofi for inviting me to speak (and helping to organize my lecture) at the House of Wisdom (Persian: "Khaneh Hekmat") in Isfahan. This lecture serves as the initial chapter of this book. Finally, I feel duty bound to express my indebtedness to all the traditional authorities, and fellow spiritual pilgrims, from whom I have learned so much. I shall always treasure the precious guidance I received when it was most needed.

Introduction

With the passing of each day, we are reminded of the ubiquitous mental health crisis facing not only the Western world, but the entire planet. Nothing in contemporary life appears to be in its proper place; as a consequence, everything around us is unstable and precarious. People are struggling with all manner of psychological problems, including addiction and self-harm, in unprecedented numbers, along with the emotional repercussions of horrific forms of violence, displacement, and various acute deprivations. At the root of all these quandaries—individual, social, political, economic, and ecological—is the grave spiritual crisis of the modern world. What does mental health look like under such compromised conditions, in which life seems to have lost all meaning and purpose?

The Western worldview has claimed a monopoly on psychology, banishing any sacred "science of the soul" as long taught by traditional cultures. Despite calls for the decolonization of modern Western psychology, this dominance continues to thwart attempts to remedy our current global mental health crisis. To suggest that there are alternative healing modalities is met with derision and resistance. Modern psychology claims supremacy for itself alone, failing to acknowledge that there are many other approaches to healing, as reflected in the diverse spiritual patrimony of humanity. These facilitate a fully integrated "science of the soul" informed by a metaphysical framework that can provide an effective and enduring response to human wholeness.

The imposition of an exclusively Western understanding of the human psyche throughout the world is nothing short of hegemonic and authoritarian, and this book demonstrates how the totalitarian agenda of modern science has given rise to the desacralized psychology we see today. The word "science" comes from the Latin *scientia*, which simply means "knowledge." All too often, we fail to ask if any kind of real wisdom is offered to us by present-day psychology. The diverse cultures of traditional humanity have their own (much more) profound insights regarding the human psyche, which are no less "scientific" even if this word may not be used to describe them.

Both the *Diagnostic and Statistical Manual of Mental Disorders (DSM)*, and the *International Statistical Classification of Diseases and Related Health Problems (ICD)*, operate on false premises that reflect the materialist prejudices of modern psychology and its aberrant view of mental psychopathology. Thus, modern sciences cannot diagnose psychiatric disorders effectively, because the psyche they are investigating is grounded in a dimension of reality that lies beyond their grasp.

There is certainly a place for modern science, but it should not stray beyond the limits of its epistemological competence by asserting a monopoly on knowledge to which it is not entitled. When it does trespass in this way, it becomes the ideology of scientism, the view that the Western scientific method furnishes the sole means of understanding reality (that is, in purely materialist terms.) This deviation has persisted since the Enlightenment project—or the Age of Reason—from the seventeenth and eighteenth centuries onward. While this movement took root in the ambiance of a growing modernity, it was not a natural outgrowth of Christianity, but rather a repudiation of its sacred tenets.

Prior to this secular trajectory, which originated in the West, the Christian worldview shared a common metaphysical understanding of reality with other spiritual traditions. This was a sacred epistemology that conferred an integrated understanding of the human person that was always connected to the Spirit. The development of modern Western psychology, as a discipline completely cut off from its more ancient precursors, stems from the profane reductionism inaugurated by the European Enlightenment—a pernicious legacy that persists to this day.

Paradoxically, psychology is considered the study of the "soul," yet its very science denies the spiritual dimension altogether—which, in turn, vitiates its ability to serve as an authentic means of fathoming the psyche. Mainstream psychology is very much limited to a truncated epistemology that cannot provide any integrated modes of healing, because it has severed its kinship with transcendent reality. Desacralized therapies fail to treat the whole person as they often just target the treatment of symptoms, not the root cause of our mental disorders. If we embrace a vision of life that is enriched by the timeless wisdom found at the heart of the world's spiritual traditions—with their penetrating sacred psychology—we may yet find the answers which we are so urgently seeking. The real cause of the global mental health crisis is that we have forgotten who we are and what it truly means to be human.

There cannot be a restoration of true mental health in a world that is bereft of meaning, and it is only through reconnecting with the transpersonal dimension of existence that an abiding wholeness in our being can begin to flourish once more. The fissures of the post-Enlightenment world are not easily remedied, even if a spiritual path and its integrated therapies were to be fully embraced today. Certain psychological problems may persist notwithstanding exposure to traditional methods of healing. This is not due to any inherent limitations in sacred psychology, but rather the result of cosmological factors whereby some people's trials in this world may require periods of psychic instability, which assist in spiritual rejuvenation. Such difficulties, though, do not come without their own compensations, one being closer proximity to divine reality.

By traditional spirituality and culture, we mean the diverse spheres of humanity that are still grounded in a spiritual understanding of human existence and the way this informs the whole of their lives. Living examples of such cultures are widespread: We can find sacred psychology embodied in both the outward teachings and mystical dimensions of the world's religions, including the sacred beliefs of indigenous communities across the globe.

In understanding these sacred ways of knowing, we may come to realize our true identity in response to the perennial question: "Who am I?" The spiritual traditions of the world embrace a sacred psychology that is fully integrated. While appearing very different from the outlook of modern psychology, they nonetheless offer effective healing for the maladies of a life that is disconnected from its transcendent source. By living in accordance with this universal and timeless wisdom, we move closer to the Divine and thus come to discern this reality within ourselves—which is what allows for a truly abiding wholeness to take root in us.

This work consists of a collection of articles that have previously been published in a variety of journals. They were originally written as self-contained essays and not conceived with a book in mind. As each essay now forms a separate chapter in this volume, a repetition of certain themes is inevitable. Authentic presentations of sacred psychology are very much needed to counter the monopoly of secular thinking in the field of mental health. Therefore, it is important to bring together a variety of themes that are key to understanding what it means to be truly human, and to make this perspective more widely known and accessible. Various terms are employed as synonyms of *sacred psychology*, such as "science of the soul," "spiritual psychology," "traditional psychology," "salvific psychology," and "pneumatology," among others that need to be distinguished from modern Western psychology.

Chapter 1 ("Modern Psychology and the Loss of Transcendence") provides an overview of how modern Western psychology has become a colonialist enterprise that asserts itself as the sole paradigm in the discipline, one that ignores or belittles traditional and non-Western ways of understanding the human psyche. Chapter 2 ("The Inner and Outer Human Being") explores the idea that human beings are a universe in miniature and that we each have an inner and outer dimension that form a unity. Chapter 3 ("Realms of Consciousness and the Real") aims to demonstrate that modern psychology has failed to understand the mystery of consciousness due to its reductionist assumptions and an uncritical reliance on Cartesian mind-body dualism. Chapter 4 ("The Enneagram's Science of the Soul") documents the growing popularity of this enigmatic symbol and its use as a sacred psychology to further our knowledge of the True Self. Chapter 5 ("Entheogens and Sacred Psychology") examines the timely theme of psychedelics and explores how secular and sacred perspectives on traditional medicine may differ. Chapter 6 ("The Nature of True Well-Being") focuses on the widespread confusion surrounding the question of self-care and explores how it contrasts with a more spiritually informed approach.

What is required now are not new psychotherapies to replace the endless proliferation of previous ones, for these are simply part of the same illness that needs to be cured. This is but an indicator of how unstable the foundations of modern Western psychology have become, thanks to its untenable assumptions that are rooted in a secular and reductionist materialism, coupled with a rejection of the sacred. While there is nothing in modern psychology that cannot be found among the sacred ways of knowing and healing in the world's diverse spiritual cultures, the reverse is certainly not the case; there is, in fact, much that sacred psychology gives us that will never be available in the former. If the hegemony of modern psychology remains unchecked, we will continue being oppressed by its spiritual myopia and cultural chauvinism, which privileges an intelligentsia that has become confounded by its own errors and persistently turns its back on a liberating wisdom that offers better ways of coming to know who we really are.

Chapter 1

Modern Psychology and the Loss of Transcendence

Since its inception, modern Western psychology has gradually cut itself off from its metaphysical and ontological roots. This is evidenced, in part, by a shift from using words such as *soul* or *psyche* to an almost exclusive use of *mind*. This process of severing the human soul from the spiritual dimension is, in large part, due to the emergence of the modern world and its secularizing outlook (which took root in the European Renaissance, continuing through the Scientific Revolution and culminating in the Enlightenment project). The concept of psychology is roughly five hundred years old, yet—as a subject of study and practice—it is much older than the word itself, which can readily be seen when we consider the worldview of ancient peoples. Curiously, having rejected transcendence and the intermediary realm of the soul, the discipline today fails to be a psychology in the best sense of the word, such that it can truly benefit humanity.

The secularizing trajectory of Western culture culminated in the twentieth century when psychology went from being a "science of the soul" to one that had become completely profane. Accordingly, it "shuts out all 'transcendence' and so also shuts out all effective spirituality."[1] Furthermore, "Modern psychology . . . dismisses . . . all that transcends it."[2] This decisive turn was championed by behaviorism and psychoanalysis—the foundational paradigms of the discipline; yet this degradation of its outlook and assumptions occurred long before these developments emerged within modern psychology. Rather, the catalyst was a declaration of psychology's independence from a metaphysical and religious perspective on what constitutes a human being. Due to the current spiritual malaise, it has been aptly observed that to comprehend humanity today, we need a sound knowledge of mental health: "To understand modern [and by extension postmodern] man, it may well be appropriate to study psychology."[3]

Among the spiritual traditions of the world, we find unanimous agreement that the tripartite constitution of the person—and of the cosmos of which we are but a mirror—comprises Spirit, soul, and body; or the spiritual, psychic, and corporeal states. The dominance of the unseen world proclaimed by the spiritual traditions (and their corresponding psychologies) was gradually overthrown and replaced by the more tangible demands of the sensorial world and its empirical modes of knowing, represented by the modern West's culture of materialism. What may be self-evident at one level is not so on a higher one, for lower levels cannot encompass what lies beyond them—only the higher can know the lower. While the reductionist position ostensibly shuns metaphysics, embedded in its argument is a hidden metaphysic of its own, one that implicitly attacks any suggestion of a reality that transcends the psychophysical order. In doing so, it has transgressed its own conceptual assumptions.

Due to the marginalization of spiritual considerations in modern psychology, there is a profound confusion between the psychic and spiritual orders. The phenomenon of psychologism has thus become unavoidable—the tendency to sublate the objective metaphysical order and thus reduce our understanding of human consciousness to the level of a purely subjective phenomenon. Furthermore, there is the aberration known as scientism, which is not an observance of the scientific method per se but an ideology that has transgressed the limits of its own inherent limitations as confined to the empirical order. The founder of the "talking cure," Sigmund Freud, declared his allegiance to scientific fundamentalism, epitomizing this overreach in the following words: "No, our science is no illusion. But an illusion it would be to suppose that what science cannot give us we can get elsewhere."[4]

There are two trends in modern psychology, with its post-Enlightenment prejudices, of which we ought to be vigilant. Both trends confuse the psychic and the spiritual, but in different ways. René Guénon explains: "In the first, the spiritual is brought down to the level of the psychic . . . in the second, the psychic is . . . mistaken for the spiritual."[5] Rūmī, a paragon of Islamic spirituality, pointed out: "The soul is one thing, and the spirit is another."[6] In verbatim agreement, Saint Augustine writes: "The soul is one thing, and the spirit . . . is another."[7]

Saint Thomas Aquinas defined the soul as "the first principle of life in those things which live."[8] Seneca says: "What else could you call [the] soul than a god dwelling as a guest in a human body."[9] Elsewhere Augustine confirms the divine origin of the human psyche and its reliance on the Spirit: "This soul which [has] its origin from the breath of God could not exist without [the] intellect [which] is the spirit."[10] Ibn 'Arabī, the Spanish-born mystic known as "the Greatest Master" (*al-Shaykh al-Akbar*), observes that our true vision requires both reason and intellect in order to "distinguish the in-between from the in-between,"[11] or what constitutes the intermediary realm of the psyche.

According to sacred psychology, the macrocosm and the microcosm reflect each other. This is conveyed in the Hermetic maxim: "In truth certainly and without doubt, whatever is below is like that which is above, and whatever is above is like that which is below."[12] In this process of cosmic mirroring, the human psyche is a miniature of the cosmos (or microcosm). The Sufi master Shaykh ad-Darqāwī writes:

> The soul is an immense thing; it is the whole cosmos, since it is the copy of it. Everything which is in the cosmos is to be found in the soul; equally everything in the soul is in the cosmos. Because of this fact, he who masters his soul most certainly masters the cosmos, just as he who is dominated by his soul is certainly dominated by the whole cosmos.[13]

The levels of reality that exist—both within and without us—are unified in the Absolute. Traditional "sciences of the soul" allow for all realms of consciousness to be known directly: "[I]n the very place where the lower worlds are, there are to be found the higher worlds and the totality of worlds. It has been said that there exist ten thousand worlds, each one like this world . . . and all of these are contained in man, without his being conscious of it."[14]

The soul is a mystery; it is immersed in time while also being rooted in the timeless. The human body participates in time and space, whereas the

Spirit transcends both. The psyche belongs to the intermediary realm between body and Spirit, but partakes of each dimension. Humanity's spiritual traditions all attest that the intermediary realm of the person is of Divine origin. Plato insists that "the soul is absolutely immortal and indestructible."[15]

According to the Abrahamic monotheisms: "And the Lord God formed man of the dust of the ground, and breathed into his nostrils the breath of life; and man became a living soul" (Genesis 2:7). The Qur'ān declares that God created Adam from clay—"I breathed into him My Spirit" (15:29)—and that the "Lord created you from a single soul" (4:1). Muslim philosopher Mullā Ṣadrā points out that "[t]he soul is *the junction of the two seas* ([Qur'ān] 18:59) of corporeal and spiritual things."[16] That the heart-intellect is the center of the human psyche was also taught in the Christian tradition by Meister Eckhart: "There is something in the soul that is uncreated and uncreatable . . . [and] this is the intellect."[17]

There are dimensions of the soul that not only bring us closer to the corporeal order, but which are also transcendent. Because it is situated between the Spirit and the body, the intermediary realm is difficult to fathom and thus requires a certain metaphysical discernment. Eckhart explains: "At the highest point of his . . . soul, man is more God than creature."[18] Plato identifies the transpersonal faculty of the Intellect as "the highest part of the soul,"[19] which is synonymous with the spiritual dimension in all beings. The Vedānta (or Brahma) Sūtras articulate a similar concept: "The soul can have a double nature, that of the supreme and that of the individual soul."[20] Correspondingly, our primordial nature or innermost Self is synonymous with the heights of the soul.

The English poet and Anglican divine Thomas Traherne declares: "As my body without my Soul is a Carcase, so is my soul without Thy Spirit, a chaos, a dark obscure heap of empty faculties: ignorant of itself, unsensible of Thy goodness, blind to Thy glory: dead in sins and trespasses. Having eyes I see not, having [ears] I hear not."[21] Every facet of reality is hierarchically ordered with its levels and modes of knowing—without recourse to the transcendent, lower orders of reality invariably become opaque and distorted.

Again, our physiology is dependent on the soul, and our bodies and souls (in turn) are grounded in the Spirit. In the same way that the body cannot function without the soul and Spirit, the same can be said for modern psychology. According to Saint Makarios of Egypt, "[T]he soul, which is a subtle body, has enveloped and clothed itself in the members of our visible body, which is gross in substance."[22] However, the human soul requires the body to manifest itself and cannot do so without it. Furthermore, throughout humanity's spiritual traditions, the human body is viewed as a theophany and is understood to be the locus of the Spirit. For example: "The body, the house of the Spirit"[23] (Chāndogya Upanishad 8:7–12) and our "bodies are temples of the Holy Spirit" (1 Corinthians 6:19).

We recall the memorable words of Eckhart, who said: "God create[d] the world . . . [so] that God might be born in the soul."[24] But this does not mean that the human psyche is independent of the Spirit; the soul is completely reliant on the spiritual domain for all things. As Titus Burckhardt has prudently observed, "[T]he psychic cannot be treated by the psychic."[25] The empirical ego or fragmented self cannot transcend or heal itself, for it needs a higher order of reality to intervene and bring about an abiding equilibrium. Similarly, psychology cannot rely on the mind alone, because it cannot objectively know itself. The Sage of Arunachala, Śrī Ramana Maharshi, remarked that "[t]he mind cannot seek the mind."[26] Likewise, our identification with the transcendent clearly implies immanence as we see in the following Patristic formula: "God became man that man might become God."[27]

The Divine immanence is recognized across all religions: "The kingdom of God is within you" (Luke 17:21), "I am the Self . . . seated in the heart of all beings"[28] (Bhagavad Gītā 10:20), or "Heaven and earth cannot contain Me, but the heart of My faithful servant containeth Me" (Ḥadīth Qudsī). This is based on a metaphysical understanding that there is a prior acknowledgment of the Divine transcendence that makes it possible to access God within oneself (in a manner not limited to the psychological level). Eckhart clarifies this distinction: "God alone is free and uncreated, and therefore he alone is like the soul with respect to being free, but not with respect to uncreatedness because the soul is created."[29]

The tripartite structure of Spirit/Intellect, soul, and body is known in Latin as *Spiritus/Intellectus, anima*, and *corpus*; in Greek as *Pneuma/Nous, psyche*, and *soma*; and in Arabic as *Rūḥ/'Aql, nafs*, and *jism*. The Arabic term *'aql* is used to denote both reason and intellect, although the distinction and interrelation between them (the first being horizontal and the second vertical) is always recognized. *Rūḥ* and *'Aql* are found to be synonymous with Spirit and Intellect. The *nafs* (soul, self, or ego) is often conflated with

Rūḥ or Spirit, as is evidenced by these terms being used interchangeably; however, they represent two very different ontological functions of the self. The "heart" and the "intellect," in a traditional context, are also synonymous with Spirit; for this reason, they are sometimes referred to as the "heart-intellect."

The Old Testament upholds the belief that human beings are a composite of Spirit, soul, and body. We see this, for example, in Genesis: "And the Lord God formed man of the dust of the ground, and breathed into his nostrils the breath of life; and man became a living soul" (2:7). Each person, according to the Jewish tradition, consists of *neshamah, ruaḥ,* and *nefesh*. During its terrestrial sojourn, our higher soul (*neshamah*) longs for its return to the Spirit, while our reasoning soul (*ruaḥ*) acts as an intermediary between the upper and lower realms, concerning itself with what is good and evil; while the animal soul (*nefesh*), our lower dimension, is linked to instincts and bodily cravings.

In the Christian tradition, references are made to the threefold constitution of the human being in Saint Paul's first epistle to the Thessalonians: "May the God of peace Himself sanctify you wholly; and may your *spirit and soul and body* be kept sound and blameless at the coming of our Lord Jesus Christ" (1 Thessalonians 5:23). Christian psychology recognizes that the human being is created in the "image of God" (Genesis 1:27) and that the Divine calls us to become "partakers of the divine nature" (2 Peter 1:4) by identifying this indwelling Spirit within ourselves with what is everlasting and "not of this world" (John 18:36). According to Saint Paul, "[H]e who is joined to the Lord is one spirit with Him" (1 Corinthians 6:17)—a reference to our chief end in this life; namely, the soul's return to its divine origin.

In the Islamic tradition, the Spirit (*Rūḥ*), while transcendent, is also immanent within the soul (*nafs*) of the human being (*al-insān*) and, when the faculty of the Intellect (*'aql*) is restored in the heart (*qalb*), our primordial nature (*fiṭrah*) can be consummated at the highest level. The intermediary realm is known within Islam as the "isthmus" (*barzakh*) between the Spirit (*Rūḥ*) and body (*jism*). Within Sufism, this tradition's mystical dimension, there are four degrees of the human psyche: ascending from the animal soul (*an-nafs al-ḥaywāniyah*); the passional soul (*an-nafs al-ammārah* or "soul that incites" to evil); the discerning or intelligent soul (*an-nafs al-lawwāmah* or "soul that blames"); and the intellective soul (*an-nafs al-muṭma'innah* or "the soul at peace," the human psyche reintegrated in Spirit or *Rūḥ*).

In the Hindu tradition, the Spirit (*Purusha*) or Self (*Ātmā*) manifests as the individual soul (*jīvātmā*), which is enveloped by five sheaths (*koshas*). The Spirit transcends each of these yet includes them at the same time. They are listed here in descending order, from the highest to the most "dense." The first envelope (*ānandamaya-kosha*) is the Spirit, the next three (*vijñānamaya-kosha, manomaya-kosha,* and *prānamaya-kosha*) pertain to the intermediary realm, and the final one (*annamaya-kosha*) corresponds to the corporeal.

Notwithstanding its nontheistic character, the Buddhist tradition also speaks of an intermediary realm. The *trikāya* doctrine of Mahāyāna Buddhism envisages the nature of reality by means of three "bodies" or *kāyas: dharmakāya* (universal body); *saṃbhogakāya* (body of bliss); and *nirmāṇakāya* (body of transformation). It is the *saṃbhogakāya* that corresponds to the intermediary realm of the human psyche. There is a cosmological corollary between the *trikāya* and the "three worlds" (Sanskrit: *triloka*) pertaining to the celestial, atmospheric, and earthly realms.

In Buddhism, each of us is said to comprise five psychophysical aggregates or "heaps" known as *khandhas* in Pāli (Sanskrit: *skandhas*): form (Pāli/Sanskrit: *rūpa*); sensation or feeling (Pāli/Sanskrit: *vedanā*); perception (Pāli: *saññā*; Sanskrit: *saṃjñā*); mental formations (Pāli: *saṅkhāras*; Sanskrit: *saṃskāras*); and consciousness (Pāli: *viññāṇa*; Sanskrit: *vijñāna*). However, the existence of these aggregates does not preclude the presence of an abiding, universal Self in all beings considered as the immanent aspect of ultimate reality (Pāli: *Attā*; Sanskrit: *Ātman*) beyond birth, old age, sickness, and death. The Buddha does not take issue with the Hindu understanding of the Self as *neti-neti* (not this, not that) which, by means of negation, conveys an apophatic understanding that transcends all determinate conceptions, leaving only the consciousness of that which is—the Self alone; all that is not this can be considered "non-Self" (*anattā*).

An integral psychology informed by metaphysics and a sacred science recognizes two aspects of human identity: one relative or horizontal, and the other Absolute or vertical (while never blurring or confusing the two.) This is made clear in Buddhist interpretations of mind. The following passage from *The Awakening of Faith in the Mahāyāna* is instructive:

> Mind, though pure in its self-nature from the beginning, is accompanied by ignorance. Being defiled by ignorance, a defiled [state of]

> Mind comes into being. But, though defiled, the Mind itself is eternal and immutable. Only the Enlightened Ones are able to understand what this means.
>
> What is called the essential nature of Mind is always beyond thoughts. It is, therefore, defined as "immutable." When the one World of Reality is yet to be realized, the Mind [is mutable and] is not in perfect unity [with Suchness]. Suddenly, [a deluded] thought arises; [this state] is called ignorance.[30]

An integrated mind sees both the mirror and the images that are reflected in it. Our original state of consciousness—unconditioned by the images of the phenomenal world—can envision an abiding unity behind all forms. Huang Po discusses this transpersonal dimension in the following passage:

> All the Buddhas and all sentient beings are nothing but the One Mind, beside which nothing exists. This Mind, which is without beginning, is unborn and indestructible. It is not green nor yellow, and has neither form nor appearance. It does not belong to the categories of things which exist or do not exist, nor can it be thought of in terms of new or old. It is neither long nor short, big nor small, for it transcends all limits, measures, names, traces and comparisons. . . . Only awake to the One Mind.[31]

Some have attempted to trace the rudiments of a sacred psychology to what Freud referred to as the "oceanic feeling"[32] in his book *Civilization and Its Discontents* (1930). Yet this venture is misplaced because the Freudian "talking cure" is, at its core, anti-spiritual and opposed to metaphysics. The "oceanic feeling" for Freud likely refers to the primary narcissistic state of union between an infant and its mother, and certainly not a unitive state with the Absolute. Although appearing to be more friendly towards the spiritual traditions and their "science of the soul," neither does the work of Carl Jung refer to the transpersonal order; rather, its perspective is altogether confined to the intermediary realm of the human psyche.[33]

Whitall N. Perry illustrates why psychic phenomena are so seductive and difficult to discern: "The confusion is between the psychic and spiritual planes of reality, where the unfamiliar, the strange, and the bizarre are mistaken for the transcendent, simply by the fact that they lie outside the ordinary modes of consciousness."[34] This recognition appears to be missing from the standard professional literature, and in any of the discussions related to understanding the intermediary realm. Guénon elaborates on these dangers:

> It is impossible to be too mistrustful of every appeal to the "subconscious" . . . in a sort of "cosmic consciousness" that shuts out all "transcendence" and so also shuts out all effective spirituality . . . but what is to be said of someone who flings himself into the ocean and has no aspiration but to drown himself in it? This is very precisely the significance of a so-called "fusion" with a "cosmic consciousness" that is really nothing but the confused and indistinct assemblage of all the psychic influences . . . these influences have absolutely nothing in common with spiritual influences. . . . Those who make this fatal mistake either forget about or are unaware of the distinction between the "upper waters" and the "lower waters;" instead of raising themselves toward the "ocean above," they plunge into the abyss of the "ocean below;" instead of concentrating all their powers so as to direct them toward the formless world, which alone can be called "spiritual," they disperse them in the endlessly changeable and fugitive diversity of the forms of subtle manifestation . . . with no suspicion that they are mistaking for a fullness of "life" something that is in truth the realm of death and of a dissolution without hope of return.[35]

All religions teach that there is an inseparable link between human beings and the Divine. Indeed, they see their task as having us awaken to our primordial nature (*fiṭrah*), the "image of God" (*imago Dei*), Buddha-nature (*Buddha-dhātu*), or Self (*Ātmā*)—our true identity *in divinis*. This traditional doctrine of identity is closely related to the image one has of Reality itself. It is the metaphysical order that restores harmony to a consciousness that has been bifurcated into mind and matter (or subject and object), which also allows for the discernment of the intermediary realm.

At the root of the crisis in modern psychology is the "Cartesian bifurcation," the dualism between mind and body (along with matter) that has plagued the mindset of the West since the seventeenth century. As a result of this myopic outlook, human beings are severed from reality and everything becomes objectified, further entrenching the psyche in a subject-object dichotomy. The Cartesian divide between *res extensa* (extended entities) and *res cogitans* (thinking entities) makes no allowance for overcoming this bifurcation, thus reducing all human experience to the private, subjective realm and destroying any notion of objective reality. This perpetuates the illusion of a fragmented worldview and an isolated self, which sunders our relationship to the sacred. This mind-body dualism lives on in modern science, especially in the fields of psychology and psychiatry, where this notion is deeply embedded in its epistemological framework. It is especially to be found in the medical model of clinical diagnosis and treatment of mental illness, which separates the psychological (*psyche*) from the biological (*soma*). It is the metaphysical order that restores harmony to a consciousness that has been distorted by dualism.

Across the diverse traditional cultures of humanity, this pernicious bifurcation does not exist, as they all recognize that we comprise Spirit, soul, and body. Within each of the world's religions—Judaism, Christianity, Islam, Hinduism, Buddhism, Taoism, and the traditions of the First Peoples—there exists a corresponding psychology that is fully integrated and grounded in the sacred. At the heart of each authentic psychology, there lies a "science of the soul" that can bring about a psycho-spiritual transformation that is essential to healing our damaged psyches: "Be ye transformed by the renewing of your mind" (Romans 12:2). The term "therapy" comes from the Greek word *therapeía* (healing). Yet, it is not only we who are in need of restoration but also the discipline of psychology as a whole, along with its mental health systems.

Although psychology today has begun, to some degree, to incorporate spiritual practices into its secular framework and is becoming more open to these approaches, it still has a long history of pathologizing religion. Furthermore, modern Western psychology continues, in large part, to view itself as the only valid way of knowing the mind, thus implicitly rejecting the validity of other approaches to this discipline. This is an acutely problematic situation that has not been fully understood, which means it cannot be properly remedied until the root causes of this crisis are clearly identified.

While one can certainly find some common ground between the spiritual psychologies and their modern counterparts, no integration between the two is possible without asking the following question: Is modern psychology able to accommodate the sacred in its worldview? As it stands, the foundations of modern psychology are vitiated by the exclusion of a spiritual dimension in its epistemology and praxis. If this trajectory continues unabated, modern psychology will never become a fully integrated "science of the soul."

Contemporary psychology had its genesis with the advent of psychoanalysis and behaviorism. All the movements and schools that came after them were simply prolongations of these two pioneering forces which have not, as many assume, disappeared into the annals of history. The question that arises is whether modern psychology and the field of mental health can be extricated from this deformed superstructure. We need to be vigilant about giving preference to the tenets of modern psychology over those of humanity's spiritual traditions if we are committed to reviving an authentic "science of the soul" as an endeavor distinct from modern psychology.

As human beings have both a body and a mind, it is important that we first attend to our corporeal nature and explore our bodily health prior to determining a mental health diagnosis. Once a physical cause has been ruled out, a person's mental health can be further assessed. At the same time, maintaining awareness of the fundamental mind-body unity and its relationship to the tripartite structure of Spirit, soul, and body at all times is central to any spiritually informed therapeutic approach. Each effective sacred psychology is sustained by the transpersonal order which facilitates an integration that does not rely on the ego. In contrast, mainstream psychology (and psychiatry) do not—by and large—take into consideration the spiritual dimension. Their attempts to reduce the human being to merely a psychophysical entity, devoid of what transcends these limitations, will only yield a fragmented understanding. This approach may, in some cases, produce a temporary cure or remove some unwanted symptoms, but it does not constitute true healing.

It is only by embracing a more spiritually integrated psychology that the discipline can be saved from itself. All spiritual traditions teach their own version of the famous inscription found at Delphi—"Know thyself" *(Gnóthi seautón)*—yet such realization is only possible if we can restore the practice of healing souls to its transcendent origins.

Chapter 2

The Inner and Outer Human Being

"[T]he *vyakti*, the outer self, is but a shadow of the *vyakta*, the inner self."[1]
—Nisargadatta Maharaj

"[T]he Heavenly is on the inside, the human is on the outside."[2]
—Zhūangzi

"[T]hough our outward man perish, yet the inward man is renewed day by day."
—2 Corinthians 4:16

"In any definition of Man, his inner and outer aspect are both to be considered."[3]
—Ibn 'Arabī

"The duality of the world, inner and outer, and things subject to causation—by distinctly understanding what they are, one is established in imagelessness [*nirābhāsa* or *anābhāsa*]."[4]
—Laṅkāvatāra Sūtra

In earlier eras when human collectivities were more anchored in their spiritual traditions, the social ambiance of the outer world reflected the sacred and permeated the culture, which nurtured and sustained the integrity of a person. In such an environment, both the horizontal and vertical dimensions of reality supported the fullness of human beings. With the loss of a sense of the sacred on a global scale, our outer dimension has gradually become eclipsed and no longer reflects the Divine. This has inevitably led to the obscuration of our inner dimension, causing the fragmentation we now see mirrored in the current global mental health pandemic and topsy-turvy state of the world. In our day, it is the outward that dominates the inward, which is an inversion of the traditional norm. Our true purpose, then, is to live in accordance with the sacred and to better integrate our outward and inward dimensions. In fact, a flourishing society depends on the human psyche remaining stable: "The state of the outer world does not merely correspond to the general state of men's souls; it also in a sense depends on that state."[5]

Among the spiritual traditions of the world, we find unanimous agreement that the tripartite constitution of the person and that of the cosmos—of which we are but a mirror—comprises Spirit, soul, and body; or the spiritual, psychic, and corporeal states. This relationship is described by Johannes Scotus Erigena as follows: "Man is the microcosm in the strictest sense of the word. He is the summary of all existence. . . . [T]here is no creature that is not recapitulated in man. . . . [T]here is nothing in the universe lower than body or higher than soul."[6] The dominance of the unseen world proclaimed by the spiritual traditions (and their corresponding psychologies) was gradually overthrown and replaced by the more tangible demands of the sensorial world and its empirical modes of knowing, represented by the modern West's culture of materialism.

Persian poet and scholar Jāmī underscores this fact as follows: "Therefore the universe is the outward visible expression of the Real, and the Real is the inner unseen reality of the universe."[7] In relying on a purely empirical approach, mainstream psychology—along with its mental health treatments—fails to recognize that it is through the visible world of forms that we can glimpse the unseen realities of the Divine. This reduction of reality to evidence-informed ways of knowing radically limits the scope of psychology to provide true healing.

If, according to contemporary science, we cannot identify the human soul or a transcendent Spirit by empirical means, then this must mean that they do not exist. A prime example of this flawed outlook is evidenced in this assertion: "If your belief conflicts with empirically confirmed knowledge, then you are not seeking meaning; you are delusional."[8] What this myopic position fails to recognize is that there are distinct levels of knowledge and modes of being.

What may be self-evident at one level is not so on a higher one, for lower levels cannot encompass what lies beyond them; only the higher can know the lower. While the reductionist position ostensibly shuns metaphysics, embedded in its argument is a hidden metaphysic of its own, one that implicitly attacks any suggestion of a reality that transcends the psychophysical order. In doing so, it has transgressed its own conceptual assumptions.

With the emergence of the European Enlightenment, psychology lost its ability to fully discern the transpersonal aspect of reality, which alone can unify all dimensions of a human being in harmony with the environment. This has been the root cause of many present-day calamities. Theodore Roszak remarked that a fundamental insight emerged "at the birth of modern science. Our knowledge of nature Out There begins with knowledge of ourselves In Here. Until we [are] freed . . . of the hidden presuppositions that stand between us and the world, we can never be certain we are in touch with reality."[9]

This debilitating secularism has fundamentally marginalized the inner dimension of the person. This is evident in this description from American psychologist James Hillman: "There is only one core issue for all [modern] psychology. Where is the 'me?' Where does the 'me' begin? Where does the 'me' stop? Where does the 'other' begin?"[10] The split between "in here" and "out there" is ultimately a play of appearances due to the superimposition of the ego on a limited comprehension reality. However, according to a traditional understanding, this bifurcation is not problematic when discerned through the transpersonal faculty of the Intellect or "eye of the heart,"[11] which confirms the distinction between the inner and outer human being—a fact acknowledged unanimously, in all times and places, by the spiritual patrimony of humanity.

It is through the gradual eclipse of the "eye of the heart" due to our fallen consciousness that the harmony between the inward and outward has been lost. Whitall N. Perry explains:

> [W]e could start by recalling the primordial state of man when he was in the terrestrial Paradise, with the inward and the outward world united in his soul. There was no schism between the inward and the outward—the subject and the object. After the Fall, the subject

> became separated from the object, so to speak, and the object has always been moving farther and farther toward the periphery, with man chasing after it and losing sight of the center and the inward self. Therefore one could say that profane knowledge is the pursuit of the outward world, with a consequent loss of the knowledge and understanding of the inward world.[12]

The mind-body dualism attributed to René Descartes is embedded in the ontological and epistemological presuppositions of mainstream psychology. This has led to inevitable consequences for how we envisage the human condition and, indeed, reality itself. Cartesian dualism—the exclusive division of the world into *res extensa* (extended entities) and *res cogitans* (thinking entities)—reduces all experience to the private and subjective realm, thus denying the demands of objective reality.

As the Scottish psychiatrist R. D. Laing points out, this dichotomy becomes evident in the therapeutic process itself, seeing as many individuals "have come to experience themselves as primarily split into a mind and a body. Usually they feel most closely identified with the 'mind.'"[13] French metaphysician René Guénon speaks to how extensively this fundamental scission has permeated today's intellectual climate: "The Cartesian duality . . . has imposed itself on all modern Western thought."[14]

The distinction between the inner and outer facets of our nature is evident in the very foundations of modern psychology. Swiss psychiatrist Ludwig Binswanger offered an acute criticism of the fragmented mentality that underlies the modern form of this discipline: "The cancer of all [modern] psychology up to now [is] . . . the cancer of the doctrine of subject-object cleavage of the world."[15] This is exemplified in its two pillars of behaviorism and psychoanalysis. Sigmund Freud observed: "Ego appears to us as something autonomous and unitary, marked off distinctly from everything else"[16] and, elsewhere, he remarks on the "boundary lines between the ego and the external world."[17]

John B. Watson took a more extreme position: "No one has ever touched a soul, or seen one in a test tube, or has in any way come into relationship with it as he has with the other objects of his daily experience."[18] B. F. Skinner calls for the eradication of our internal dimension altogether: "It is . . . inner man who is abolished, and that is a step forward."[19] He continues by reducing the human being exclusively to its corporeal or physical order:

> The picture which emerges from a scientific analysis is not of a body with a person inside, but of a body which *is* a person in the sense that it displays a complex repertoire of behavior. . . . What is being abolished is autonomous man—the inner man, the homunculus, the possessing demon, the man defended by the literatures of freedom and dignity. His abolition has long been overdue. . . . Science does not dehumanize man, it de-homunculizes him.[20]

It cannot be stressed enough that unless this disjunction is overcome, there cannot be a true "science of the soul." We need to examine the causes that have led to this dire predicament, as Victor Danner notes: "One thing is certain: the modern world has generated a permanent separation between man's inner and outer nature."[21]

Furthermore, modern philosophy goes as far as denying the interior life altogether, as the well-known words of Maurice Merleau-Ponty reinforce: "There is no inner man."[22] As a response to this reductionist perspective, we turn to a paragon of Islamic spirituality, Rūmī , who writes: "For the common people are not able to see the inward—they only see the outward."[23] He further adds: "The body is outward, the spirit hidden."[24] This vision reflects the metaphysical levels of existence, and the corresponding ways of knowing reality.

In stark contrast, *Duo sunt in homine* ("There are two [natures] in man")[25] was an axiom in the West—prior to the emergence of the Renaissance—which recognized an inner and outer aspect to our being. Plato also acknowledges this doctrine of the two natures within us: "[When] there are two opposite impulses in a man at the same time about the same thing, we say that there must . . . be two [natures] . . . in him."[26] All religions take for granted that we are one essence that comprises two natures: an outward form connected to the psychophysical, and an inward dimension, being our spiritual constitution. Kurt Almqvist writes:

> One of the most important themes in religion—*the* most important—is the confrontation between the two "selves" in man: the inner, which partakes of God's unconditional, infinite nature and is identical with his "kingdom," and the outer self, or human personality with a certain name. It is the intersection of these two dimensions that comprises the religious life. One sees man horizontally from the earthly side;

> the other vertically as a vehicle of divinity. The crossing point may be multiplicated both horizontally and vertically, making a cosmic web formed in one direction of layered worlds or conditions and, in the other, of the beings embodied in them—horizontal and vertical, woof and warp.[27]

Throughout the traditional cultures of the world, it is recognized that "your outward is the analogy of your inward"[28]—these two natures unified in the transpersonal Self.

The diverse religions all express the immanence of this transpersonal dimension found in human beings: "The kingdom of God is within you" (Luke 17:21); "I am the Self . . . seated in the heart of all beings"[29] (Bhagavad Gītā 10:20); or "The heavens and the earth cannot contain Me, but the heart of my believing servant does contain Me" (Ḥadīth Qudsī). It is through the primacy of the vertical dimension that immanence—or the horizontal dimension—is possible. Isaac the Syrian gives a compelling description of our inner treasure-house and its connection to the celestial treasure-house that transcends each person:

> Be zealous to enter the treasury within thee; then thou wilt see that which is in heaven. For the former and the latter are one, and entering thou wilt see both. The ladder unto the Kingdom is hidden within thee and within thy soul. Dive into thyself [freed] from sin; there thou wilt find steps along which thou canst ascend.[30]

Our theomorphic essence is unconditioned and unaffected by the activities of the world: "Everything a man does in the lower part of active life is necessarily exterior to him, so to speak, beneath him."[31] This was expressed slightly differently by the great art historian Ananda Coomaraswamy: "Our Inner Man is in the world but not of it, in us but not of us, our Outer Man both in the world and of it."[32] Mainstream psychology exclusively focuses on the diagnosis and treatment of the outer human being, unaware that its materialistic science excludes, perforce, the "inward man" (Romans 7:22), and thus has no framework by which to bridge the traditional doctrine of our two natures.

According to Frithjof Schuon, "It is necessary to make a distinction in the human being between the outer and inner man: the former is turned toward the outward and lives in the 'accidental'; the latter looks inward and lives on Substance."[33] Similarly, Buddhist writer Marco Pallis observes: "As between the outer and inner man, only the latter is the Man (the image of God), the outer man being the 'shadow' or 'vehicle' or 'house' or 'garment' of the inner, just as the world is the Lord's 'garment.'"[34] Martin Lings remarked that "[t]he perfect balance of the primordial soul depends on the harmonious union of the domains of inner and outer man."[35] This distinction was understood by the traditional world, yet it has been forgotten—if not altogether subverted—by our contemporaries: "The Inner Man, who in traditional terms is considered as a spiritual being, endowed with mind and body, is thus reduced to the Outer Man."[36]

In the Hindu tradition, also known as *sanātana dharma* (eternal religion), there are several texts that speak of the "two birds who dwell on the same tree"[37] (Muṇḍaka Upanishad 3:1:1; Shvetāshvatara Upanishad 4:6). One oft-quoted passage is the following: "Two birds, inseparably united companions, dwell in the same tree; the one eats of the fruit of the tree, while the other looks on without eating"[38] (Muṇḍaka Upanishad 3:1:1; Shvetāshvatara Upanishad 4:6). These birds illustrate the nature of the human being: One of them eats the fruit of the tree, meaning that it engages in the world of phenomena, while the other looks on without eating—witnessing the transitory nature of all things with equanimity. This describes the distinction between the corporeal and spiritual nature that exists in us all and presents a fully integrated understanding of the person. The higher Self and lower self are described here: "The mind is said to be twofold: The pure and also the impure; Impure—by union with desire; Pure—from desire completely free!"[39]

The great Dominican mystic Meister Eckhart exhorts us to "harmonise [the] inner and . . . outer man."[40] He observes:

> In every man there are two kinds of man: One is called the outer man, which is our sensuality, with the five senses serving him, and yet the outer man works through the power of the soul. The second man is called the inner man, which is the man's inwardness. Now you should know that a spiritual man who loves God makes no use in his outer man of the soul's powers except when the five senses require it; and his inwardness pays no heed to the five senses, except as this leads and guides them, and protects them, so that they are not employed for beastly purposes, as they are by some people who live for their carnal

> delight, as beasts lacking reason do. Such people deserve to be called beasts rather than men.[41]

Influential early Christian theologian and scholar Origen observes: "[T]here are two men in every one of us. Of these two men he [Solomon] tells us that the one, namely, the inner man, is renewed from day to day; but the other, that is, the outer, he declares to be corrupted and weakened."[42] German priest and physician Angelus Silesius explains: "There are two men in me; one wants the will of God, / The other the will of the world, the devil, and of death."[43] The renowned Sufi al-Ḥallāj tells us: "We are two spirits dwelling in one body,"[44] and Ḥāfiẓ writes: "Look not at the outward poverty of Ḥāfiẓ, for his inner self is a treasure-house of the Divine love."[45]

Plotinus asserts that because we lack discernment, our lives are driven by the outward: "[U]ndisciplined in discernment of the inward, knowing nothing of it, we run after the outer, never understanding that it is the inner which stirs us; we are in the case of one who sees his own reflection but not realizing from whence it comes goes in pursuit of it."[46] The spiritual traditions teach that there is a part of us that is always firmly rooted in divine reality. The dimension of ourselves that is caught in dysfunctional patterns, or addictive tendencies, can never compromise our primordial nature. Whatever transpires outwardly, it can never destroy the inward, as Johannes Tauler explains: "Even though thy outward man grieves, or weep[s] . . . thy inner man remain[s] at peace."[47]

According to Zhūangzi, "[B]y [the] cultivation of the inner man there is no failure in Tao."[48] Likewise, Jakob Böhme notes: "As the power of the inner man over the outer man increases, the former changes the qualities of the latter."[49] An approach to mental health informed by metaphysics and a sacred science recognizes two distinct facets of human identity: one relative or horizontal, and the other Absolute or vertical (while never conflating these two dimensions). In order to understand the fullness of what it means to be human, Paracelsus points out: "If we would know the inner nature of man by his outer nature,"[50] a properly ordered metaphysical framework is required.

Each "science of the soul" provides spiritual teachings and methods to integrate our outer and inner selves. Again, in our true identity as the primordial nature (*fiṭrah*), the "image of God" (*imago Dei*), Buddha-nature (*Buddha-dhātu*), or the Self (*Ātmā*), we are the eternal witness that does not partake in the activities of the temporal world. No matter how many transgressions we may incur in this life, it must never be forgotten that our primordial nature can never be lost or destroyed, as it contains within itself the transpersonal human archetype. It is our essential identity in the Divine that prevents our fallen or *saṃsāric* state from becoming absolute or terminal.

The obscuration of the Intellect or "eye of the heart" has distorted our vision of reality, which inevitably leads to innumerable problems and immense suffering: "Where there is no vision, the people perish" (Proverbs 29:18). Because of this, our noetic faculty is reduced to a one-dimensional or tunnel-like vision, which makes us forget who we truly are, and what our relationship should be with all that is. It is only the perspective of the outward that denies the inward, and not the other way around: "Who is it then who is calling it 'nothing?' Our outer self, to be sure, not our inner. Our inner self calls it 'All.'"[51] The limited scope of our vision has been described as such in the Qur'ān: "They know only an outward appearance of this lower life" (Qur'ān 30:7). This ubiquitous darkening of the "eye of the heart," coupled with an exclusive reliance on reason alone, has caused us to see only the outward at the expense of the inward.

A central tenet of any "science of the soul" is affirmed by the Sufi Abū Naṣr as-Sarrāj: "The outward cannot get by independent of the inward."[52] Without the inner self to ground the outer, we become diffused into our environment without orientation. This requires adherence to one of the time-tested spiritual paths of the great world religions or the First Peoples. Each of these revealed traditions provides theory (doctrine) and practice (methods) to integrate the outer with the inner, and to ground the ego into its transcendence source. Failing to do so will have adverse consequences to human well-being and flourishing. Zhūangzi admonishes that "you let outside considerations weigh on your mind. He who looks too hard on the outside gets clumsy on the inside."[53]

Philip Sherrard explains: "The higher or spiritual consciousness perceives and experiences things as they are in themselves, inner and outer, spiritual and material, metaphysical and physical interpenetrating and forming a single unsundered and unsunderable reality."[54] Through the transpersonal order, human beings can obtain a lasting equilibrium, because the body and soul are contingent on what surpasses them. For this reason, only what transcends the psychophysical order can bring balance to the physical body and its human soul.

We cannot overlook the complexity involved in understanding and healing the human psyche. As the soul is inseparable from the spiritual dimension of existence, treating it requires knowledge of humanity's spiritual traditions. This is something that modern Western psychology does not appear to comprehend. Each person consists of Spirit, soul, and body, and has an inner and outer facet; the inward is linked to the spiritual dimension, and the outward to the psychophysical order. Neither of these dimensions can be ignored without causing grave harm to our equilibrium.

The soul is a mystery; it is immersed in time while also being rooted in the timeless. The human body participates in time and space, whereas the Spirit transcends both. The human psyche belongs to the intermediary realm between body and Spirit but partakes of both dimensions. The spiritual traditions all attest that the intermediary realm of the person is of Divine origin. We see this, for example, in the Islamic tradition—the "Lord who created you from a single soul" (Qur'ān 4:1). Muslim philosopher Mullā Ṣadrā points out: "The soul is *the junction of the two seas* ([Qur'ān] 18:59) of corporeal and spiritual things."[55]

If we are going to authentically address the harm caused by the Cartesian mind-body dualism that continues to handicap modern Western psychology, the discipline needs to return to its rightful foundations in metaphysics, sacred science, and spiritual principles. The demarcations of inside and outside correspond to the center and the circumference, as well as to the vertical and horizontal among all levels of reality and modes of knowing. We recall the Qur'ānic verse: "He is the First and the Last, the Outward and the Inward" (57:3).

Ultimately all distinctions are unified in the Ultimate Reality or the Absolute. Paracelsus explains that "form . . . is also the essence, and thus the form reveals the essence."[56] Within the Buddhist tradition, this idea is expounded in the Heart Sūtra (*Prajnāpāramitā-hridaya-sūtra*): "Form is emptiness . . . emptiness is form."[57] Joseph Epes Brown discusses the power of traditional spiritual practices for transforming "these 'inner' and 'outer' worlds into one."[58] Fundamentally, as Paracelsus again notes: "The outer and the inner are *one*."[59] It is worth recalling the pertinent words in *The Gospel According to Thomas*: "When you make the two one, and when you make the inner as the outer and the outer as the inner and the above as the below . . . then shall you enter the Kingdom."[60] Śrī Rāmakrishna, the Paramahamsa of Dakshineswar, recognizes this non-dual dimension: "There is inner and outer harmony between Purusha [Spirit] and Prakriti [universal substance]."[61] In Ultimate Reality or the Absolute, there are no distinctions between the inner and outer for they are all one in the Divine.

The Sufi master 'Ayn al-Quḍāt points toward a pure metaphysics that resolves and transcends the dialectics of the Cartesian mind-body dualism:

> The spirit is inside and outside the body and is inside and outside the world. The spirit is also neither inside nor outside the body and is neither inside nor outside the world. Alas! Understand what has been spoken: the spirit is not connected to the body but is not disconnected from it. God is not connected to the world but is not disconnected from it.[62]

Without returning to its metaphysical and ontological foundations, the discipline of psychology is unable to acknowledge either the tripartite division of the Spirit, soul, and body, or the inner and outer dimensions of the human being and its integrative healing modalities. True wholeness flows from the transpersonal order, yet only the outer self requires therapy, as the inner self is already intrinsically whole. The "science of the soul," as informed by the spiritual traditions, supports the human psyche in becoming fully integrated in all its modes of knowing and corresponding ways of healing: "The soul's apprehension of the nature of things changes in accordance with its own inner state."[63] In the same way that sages have emphasized the existence of the inner teacher—"the Guru is always within you"[64]—there is also an inner therapist, along with the medicine to heal us within. But this first requires the spiritual guidance of a valid tradition to help prevent us from going astray and becoming lost in our turbid subjectivity.

A true "science of the soul" ensures that the assessment, treatment, and healing of a person is informed by the transpersonal dimension—this is confirmed when we discern the intrinsic wisdom reflected in the human body.[65] Therefore, being a wayfarer on a spiritual path is indispensable. Paracelsus speaks about the "inner physician" hidden within each person and that "[e]ach . . . disease bears its own remedy within itself."[66] Rūmī states something similar: "The physician comes to the sick man and questions the inward physician; for within you there is a physician."[67] Saint John Cassian writes: "The Doctor of our souls has also placed the remedy in the hidden regions of the soul."[68] According to 'Alī ibn Abī Ṭālib: "Your cure is within you, but you do not know."[69]

The overthrow of metaphysics in the modern West by scientific materialism has led to human beings being rendered one-dimensional. To deny that "[m]an is both inner and outer"[70] or that "there is within every man both an outer and an inner man"[71] is to perpetuate the fissure in consciousness that has severed the human soul from its transpersonal center. This bifurcation has created a void in the human psyche that has proven to be profoundly traumatic. Furthermore, by recognizing as valid only the empirical order, which is measured and verified solely by the five senses, human beings become caricatures of their own captivity, "immersed in the maze of phenomena."[72] A metaphysical framework integrating the Spirit, soul, and body—and its diverse modes of knowing—is urgently needed to reconcile all facets of a person with a view to offering fully efficacious mental health treatment. It is through our immanent and sacred center, connecting us to transcendence, that authentic action in the outer world can occur: "No outward act however perfect but hinders the interior life."[73]

While there is a boundary that divides our inner and outer selves, they are not impervious to one another as one might think; in fact, through the Intellect, or the "eye of the heart," the outward can be illuminated by the inward, thus establishing a proper equilibrium in our lives that is key to our vocation as human beings. Modern science is restricted to the phenomenal world, but the sacred science of the world's spiritual traditions provides the keys to unlock knowledge of both the human microcosm and the universal macrocosm, as it applies to the spiritual, psychic, and corporeal orders. Only in returning psychology to a true "science of the soul," can humanity become fully integrated, and thus faithful to its true vocation: "May the inward and outward man be as one."[74]

Chapter 3

Realms of Consciousness and the Real

"Man is in this world already in heaven or hell."[1]

—Jakob Böhme

"*Samsara*, the transmigration of life, takes place in one's own mind. Let one therefore keep the mind pure, for what a man thinks that he becomes: this is a mystery of Eternity."[2]

—Maitrī Upanishad 6:24

"The manifestations of mind outnumber the / myriads of dust-motes / In the infinite rays of sunlight."[3]

—Milarepa

"[T]he whole world of existence is imagination within imagination."[4]

—Ibn 'Arabī

While modern Western psychology has occasionally acknowledged the importance of the transpersonal realm and other dimensions of reality, it nevertheless remains afflicted by a reductionist *Weltanschauung* that thwarts its clinical efficacy and treatment modalities. We are reminded that "the materialistic consensus which undergirds practically all of current mainstream psychology, neuroscience, and philosophy of mind is fundamentally flawed [and that] current mainstream opinion in psychology *must* change."[5] It is important to bear in mind that an early (and widely accepted) definition of psychology developed by influential American psychologist George Trumbull Ladd refers to "the description and explanation of the states of . . . consciousness, as such,"[6] yet the discipline in the present-day does not know what consciousness is and for the most part has lost all connection to higher orders of reality. By contrast, holistic psychologies rooted in the spiritual traditions have fuller access to the realm of consciousness—in the multiplicity of its forms—along with their corresponding epistemological modes that ground humans in the collective, the sacred, and in right relationship with the natural world. Across the world's religions, "Mind" is the source of all things because it exists prior to the created order and pervades all of reality.

The life of the mind is often taken for granted and when a thought enters it, without fully realizing its power, we can find ourselves propelled into very confused and dark spaces. The basis of a thought's validity is seldom considered anymore. The notion that because thoughts arise, they must somehow reflect reality, is very deceptive and can in most cases be totally false. If a thought has no foundation in what is real, then what is the point of occupying our minds with it? Yet, our ordinary minds are disconnected from their centers, such that what is higher within them is lost to the onslaught of mental white noise that we all generate.

For most people in the present day, the consciousness that we inhabit is not a friendly one; rather, it betrays a myriad of hostilities that serve to undermine our vision of the transpersonal Self. In such cases, our mind is our worst enemy. By means of the contemplative practices found in humanity's spiritual traditions, we can glean ways of grounding our thoughts and emotions in our moment-to-moment experience through an abiding connection to the sacred. Without a vertical perspective on the metaphysical basis of consciousness, we will become captive to the fragmented outgrowth of our cognition. To ignore this is, in a sense, to throw ourselves out to sea in the midst of a storm, the consequences of which can be deleterious to our psychological well-being.

Modern Western psychology has failed to understand the enigma of consciousness due to its reductionist assumptions and its uncritical reliance on Cartesian bifurcationism. A proposed remedy for this failure is to adopt a proper "science of the soul," which is found in all of the world's religions, where the sacred remains pivotal to an authentic understanding of the person. By returning psychology to its sacred foundations in metaphysics and ontology, it can provide us with the traditional knowledge and modes of healing that are rooted in immutable principles that empirical epistemologies have long rejected: "[T]he best way in which we can facilitate their advent is to understand how great is the darkness in which we grope, and never to forget that the natural-science assumptions with which we started are provisional and revisable things."[7]

The genesis of the desacralized and reductionist outlook that dominates psychology today is likely to be found in the ideas of John Locke, one of the most influential thinkers of the European Enlightenment. To him was attributed the theory of empiricism and the associated notion of *tabula rasa*, whereby human beings are born with a "clean slate" or "blank canvas" rather than as an image of the Divine. The foundations of modern psychology—especially behaviorism and psychoanalysis—need to be understood for what they are: namely, an unbridled assault on what it means to be fully human. Any so-called psychology that abolishes the soul and Spirit, and regards the mind or consciousness as a mere epiphenomenon, is not a true "science of the soul." In the winter of 1913, John B. Watson, known as the "father of behaviorism," delivered a lecture at Columbia University entitled "Psychology as the Behaviorist Views It," which became widely known as the "behaviorist manifesto."[8] This address inaugurated one of the most powerful currents in twentieth-century psychology. Watson's attack on the "science of the soul" is usefully encapsulated as follows:

> The time seems to have come when psychology must discard all reference to consciousness; when it need no longer delude itself into thinking that it is making mental states the object of observation. . . . This suggested elimination of states of consciousness as proper objects of investigation in themselves will remove the barrier from psychology which exists between it and the other [modern] sciences.[9]

Sigmund Freud also had a reductionistic interpretation of the mind:

> [T]he "essential nature" of consciousness: we see the process of a thing becoming conscious as a specific psychical act, distinct from and independent of the process of the formation of a presentation or

> idea; and we regard consciousness as a sense organ which perceives data that arise elsewhere.[10]

Freud's one-time protégé Carl Jung is often considered a pioneer of transpersonal psychology who recognized the need to include the spiritual dimension in psychology. Nevertheless, his own interpretation of consciousness is limited to the empirical ego and does not encompass anything that is transcendent to it:[11] "Consciousness is the function or activity which maintains the relation of psychic contents with the ego"[12] or "Consciousness can only exist through continual recognition of the unconscious."[13]

In this context, Cyril Burt offers this assessment of the discipline: "Psychology, having first bargained away its soul and then gone out of its mind, seems now, as it faces an untimely end, to have lost all consciousness."[14] Since its emergence, modern Western psychology has not been able to establish a healthy epistemological pluralism to support both the ordinary and transpersonal dimensions of mind, seeing as it has abandoned its roots in metaphysics and spiritual principles. When souls are living in a state of forgetfulness, their consciousness is obscured. This prevents them from truly knowing themselves, as they fail to see that the endless stream of thoughts in the mind has an ontological status that is only contingent or provisional. What is required for a proper and abiding psychological orientation is to stabilize one's psychic center by having it anchored in a reality that is transmundane.

According to traditional thought, the macrocosm and microcosm mirror each other. Levels of reality exist both within and outside us given our fundamental unity in the Absolute. According to Islamic spirituality, "Man is a little cosmos, and the cosmos is like a big man."[15]

Not only are we in the cosmos, but the cosmos dwells in us. Similarly, there is a correspondence between the soul and the cosmos, including our posthumous states and consciousness in this life. For in the deepest recesses of the human microcosm there reverberates another world—more real and enduring than this one, yet fully present, here and now, at the very heart of existence. As Muhammad is recorded to have said: "Paradise is closer to you than the thong of your sandal, and the same applies to hell."[16] The Divine is an irreducible whole that cannot be artificially sundered into disjointed parts—every dimension of existence reflects the whole of Reality, and each realm of cognition is permeable to the whole.

If we pay attention to our minds and their fluctuating states, we can see how much of our experience in this life is susceptible to momentary cognitions. Although we cannot underestimate the power of consciousness, we need to also emphasize that "[m]ind is indeed the source of bondage and also the source of liberation"[17] (Maitrī Upanishad 6:24). Indeed, the tradition of Vedānta—one of the six perspectives (*darśana*) of Hindu philosophy—teaches that the mind (*manas*) according to the Vedānta is the by-product of illusion (*māyā*).

The mind cannot know itself through its own efforts, as it requires the agency of what lies beyond the empirical ego in order to do so. Just like the "ordinary" self, consciousness itself cannot be understood at its own level. The discipline of modern Western psychology has yet to grapple with this fundamental predicament, something that Ladd discerned early on when he observed: "You cannot, by so-called introspection, analyze your own states of consciousness."[18] Our minds create a dreamlike reality that can appear to be quite vivid and all-encompassing, but this is a chimera. In such a state, we are captured by distorting mental fragments that prevent us from discerning the whole, which is why we are often apt to be deceived. For this reason, the life of the mind can become a quagmire of distress and confusion.

It ought to be obvious that existence as a whole cannot simply be reduced to the functions of our precarious cognition. So, while the mind is unable to create reality as such, our perspective on life can still have a powerful impact on our psychophysical flourishing. The endemic relativism that has undermined the discipline of modern Western psychology is underscored by American psychologist Carl Rogers: "The only reality I can possibly know is the world as *I* perceive and experience it at this moment. . . . And the only certainty is that those perceived realities are different. There are as many 'real worlds' as there are people!"[19] A similar view was held by Freud: "Fundamentally, we find only what we need and see only what we want to see."[20]

By expunging the very notion of truth, we become imprisoned in a solipsistic cul-de-sac. As the New Age mantra proclaims: "You create your own reality."[21] For this reason, René Guénon observed that an experience of existence that excludes higher orders of reality can only give rise to "the illusion of 'ordinary life.'"[22]

Our thinking about the world and ourselves is rooted in our state of mind, which is situated in a particular individual perspective. This varies from moment to moment in each person. Our thoughts can also conflict among themselves. Without an awareness of this, our attention is often diffused outwardly into the world, and we lose touch with our sacred center—which is a direct reflection of Reality. It is through a comprehensive "science of the soul," as taught by spiritual traditions, that we can distinguish the psychic from the Spiritual, as well as the relative from the Absolute. According to the Māṇḍūkya Upanishad: "Two kinds of knowledge must be known—that is what the knowers of Brahman tell us. They are the Higher Knowledge and the lower knowledge"[23] (1:1:4). This discrimination cannot be found in most modern Western psychology, as it has rejected its metaphysical and spiritual foundations.

Throughout all spiritual traditions, we find examples of how both heaven and hell—and everything in between—are present within the human psyche. The Anglican divine William Law writes: "There cannot be the smallest Thing, or the smallest Quality of any Thing in this World, but what is a Quality of *Heaven* or *Hell*, discovered under a temporal Form."[24] The English poet John Milton confirmed this in his famous poem, *Paradise Lost*: "The mind is its own place, and in itself / Can make a Heaven of Hell, a Hell of Heaven."[25]

The Māṇḍūkya Upanishad describes four states (*avasthā*) of consciousness that are central to human beings: waking (*jāgrat*), dreaming (*svapna*), deep sleep (*sushupṭi*), and the underlying substratum of all three states corresponding to the gross, subtle, and causal realms (*turīya*). The Self (*Āṭmā*) is the principle of all states of consciousness and all degrees of its manifestation. Typically, the perspective of modern Western psychology begins and ends with the waking state of consciousness, meaning that all facets of life are analyzed from the waking state with other realms being, for the most part, disqualified, as they cannot be empirically verified.

Contrary to the belief that "the psyche is a self-regulating system that maintains its equilibrium,"[26] what we find, in fact, is that consciousness alone regulates all levels of a human being. A "science of the soul," grounded in metaphysics and ontology, sees the waking state as a relative point of reference, not one that is absolute. For this reason, it can account for multiple realms of consciousness. In Sāṇkhya-Yoga, we find the cosmological principles of the three *guṇas* and their psychic correspondences: "When *sattva* predominates, consciousness is calm, clear, comprehensible, virtuous; dominated by *rajas*, it is agitated, uncertain, unstable; overwhelmed by *tamas*, it is dark, confused, passionate, bestial."[27]

In Buddhist cosmology, there are six realms that constitute life in *saṃsāra* (the cycle of birth and death): hell beings, hungry ghosts, animals, humans, fighting spirits, and gods. If we conceive of these worlds—not only as posthumous states that we experience after death—but as realms in which we can become immersed here and now, we can better understand not only the nature of the mind, but also extreme cognitive states and their relationship to mental health. By having recourse to a proper metaphysical perspective, we can make sense of the well-known insight by Ādi Śaṅkara, the eighth-century sage of the Advaita Vedānta tradition: "There is in reality no transmigrating soul different from the Lord."[28]

Beyond the corporeal and psychic realms, traditional forms of wisdom maintain that human beings can occupy multiple states of consciousness. Buddhist writer Marco Pallis explains: "Man is but one of an indefinite number of states of the being."[29] William James, the "father of American psychology," notes a similar idea:

> [O]ur normal waking consciousness . . . is but one special type of consciousness, whilst all about it, parted from it by the filmiest of screens, there lie potential forms of consciousness entirely different. We may go through life without suspecting their existence; but apply the requisite stimulus, and at a touch they are there in all their completeness. . . . No account of the universe in its totality can be final which leaves these other forms of consciousness quite disregarded. How to regard them is the question. . . . At any rate, they forbid a premature closing of our accounts with reality.[30]

The sacred psychologies of diverse cultures throughout the world provide us with a context for understanding these other states of mind. Due to their limited scope, empirical epistemologies fail to discern these realms of consciousness, as they only consider horizontal dimensions of reality. We are reminded that "Heaven or Hell . . . comprise regions and degrees—in both the 'horizontal' and 'vertical' dimensions—but the 'life' or 'movements' in these abodes cannot be penetrated by earthly understanding, unless it be through rare and fragmentary images."[31] For this reason, Toshihiko Izutsu points out:

> Such a vision of reality, however, is not accessible to human consciousness as long as it remains at the level of ordinary everyday experience. In order to have access to it . . . the mind must experience a total transformation of itself. The consciousness must transcend the dimension of ordinary cognition where the world of being is experienced as consisting of solid, self-subsistent things, each having as its ontological core what is called essence. There must arise in the mind a totally different kind of awareness in which the world is revealed in an entirely different light.[32]

That at any given moment we are in a particular state of mind or realm of consciousness, including extreme states, does not mean that they are not real. They can be just as vivid as our experiences in the external world of matter—seeing as all realms coexist in reality—but it must be remembered that our current temporal existence is subject to impermanence and countless vicissitudes. No matter how real the contents of the mind may appear, they are grounded in an order of reality that is individual and highly conditioned, rather than in the transpersonal.

Our cognition is instrumental in traversing the multifarious states of consciousness and can act as a support to the spiritual path when rooted in a sacred ambiance. This is attested to in the Ashtāvakra Gītā of the Hindu tradition: "You are what you think"[33] (1:11); in a Buddhist text, the Dhammapada: "All that we are is the result of what we have thought"[34] (1:1); in Jewish scripture: "As he thinketh in his heart, so is he" (Proverbs 23:7); in the New Testament: "We . . . beholding . . . are changed into the same image" (2 Corinthians 3:18); and in the Islamic tradition: "You are your thought."[35] By contrast, an early exponent of the discipline upholds that, devoid of transcendence, "belief creates its verification."[36] Both a horizontal and vertical understanding of existence are needed to fully grasp the nuances of the human psyche, yet mainstream psychology, for the most part, confines itself to a purely secular outlook.

Without opening the "eye of the heart" (or the transpersonal Intellect) we cannot discern the true nature of reality. According to the Bhagavad Gītā: "The unreal never is; the Real never is not. This truth indeed has been seen by those who can see the true"[37] (2:16). In the same way that a Hindu proverb speaks of a "rope . . . mistaken for an illusory snake,"[38] human beings superimpose a separate ego onto the transpersonal Self, giving rise to a plethora of confusion and suffering. For this reason, discernment is essential for our mental health.

Time and time again, spiritual traditions call us to "remember that thou goest in the midst of snares" (Ecclesiasticus 9:13). In Plato's allegory of the cave, people mistake shadows for the real world. The experience of being shackled in a cave can be likened to a psychosis of delusional thinking or hallucinations about the reality of the shadows in our minds. To face the real world beyond the "cave" requires entering a spiritual path in order to restore true vision through the "eye of the heart." From the aspect of ultimate reality, we need to "see through" the phenomenal world of fleeting appearances to behold the transpersonal order:

> It is like a cinema show. There is light on the screen and the shadows flitting across impress the audience as the acting of some story. Now suppose that in this film story an audience is also shown on the screen. The seer and the seen will then both be on the screen. Apply this to yourself. You are the screen, the Self has created the ego, the ego has its accretions of thoughts, which are displayed as the world, trees, plants, etc., about which you are asking. In reality all these are nothing but the Self. If you see the Self it will be found to be all, everywhere and always. Nothing but the Self exists.[39]

From this metaphysical perspective, we can understand the Buddha when he remarked, "Our life is the creation of our mind."[40] The eighth-century Buddhist yogi Saraha observed: "Mind is the seed of everything, from which sprouts both [*saṃsāra*] and *nirvāṇa*."[41] The Sage of Arunachala, Śrī Ramana Maharshi, explains: "You carry heaven and hell with you."[42] John Smith, one of the Cambridge Platonists, writes: "The foundation of heaven and hell is laid in men's own souls."[43] Boethius stated: "Nothing is miserable unless you think it so; and on the other hand, nothing brings happiness unless you are content with it."[44] Within the Jewish tradition, this insight is framed as: "A man is shown in a dream only what is suggested by his own thoughts."[45] The Persian poet Sanā'ī expressed this thought as follows: "Your heaven and hell are within yourself: Look inside!"[46] Ralph Waldo Emerson also proposed a similar view: "To different minds, the same world is a hell, and a heaven."[47]

According to the diverse spiritual traditions of the world, there is a transpersonal dimension in human beings that is both transcendent and immanent. It lies beyond the compass of conventional ratiocination and integrates all the multifaceted dimensions of a person—with all the epistemological consequences that this entails. Rabbi Israel of Ruzhin points out: "Thought may be utilized for holy or unholy purposes. Should not a man's intellect elevate his thoughts to the Supreme Mind?"[48] The perspective of two minds, one ordinary and the other transpersonal, is captured in *The Laws of Manu*: "From himself he also drew forth the mind, which is both real and unreal"[49] (1:14). Śrī Rāmakrishna declares: "Through His Consciousness one becomes conscious of everything."[50] In Hindu thought, the "mind is Brahman"[51] (Chāndogya Upanishad 7:3:1). A corresponding idea was noted by Fu-Ta-shih who stressed that "[m]ind is Buddha."[52] Saint Nikitas Stithatos writes: "God is . . . Intellect"[53] and as Moses Maimonides also observed, "God is the *intellectus*."[54] This metaphysical understanding can be summarized as follows: "Brahman [is] mind: for from mind all beings have come, by mind they all live, and unto mind they all return"[55] (Taittirīya Upanishad 3:4:1). Ādi Śaṅkara taught the supra-individual aspect of cognition: "The universe is an unbroken series of perceptions [cognitions] of Brahman."[56]

In the traditional or premodern world, there were modes of knowledge, with corresponding levels of reality, by which one could realize ultimate reality. Parmenides acknowledges that to be is to know: "The same thing is there for thinking and for being."[57] Rabbi Nachman of Bratslav has this to say: "The thought of man is his being: he who thinks of the upper world is in it."[58] The unity of the knower and the known needs to be realized through direct awareness:

> [M]etaphysics or ontology is inseparably connected with the subjective state of man, so that the self-same reality is said to be perceived differently in accordance with the different degrees of consciousness . . . the highest degree of knowledge is always achieved when the knower, the human subject, becomes completely unified and identified with the object so much so that there remains no differentiation between the two.[59]

Through *metanoia*, or radical transformation, which appears in all sapiential traditions, we can restore the "eye of the heart" to safely navigate the overwhelming complexity of consciousness. This was Saint Paul's instruction: "Be renewed in the spirit of your mind" (Ephesians 4:23). However, we need to undergo a phase of purification prior to any abiding union with the Absolute; otherwise, our minds will remain akin to "a venomous snake or scorpion"[60] according to the Japanese Pure Land Buddhist master Shinran. This is how we can begin to make sense of that famous line by the English poet William Blake: "If the doors of perception were cleansed, everything would appear to man as it is, infinite."[61]

"In a pure mind shines the light of the Self" according to the Māṇḍūkya Upanishad.[62] Put differently, Meister Eckhart points out that the goal is for "the human mind [to] be united to God."[63] Additionally, we read: "When the mind is silent . . . it can enter into a world which is far beyond the mind: the highest End"[64] (Maitrī Upanishad 6:24). The Taoist tradition states: "When body and mind are both quiet, Heaven and Earth merge"[65] and the Psalms declare: "Be still, and know that I am God" (46:10).

When the mind is not anchored in the transcendent, it cannot properly discern the nature of its fluctuating thoughts or unstable states. Jung once asked: "By what criterion do we judge something to be an illusion? Does there exist for the psyche anything which we may call 'illusion'? . . . the psyche does not trouble itself about . . . categories of reality . . . It is highly probable that what we call illusion is actual for the psyche."[66] For this reason, "distraction is the cause of the intellect's obscuration"[67] and "if you do not put an end to delusions prompted by external things, you will not overcome those that ambush you from within."[68] Accordingly, we need to remember that no matter how sullied our consciousness may appear to be, there is always an indwelling connection to the Spirit that can never be erased. Every human being, no matter what their circumstances, is born with an innately pure mind. The following passage from *The Awakening of Faith in the Mahāyāna* is instructive:

> Mind, though pure in its self nature from the beginning, is accompanied by ignorance. Being defiled by ignorance, a defiled [state of] Mind comes into being. But, though defiled, the Mind itself is eternal and immutable. Only the Enlightened Ones are able to understand what this means.
>
> What is called the essential nature of Mind is always beyond thoughts. It is, therefore, defined as "immutable." When the one

> World of Reality is yet to be realized, the Mind [is mutable and] is not in perfect unity [with Suchness]. Suddenly, [a deluded] thought arises; [this state] is called ignorance.[69]

There is Suchness as it pertains to the Mind that apprehends directly, and there is a cognition that is contingent, and thus restricted to its own domain. Tennō Dōgo (T'ien-huang Tao-wu) instructs: "If you want to see, see right at once. When you begin to think, you miss the point."[70]

An integrated mind sees both the mirror and the images that are reflected in it, as Zhūangzi notes: "[T]he perfect man employs his mind as a mirror."[71] Frithjof Schuon writes, "[W]hen the *mind* is perfectly calm—or perfectly simple—Truth is mirrored in it just as objects are reflected in calm water."[72] Eighth-century Indian tantric master Padmasambhāva illustrates how our original state of the mind, which is unconditioned by the images of the phenomenal world, can envision an abiding unity behind all forms:

> In its true state, mind is naked, immaculate; not made of anything, being of the Voidness; clear, vacuous, without duality, transparent; timeless, uncompounded, unimpeded, colourless; not realizable as a separate thing, but as the unity of all things, yet not composed of them; of one taste, and transcendent over differentiation.[73]

The ultimate purpose of human life is to return consciousness to our primordial nature (*fiṭrah*), the "image of God" (*imago Dei*), Buddha-nature (*Buddha-dhātu*), or Self (*Āṭmā*) that surpasses the name and form (*nāma-rūpa*) of all appearances. The ordinary mind remains ensnared in the world of phenomenal appearances, and longs to return to its transpersonal source. There is but one consciousness that dwells at the heart of all beings—that is what we seek as the goal of our spiritual odyssey during our transient sojourn in this world.

It is in the nature of the ordinary mind to be unstable yet, when restored to its center in the Spirit, it can reach its natural composure. In returning our thoughts and emotions to the very source of consciousness itself, we are able—as Saint Francis de Sales shows—to navigate the flux of the ordinary mind: "Do not lose your inward peace for anything whatsoever, even if your whole world seems upset."[74] Through abiding in consciousness, we can find the kind of peace in which Julian of Norwich was able to say: "All will be well, and all will be well, and every kind of thing will be well."[75] According to the "science of the soul," as known across all spiritual traditions, it is the way in which the mind perceives that either supports our inner peace or disturbs it, rather than events in themselves. According to William Shakespeare, "There is nothing either good or bad, but thinking makes it so."[76]

As all perturbations of mind are ephemeral, we are concerned with what lies beyond (while fully embracing) this realm of transience. As Guénon writes, "[T]he unconditioned state . . . is superior to all the conditioned states."[77] Union with Ultimate Reality or the Absolute is described in the Hindu and Islamic traditions as "being-consciousness-bliss" (Sanskrit: *sat-chit-ānanda*; Arabic: *wujūd-wijdān-wajd*). As the Divine is immanent as well as transcendent, consciousness not only surpasses the psychophysical realm but also includes the human psyche. The antidote to our endless distractions—to our dispersed attention resulting from the overwhelming stimulus of the outer world—is, according to a host of saints and sages, to return to our sacred center where we can access a deeper, undefiled consciousness. This deeper consciousness helps us bring an equanimity to the topsy-turvy nature of our inner life, while allowing us to discern unity in multiplicity, and multiplicity in unity.

A few exponents of modern Western psychology have acknowledged—as William James did—that "our normal waking consciousness . . . is but one special type of consciousness."[78] While this admission is certainly welcome, it is by no means a new discovery. This truth has long been recognized by the holistic psychologies of spiritual traditions. All true forms of the "science of the soul" accept that there are distinct realms of mind—and corresponding modes of knowing—that do not fit the mold of quotidian thinking.

It is high time that we reevaluate the pernicious assumptions on which the post-Enlightenment world has been constructed. By grounding the discipline of psychology in traditional metaphysics, we might begin to restore our consciousness of the Divine in all things, including ourselves. There are severe limitations to modern Western psychology comprehending the enigma of consciousness. By stressing the need to turn to forms of therapy that are founded on an authentic epistemological pluralism, we will come closer to restoring a true sense of wholeness in our healing modalities. In particular, we may also be able to finally repair the tragically broken bond between the sacred and the treatments that are now sorely needed in the crucial area of mental health, which is undergoing a profound crisis today.

Chapter 4

The Enneagram's Science of the Soul

"We shall show them Our signs upon the horizons and within themselves, until it be manifest unto them that it is the truth."
—Qur'ān 41:53

"Each of the Nine Points is represented by one of nine saints who are at the highest level in the Divine Presence. They are the keys to unfold powers within the human being, but there is no permission to use these keys."[1]
—Shaykh 'Abd Allāh al-Fā'iz ad-Dāghestanī

"[I]f an idea is true, it belongs equally to all who are capable of understanding it; if it is false, there is no credit in having invented it. A true idea cannot be 'new,' for truth is not a product of the human mind; it exists independently of us, and all we have to do is to take cognizance of it; outside this knowledge there can be nothing but error."[2]
—René Guénon

The enigmatic origins of the nine-pointed symbol known as the Enneagram (*ennea* in Greek means "nine," and *gram* means something "written" or "drawn")—consisting of a circle, an inner triangle (connecting 3-6-9), and an irregular hexagon (connecting 1-4-2-8-5-7)—has captivated and perplexed people ever since its first appearance in the West around

1916.[3] At the same time, there are few more prominent examples of a blatant appropriation of esoteric knowledge by popular culture as we find with the Enneagram. That the nine-pointed figure of the Enneagram has entered the mainstream illustrates its strange fate and perhaps the fate of all things of a spiritual nature. Helen Palmer, one of its key popularizers, writes: "[T]he enneagram was arguably the worst-kept secret in spiritual history."[4]

There has been a great deal of speculation about the origin and application of the Enneagram, but its true nature remains elusive. What part of it is fact and what part fiction or allegory? The Enneagram may go back as far as the Babylonian civilization, but even contemporary efforts to unveil this ancient symbol remain inconclusive. British scientist and mathematician John G. Bennett recounts: "I concluded . . . that this symbol and the ideas for which it stands, originated with the Sarmān society about 2500 years ago and was revised when the power of the Arabic numerical system was developed in Samarkand in the fifteenth century."[5]

The Enneagram has migrated from the fringes of pop psychology or New Age fads to the mainstream. Its new status has been described as follows: "[T]he Enneagram is being popularized in America and used as a new psychological parlor game—'Want to find your Self? Take a number!'—which is very unfortunate."[6] Given its wide-ranging utility, we can see how the Enneagram is "a sleeping giant, awakened in our times."[7]

This study has been undertaken to rectify some widespread misconceptions. Although the Enneagram remains largely enigmatic, this does not prevent us from making useful observations regarding its meaning and use. First, interpreting the Enneagram through a secular lens that ignores sacred tradition cannot fully fathom its significance because this approach fails to see how it can be used as an adjunct to spiritual growth. Furthermore, reductionist attempts to comprehend the nine-pointed symbol through modern psychology also fall short for the same reason. Laleh Bakhtiar's ground-breaking research—which adopted a spiritual hermeneutic (*ta'wīl*)—has given a renewed focus on the traditional origins of the Enneagram within Islamic spirituality.[8] Thus, through a discernment that is properly metaphysical, the Enneagram may be viewed as a universal symbol that can support wayfarers on any path.

This study argues that only when the Enneagram is situated within humanity's spiritual traditions can we comprehend its meaning and utility as a sacred psychology. It is through a "science of the soul" grounded in metaphysics and cosmology that the nine-pointed symbol becomes operative for the purposes of healing and transformation. From the perspective of sacred symbolism, the Enneagram reveals a spiritually "operative" aspect. René Guénon writes, "[T]he whole of nature amounts to no more than a symbol of the transcendent realities"[9] and "the entire natural order can in its turn be a symbol of the divine order."[10] Everything in the manifest world of the five senses pertains to symbolism. Frithjof Schuon observes that "to exist is to be a symbol"[11] and that we need sacred tradition to supply us with "wisdom . . . to perceive the symbolism of things."[12] Our identity as human beings, and the meaning of our lives, are inseparable from symbolism and its metaphysical significance. In learning again to discern the "signs of God" (Latin: *vestigia Dei*; Arabic: *āyāt Allāh*), we can reintegrate the science of the cosmos with a "science of the soul," a unitive knowledge that had never been sundered prior to the modern age.

Awakening to our True Self is to recognize our fundamental identity in the Divine. In contrast, modern psychology is confused as to what comprises our fundamental personhood. The relative reality of the ego is perceived to be who we really are, but the true dimension of our being has transcendent origins. For this reason, Clement of Alexandria said: "[I]f one knows himself, he will know God."[13] Phenomenology, as contextualized in the epistemological pluralism of the sacred, serves as the interpretive framework in understanding the Enneagram. Henry Corbin suggests we study phenomenon by "tracing a thing back to its source, to its archetype."[14] Corbin translated "phenomenology" as *kashf al-maḥjūb* or "unveiling of the hidden" as informed by the spiritual hermeneutics (*al-ta'wīl*) of Sufism.[15] In the same way, a phenomenological approach is taken here as a method of studying the essence (or essential meaning) of phenomena in a way that is not limited to a given religious or spiritual form.

Without knowing its origins, one cannot account for the Enneagram, and its meaning will thus be left to the winds of conjecture and subjective whim. Oscar Ichazo explains: "[T]hey have created an unending labyrinth over the descriptions and suppositions of each type with no other foundation, except for the wit of their own opinion. No wonder the contradictions mount, and there is no way they will ever get into any agreement."[16] What fundamentally distinguishes a sacred from a modern perspective—not only with respect to the Enneagram—is the attribution of a divine origin to all traditional symbols, rather than to a source based solely on human contrivance. It is a traditional understanding of symbols alone that provides the integrated knowledge necessary to situate them beyond a purely psychological point of view. The world's sapiential traditions unanimously recognize that "symbolism is of 'non-human' origin."[17]

We must therefore distinguish two ways of comprehending the Enneagram: a traditional interpretation rooted in divine revelation, and a modern approach that is divorced from the sacred. The Enneagram has profound implications for our understanding of the human psyche and its spiritual potential, yet this is not to suggest that its purpose is merely "psychological." Such an outlook can only lead to psychologism—the reduction of reality exclusively to the domain of the psyche, which is to fundamentally confuse ontological levels. In the same way that the human microcosm is a tripartite entity—consisting of Spirit, soul, and body—so too the cosmos at large, according to traditional cosmologies, has a three-fold structure, comprising realms that are spiritual, psychic, and corporeal. Titus Burckhardt observes that "man in his integral nature . . . is not only a physical datum but, at one and the same time, body, soul, and spirit."[18]

An exclusive use of the Enneagram for the sole purpose of understanding the empirical personality, at the expense of what transcends it, is to radically curb its metaphysical scope and integrative potential. Such reductionism not only undermines a profound understanding of this nine-pointed symbol, but of everything pertaining to the transcendent order. What is needed is a deeper discernment that differentiates New Age parodies from authentic expressions of the sacred. This degeneration is what Guénon refers to as "a parody of spirituality, imitating it so to speak in an inverse sense, so as to appear to be its very opposite."[19]

Gurdjieff and the Introduction of the Enneagram to the Modern West

The Enneagram became largely known in Western circles through contacts made with the Naqshbandī Sufi order, founded by Bahā ad-Dīn Naqshband Bukharī. G. I. Gurdjieff learned about the Enneagram through his association with the Naqshbandī Shaykh 'Abd Allāh al-Fā'iz ad-Dāghestanī.[20] As noted by James Moore, a highly regarded biographer of Gurdjieff: "[T]he enneagram is *sui generis* and G. I. Gurdjieff, if not its author, is at least its first modern proponent."[21] He initially presented the nine-pointed figure to his Russian pupils in Moscow and Petrograd (Saint Petersburg) in 1916. The first book to discuss the Enneagram did not appear until 1949, when Russian mathematician and esotericist P. D. Ouspensky, a distinguished disciple of Gurdjieff, released his work *In Search of the Miraculous: Fragments of an Unknown Teaching*. Ouspensky, who first met Gurdjieff in Moscow in 1915, recounts Gurdjieff's words on the significance of the nine-pointed figure:

> Speaking in general it must be understood that the enneagram is a *universal symbol*. All knowledge can be included in the enneagram and with the help of the enneagram it can be interpreted. And in this connection only what a man is able to put into the enneagram does he actually *know*, that is, understand. What he cannot put into the enneagram makes books and libraries entirely unnecessary. *Everything* can be included and read in the enneagram.[22]

The following underscores the centrality of the Enneagram to Gurdjieff's "Fourth Way":

> The most important use which Gurdjieff made of number symbolism is the figure of the enneagram, which he said contained and symbolized his whole System. His enneagram consists of a circle with the circumference divided into nine points which are joined to give a triangle and an irregular six-sided figure. Gurdjieff said that the triangle represented the presence of higher forces and that the six-sided figure stood for man. He also claimed that the enneagram was exclusive to his teaching. "This symbol cannot be met with anywhere in the study of 'occultism,' either in books or in oral transmission," Ouspensky reports him as saying. "It was given such significance by those who knew, that they considered it necessary to keep the knowledge of it secret." Because of the emphasis which Gurdjieff placed on this diagram, his followers have sought high and low for the symbol in occult literature. Bennett claims that it cannot be found anywhere; and if disciples of Gurdjieff have in fact discovered the figure, they have kept it very quiet.[23]

Oscar Ichazo, Claudio Naranjo, and the Enneagram of Personality Types

Although Gurdjieff made the Enneagram known in the contemporary West, it was Oscar Ichazo, the Bolivian-born founder of the Arica Institute (*arica* is a Quechua word meaning "open door")—established in New York in 1971—who is recognized as having developed the system of the psychological typology of the Enneagram.[24] Because of his codification of personality types, some refer to Ichazo as the "father of the Enneagram." Prior to establishing the Arica Institute, Ichazo founded the Instituto de Gnoseologia in 1968, where he gave instruction in the *enneagon* (Ichazo's term for the Enneagram), and taught protoanalysis (his word for the knowledge obtained from analysis of human personality through the Enneagram) in 1969 at the Instituto de Psicología Aplicada in Santiago, under the sponsorship of the Chilean Psychological Association.[25]

Ichazo discusses the process of how he became a spiritual teacher, and what lay behind his instruction of others, as follows: "I went into a divine coma for seven days. When I came out of it I knew that I should teach; it was impossible that all my good luck should be only for myself. But it took me two years to act on this decision. Then I went to Santiago and started lecturing in the Institute for Applied Psychology."[26]

Due to the many unknown details of Ichazo's life, one could draw interesting parallels between Ichazo and the Peruvian-born Carlos Castañeda, who was himself a New Age icon, even dubbed the "godfather of the New Age."[27] Ichazo's notoriety spread throughout the counterculture movement following his involvement in the 1973 cult classic film *The Holy Mountain*, directed by Alejandro Jodorowsky, a Chilean-French filmmaker. All the actors, including Jodorowsky himself, are reported to have participated in Arica training before shooting the movie.

Jodorowsky invited Ichazo, whom he recognized as a spiritual master, to come to Mexico where the film was going to be made so as to receive his instruction. Ichazo accepted this invitation by initiating Jodorowsky into his first psychedelic experience through LSD, which was instrumental in the development of his perspective. Jodorowsky was also introduced to the sensory deprivation tank by a pupil of Ichazo's in November 1973, along with a host of other representatives of the counterculture and Human Potential movements.[28] It has been suggested that the use of psychedelic drugs was a common feature of the Arica training, and Ichazo himself was exposed to these early on in his life when he had contact with indigenous peoples in South America who used mind-altering substances for ceremonial purposes. He said: "I had contact with Indians and they introduced me to psychedelic drugs and shamanism while I was in my early teens."[29]

Claudio Naranjo, a Chilean psychiatrist regarded as a pioneer of the Human Potential Movement, was another innovator of the Enneagram of personality types.[30] Naranjo sought to further his understanding of both psychology and spirituality, having visited the Esalen Institute in Big Sur, a leading center for the Human Potential Movement. While at the institute, he encountered Fritz Perls, the German-born psychiatrist and psychotherapist known as the "father of Gestalt therapy," which influenced his theoretical outlook. Perls's impact upon the Human Potential Movement and modern psychology itself may be summarized best in his own words: "Freud took the first step . . . I accomplished the next step after Freud in the history of psychiatry."[31] Naranjo apprenticed under Perls and was considered one of his three successors at the Esalen Institute.

Naranjo initially learned about Ichazo in 1969, through various Chilean students who shared their experiences with him about Ichazo. Initially, Naranjo corresponded with Ichazo but then decided to visit Chile to meet him in person. Following his return to California, Naranjo spread the word to others about Ichazo and the Arica training. Soon thereafter, Naranjo, along with John Lilly—a physician and psychoanalyst—were part of the first group of fifty-four Americans (many of whom were from the Esalen Institute and Big Sur) who traveled to Arica in Chile during July 1970 to study with Ichazo.

What precisely took place between Ichazo and Naranjo is unknown and will likely remain a mystery. However, we do know that Naranjo decided to leave Ichazo after several months of training with him and returned to the United States. By Ichazo's own account, he had no dispute with Naranjo. Upon returning to the San Francisco Bay Area, Naranjo began to teach the Enneagram of personality types (or ego fixations) that he had learned from Ichazo. Consequently, Ichazo's influence on the Esalen Institute was legendary, and many of the early disciples who studied under him in Chile returned to propagate the Arica training at Esalen, which was reflected in *The Esalen Catalog* (Winter 1972).[32]

In September 1971, Naranjo established the SAT ("Seekers After Truth," a phrase borrowed from Gurdjieff) Institute in Berkeley in order to amalgamate his knowledge of modern psychological theories from the *Diagnostic and Statistical Manual of Mental Disorders* (*DSM*) and to correlate them with the Enneagram and an assortment of other spiritual methods (for example, Buddhist meditation, Gurdjieffian attention exercises, and Sufi stories). It is important to note the SAT Institute predated, by a decade, the flurry of interest in the Enneagram as it relates to personality types within the New Age movement and mainstream psychology.

Claudio Naranjo, the "Breach of Secrecy," and the Enneagram for Mass Consumption

Several figures who had trained directly with Naranjo (or received instruction from those who studied under him) are responsible for the mass dissemination of the Enneagram as most people understand it today. Some of those exposed to Naranjo's early teaching on the Enneagram have gone on to become teachers themselves, such as Robert Ochs, Helen Palmer, Kathy Riordan Speeth, A. H. Almaas (also known as A. Hameed Ali), Sandra Maitri, Peter O'Hanrahan, and Reza Leah Landman. Naranjo's commitment to complete secrecy regarding the teachings of the Enneagram of personality types was something that he felt very strongly about, as we can see from his admission:

> Let me just say that the teaching I did in 1971/73 was restricted to two groups. One met during one and a half years, and the other for only six months, I believe. Both were subject to a considerable reserve. This reserve was made explicit through a signed commitment that nobody was to teach this, which I felt necessary because I was under a commitment of reserve with Ichazo at the time.[33]

Robert Ochs, a Jesuit priest who attended the SAT Institute, took extensive notes during Naranjo's teaching on the Enneagram and taught it to other Jesuits at Loyola University in Chicago, making these teachings available to the Jesuit community at large. Those who had access to these teachings were Patrick H. O'Leary, Paul Robb, and Jerome Wagner. Before long, these notes on the Enneagram teaching had spread throughout North America.

Considering the popularity of the Enneagram within Catholic circles, it is significant to consider this interest in light of the events following the Second Vatican Council (1962–1965), which have fundamentally compromised Western Christianity, as these desacralizing forces also inevitably spread to Protestant denominations leading to the pervasive secularism that is found throughout the West today.[34] The faithful have been cautioned: "For the time will come when they will not endure sound doctrine; but after their own lusts shall they heap to themselves teachers, having itching ears; And they shall turn away their ears from the truth, and shall be turned unto fables" (2 Timothy 4:3–4). While efforts have been made to claim Christian origins for the Enneagram,[35] some have become very critical of its application to personality types and lament its ties to the New Age movement within Christian circles.[36]

September 1984 saw the first book published on the nine-pointed symbol: *The Enneagram: A Journey of Self Discovery* by Maria Beesing, Robert J. Nogosek, and Patrick H. O'Leary. While in Jesuit seminary in Toronto, Don Richard Riso encountered the early Enneagram material made available by Ochs in 1974, through one of Ochs's initial students by the name of Tad Dunne. In 1987, Riso published his first book on the Enneagram, *Personality Types*. Helen Palmer, psychic and self-proclaimed "queen of the Enneagram,"[37] published her first book on the subject in 1988.

According to Palmer, she did not breach Naranjo's pact of secrecy, as this was not a requirement within the SAT group in which she participated: "I did attend nine sessions of a public enneagram class with no 'secrecy' requirement."[38] Palmer has no qualms over having aided the popularization of the Enneagram, as long as it has been in the service of consciousness expansion: "I'm happy to be a popularizer, as long as what I've accomplished stands for popularization of the fact that type plays a part in accessing higher consciousness."[39] Shortly after Palmer's book hit the marketplace, Naranjo published his *Ennea-Type Structures: Self-Analysis for the Seeker* in 1990. From this juncture on, interest in the Enneagram has spread like wildfire. Naranjo laments the fact that his early teachings on the Enneagram were released and that his students did not honor his request for secrecy:

> I want to only say parenthetically that I was not happy with the fact that the commitment to secrecy was not kept, that the enneagram came to the streets a little prematurely. I felt critical of people taking

> initiative in writing about information that had not been originated by them, and who were acquainted with only a fragment of a traditional body of knowledge that is considerably more complex.[40]

Ichazo makes a thought-provoking and no less sobering assessment of the explosion surrounding the Enneagram of personality types on the global marketplace: "The types that have become popular are 'mind games,' with rather no foundation whatsoever."[41] Gurdjieff makes a cautionary remark concerning the popularization of the Enneagram, and of its limitations when devoid of the esoteric knowledge that is necessary to access its inner dimensions: "The knowledge of the enneagram has for a very long time been preserved in secret and if it now is, so to speak, made available to all, it is only in an incomplete and theoretical form of which nobody could make any practical use without instruction from a man who knows."[42]

Oscar Ichazo, Claudio Naranjo, and the Fourth Way teaching

It is important to note the connection between Ichazo and Naranjo, in relation to the teachings of Gurdjieff, as both were very familiar with the latter's Fourth Way system. Ichazo confirmed that he came in contact with the ideas of Gurdjieff in the early 1950s through Ouspensky's book, *In Search of the Miraculous*. An early exponent of both Gurdjieff's teaching and the Enneagram to the Spanish-speaking world was Rodney Collin, a British disciple of Ouspensky's. Rodney and his wife immigrated to Tlalpan on the outskirts of Mexico City in 1948, accompanied by a number of Ouspensky's followers and, in 1952, he published *The Theory of Celestial Influence* (*El Desarrollo de la Luz*).

Although it is suggested that Ichazo appropriated the teachings of the Enneagram from Gurdjieff without giving him due credit, Ichazo denies such claims. The Gurdjieff Foundation of California has stated the following about Ichazo and his institute: "The Bolivian founder of Arica expounds his system, a popular psychological training which draws—usually without acknowledgment—on several of the Gurdjieff ideas, especially the symbol of the enneagram (called here the 'enneagon')."[43] Palmer links Ichazo's "new tradition" with New Age thought because of his theoretical departure: "He [Ichazo] has moved the Enneagram from a Sufi context, from a Christian esoteric context, from the Gurdjieff context, and couched his 'new discovery' in an eclectic, new age spiritual growth context."[44] Others suggest that "the enneagram is a teaching device used by the Sufi school and developed by Ichazo."[45]

While Ichazo admitted to having read all Gurdjieff's books (and those of his disciples), he responded to the accusation of having borrowed from his work, and not giving him due credit, as follows: "In synthesis, though I have gone through all of Gurdjieff's material, as well as all the important literature about him, I have never come to an 'idea' that I can call the unique apport [a term indicating the paranormal transference or appearance of an object] of Mr. Gurdjieff."[46] Here Ichazo appears to adopt Gurdjieff's concepts without giving him credit for them.

Ichazo alludes to the syncretic underpinnings of the Arica Institute: "Arica is not as much my invention as it is a product of our times. The knowledge I have contributed to the school came to me from many sources I encountered in my peculiar quest."[47] Although Ichazo has studied the numerous religious and mystical systems of the world and warns against *syncretism* (the indiscriminate mixing of heterogeneous ideas in an attempt to fashion a synthesis), it is not clear if Ichazo had a traditional spiritual affiliation or whether he offered a more nuanced version of the piecemeal approaches found in the New Age movement:

> You cannot make a cocktail of traditions. That is totally false. I was not doing that at all. At any time I would teach one distinct path, just that path without including any elements of a different path. Or more clearly, suppose: If we were doing some Sufi exercise we would be working that Sufi exercise exclusively, not mixing Sufism with yoga, or yoga with Zen, etc. We worked them as separate units and never really mixed them. We were studying these traditions, just as you can study geography, mathematics, or history, and yet you don't confuse them: each is a different science with a different method.[48]

Ichazo went as far as to say: "Since I am proposing a completely new method, I am certainly correct when I say 'I am the root of a new tradition.'"[49] According to Naranjo, "[H]e [Ichazo] asserts that he received the enneagram of character-fixations by direct inspiration."[50] What was the source of this "inspiration?" Ichazo claims to have received his instruction from the Metatron of the Kabbalah—the prince of the archangels—and from the mysterious "Green Qu'Tub" (likely referring to Khaḍir, meaning "the Green One" in the Islamic tradition), and claims that both entities are in theory available to all Aricans. Indeed, a person "may receive instructions from the higher entities such as Metatron, the prince of the archangels, who has given instructions to Ichazo."[51] Furthermore, "The interior master of all Aricans is called the Green Qu'Tub. He may or may not make himself known to individual Aricans, depending on the stage of development of the student."[52] Ichazo emphasizes that the Enneagram came to him as in a vision, and its development into a system is his alone:

> They came to me, 108 in all, as in a vision, showing their internal relations with complete clarity, in 1954 in Santiago, Chile. Not only am I the holder of the beginning of this tradition, but also, as can be absolutely and concretely proven, the 108 enneagons and the entire system in all its terms have been developed by me, only and exclusively, and I am more than ready to contest it publicly.[53]

Naranjo informs us that he first learned about the Enneagram through the Fourth Way teaching in his early youth: "I was first acquainted with the enneagram by reading Ouspensky's *In Search of the Miraculous* when I was in my late teens."[54] It was this early exposure to the Fourth Way teaching of Gurdjieff that led Naranjo to study with Ichazo. "[M]y main interest in learning from Oscar Ichazo was a conviction that he was a link to the Sarmouni—the school behind Gurdjieff."[55] Naranjo has stated that Ichazo had, on several occasions, alluded to his affiliation with the Sarmouni or the "School of the Bees"—the same ancient source from which Gurdjieff obtained certain Sufi teachings, which is what drew Naranjo to Ichazo: "As we worked with Oscar [Ichazo], I had no doubt about regarding him as a link with that tradition which had been the main element in Gurdjieff's own background."[56]

Yet Ichazo later appears to have denounced Gurdjieff's influence on the formation of the Arica system, as Naranjo explains: "Originally, Oscar Ichazo claimed that the enneagram was passed on to him orally by the Sarmouni, a Sufi brotherhood. In a recent interview, he said that he had never met a single Sufi who knew about the enneagram."[57] We need to take heed of Moore's intimation regarding Gurdjieff's encounter with the Sarmouni:

"Gurdjieff's provocative claim to have found and entered 'the chief Sarmoung Monastery' is in effect a litmus test, differentiating literal minds from those preferring allegory."[58]

Naranjo initially gave credit to his teacher for the psychological typology of the Enneagram, admitting that it was "Oscar Ichazo, through whom I first became acquainted with the 'enneagrams of personality' during a series of lectures dictated [by Ichazo] at the Instituto de Psicología Aplicada (Santiago) in 1969, under the sponsorship of the Chilean Psychological Association."[59] In 2010, however, he recanted this in two separate interviews, claiming that he did not in fact learn ennea-types from Ichazo. Naranjo stated that he intentionally gave authorship to Ichazo, who was more famous than he, in order to draw people to the Enneagram and thus establish a correlation between the ancient Sufi origins of the Enneagram—purportedly brought to the modern West through Gurdjieff—and Ichazo leading up to him. Palmer gives credit to Ichazo by way of the Fourth Way teachings: "The correct placement of the emotional passions was produced by Oscar Ichazo, and with that deceptively simple arrangement of what Gurdjieff called Chief Feature, the Enneagram code became available to us."[60]

Naranjo stated that under his tutelage, Ichazo spoke minimally about the Enneagram and said nothing about the specific ennea-types he later developed: "He didn't talk about the enneagrams of personality more than two hours during our year with him."[61] Incidentally, Naranjo credits E. J. Gold, who was also influenced by Gurdjieff, for coining the term "ennea-type." Naranjo then tells us that he obtained his theories about the psychological types of the Enneagram through "automatic writing" or "psychography," before verifying them through observation.[62] We must not neglect the fact that Naranjo himself never completed his tutelage with Ichazo before taking on students himself: "Claudio [Naranjo] broke with Oscar [Ichazo] very early on, before completing Oscar's training. Claudio took the enneagram with him, thus starting a tradition within the enneagram community."[63]

Naranjo affirms the significance of his instruction under Ichazo in understanding personality types and the structure of the personality: "To this awakening of a 'clinical eye' I owe everything that I was able to learn about personality types and personality in general from then on, and for the intellectual experience of an increasing coalescence of what information on the subject I acquired."[64] Palmer emphasizes what she considers Ichazo's chief contribution to the Enneagram of personality types: "Most important, Ichazo had placed the types correctly on the nine-pointed star."[65] Naranjo dually credits the impact of Gurdjieff's introduction of the Enneagram: "I could say that the enneagram of the Sarmouni acted as a magnet in my mind to bring together the pieces of psychological lore that, until then, were separate, an organizing catalytic factor causing the relative chaos of the information to come into a more precise pattern."[66] Naranjo was initially going to call his first book on the Enneagram *Character Structure and Psychodynamics in the Light of the Enneagram of the Sarmouni*, in order to illustrate his indebtedness to the Sarmouni in its title; but he later renamed it.[67]

An additionally important influence upon Naranjo's outlook is the influence of the pseudo-Sufi teacher Idries Shah: "I should interpolate here for the sake of context that, as many who were deeply affected by the Gurdjieff heritage, I had been disappointed in the extent to which Gurdjieff's school entailed a living lineage. I had turned in my search towards Sufism and had become part of a group under the guidance of Idries Shah."[68] Although (to our knowledge) Shah only references the Enneagram in one book,[69] he was a key source for the popularization of Sufism in the West that has filtered into modern psychology.[70] However, it has been well demonstrated that Shah's brand of Sufism is highly distorted and does not reflect the authenticity of traditional Islamic spirituality.[71]

Riso insists that the Enneagram of personality types is a contemporary innovation, and the credit needs to go to Ichazo and Naranjo, not to any ancient origins. He has called those within the "enneagram community" to stop *romancing* the Enneagram; however, this appears to be a change from his initial position as reflected in an earlier publication: "I not only have much to learn but also much for which to give thanks, especially to those ancient masters who have handed down to us the profound wisdom of the Enneagram."[72]

Kathleen Riordan Speeth, who was raised in the milieu of Fourth Way teachings (seeing as her parents were disciples of Gurdjieff), firmly asserted that the nine-pointed figure derived from Islamic esoterism: "The central symbol of the Gurdjieff work, the enneagram, is almost certainly of Sufi origin—an indication of the importance of these teachings in the system Gurdjieff developed."[73] Palmer, who also avows that the origins of the Enneagram are to be found in the mystical dimension of Islam, dedicated her first book on the Enneagram to Lord Pentland (Henry John Sinclair), a prominent disciple of Ouspensky and Gurdjieff who became the president of the Gurdjieff Foundation in both New York and California: "The Enneagram is an ancient Sufi teaching."[74] Ichazo nevertheless questions the Sufi origins of the Enneagram: "I know Sufism extensively—I've practiced traditional *zhikr*, prayer, meditation—and I know realized Sufi sheiks. It [the Enneagram] is not part of their theoretical framework. They couldn't care less about the Enneagon."[75] A. H. Almaas, who took part in the early SAT group under Naranjo, presents the connection between Gurdjieff, Ichazo, and Naranjo in a summary fashion that sheds light on contemporary understandings of the Enneagram:

> The nine-pointed symbol of the Enneagram first made a significant appearance in the modern West through the teachings of G. I. Gurdjieff, an Armenian mystic, around the turn of the century. Gurdjieff appears to have learned it from a secret school in the Middle East, a school steeped in a spiritual tradition that is at least two thousand years old. He did not, as far as we know, teach the Enneagram of personality fixation, which is currently the most widely known Enneagram. This Enneagram, which has become popular in recent years, came mostly from Claudio Naranjo, a Chilean psychiatrist and teacher, who learned it from Oscar Ichazo, a South American spiritual teacher. It is not clear which parts of this Enneagram teaching originated with Ichazo and which were added to or elaborated upon by Naranjo in the context of his extensive knowledge of depth psychology. Naranjo, from whom we learned the body of knowledge associated with the Enneagram, related it to the Middle Eastern school with which Gurdjieff was associated, but clearly stated that he received the basic knowledge of the Enneagram from Oscar Ichazo.[76]

We will defer to Naranjo's assessment of the current state of the "enneagram community" that he was instrumental in launching: "I see the movement as pervaded by a combination of greed and arrogance, and by a great disrespect toward the sources of the knowledge."[77] Naranjo again: "I will finish by saying that I have been ambivalent about the enneagram movement that I have unwittingly fathered . . . looking in retrospect, we may say what Oscar [Ichazo] used to say concerning the excitement of the enneagram movement (and this was one of his most favorite slogans): 'the devil doesn't know for whom he works.'"[78]

Origins of the Enneagram and Islamic Spirituality

Although the Enneagram is known to have several different origins, a primary source can be found within the esoteric tradition of Islam. Yet this does not detract from the universal dimension of this symbol as it applies to all revealed religions and their "science of the soul." As previously indicated, a significant encounter—that reveals the traditional genesis of the Enneagram—took place between Gurdjieff and Shaykh 'Abd Allāh al-Fā'iz ad-Dāghestanī, who was raised and trained by his maternal uncle, Shaykh Sharafuddīn ad-Dāghestanī of the Naqshbandī Sufi order. It was this meeting, along with several key Sufi works, that not only provide a richer context for the Enneagram—or the "face of God" (*wajh Allāh*) as it is known in Sufism—but unveils its esoteric depth as well. Bennett also made the acquaintance of Shaykh 'Abd Allāh.[79] I cite the following account of this encounter at length to show that the *wajh Allāh* is clearly a spiritual symbol connected to a major divine revelation.

As soon as they met, Shaykh 'Abd Allāh said, "You are interested in the knowledge of the Nine Points. We can speak on it in the morning after the dawn prayer [*fajr*]. Now you eat something and rest." At the time of the dawn prayer, Shaykh 'Abd Allāh called Gurdjieff to come and pray with him. As soon as the prayer finished, the shaykh began to recite *Surah YaSin* from the Holy Qur'ān. As he finished reading, Gurdjieff approached him and asked if he could speak of what he had just experienced. Gurdjieff said:

> As soon as you finished the prayer and began to recite, I saw you come to me and take my hand. We were transported to a beautiful rose garden. You told me that this garden is your garden and these roses are your disciples, each with his own color and perfume. You directed me to one particular red rose and said, "That one is yours. Go smell it." As I did, I saw the rose open and I disappeared within it and became the rose. I entered its roots, and they led me to your presence. I found myself entering into your heart and becoming a part of you. Through your spiritual power I was able to ascend to the knowledge of the power of the Nine Points. Then a voice, addressing me as Abd an-Nur, said, "This light and knowledge have been granted to you from the Divine Presence of God to bring peace to your heart. However, you must not use the power of this knowledge." The voice bid me farewell

> with the salutation of peace and the vision ended as you were finishing the recitation from the Quran.

Shaykh 'Abd Allāh replied:

> *Surah YaSin* was called "the Heart of the Quran" by the Holy Prophet and the knowledge of these Nine Points was opened to you through it. The vision was by the blessings of the verse, "*Peace! A World (of salutation) from a Lord Most Merciful*" (36:58). Each of the Nine Points is represented by one of nine saints who are at the highest level in the Divine Presence. They are the keys to untold powers within the human being, but there is no permission to use these keys. This is a secret that, in general, will not be opened until the Last Days when the Mahdi appears and Jesus returns."[80]

Others have traced the Enneagram to the influence of the Kabbalistic *sefirot* through Medieval Christian philosopher Ramón Lull and the German Jesuit scholar Athanasius Kircher, who published *Arithmologia* in 1665—containing the Enneagram on the frontispiece of the volume—who was reported to have influenced Gurdjieff's ideas on the nine-pointed symbol.[81] Gurdjieff is also recorded as having said that another one of its origins is in "esoteric Christianity."[82] Ichazo alludes to the ancient sources of the Enneagram as follows:

> The enneagon figure, which the Gurdjieffians affirm that I took from their Master, is in fact one of the forms known as "seals," which were produced by the Pythagorean school (500 BC), and the Platonic mathematicians (300 BC) who studied the internal relation of numbers with geometrical forms, giving to each number, not only their characteristics, but their internal interrelations.[83]

Although the Enneagram contains a sacred psychology, it is essentially a method of spiritual transformation. However, contemporary Enneagram proponents typically overlook or misunderstand this aspect because they invariably confuse the domain of the psyche with that of the spiritual. To reduce the Enneagram solely to a system of psychology, or a codification of personality types, serves to distort our understanding of this sacred symbol by undermining its ontological and cosmological foundations.[84]

The human psyche is subordinate to what is higher than itself (i.e. the Spirit). This principle has been, for the most part, rejected by modernity, which has cut itself off from transcendence thanks to the secularizing tenets of the Enlightenment project. The main danger to which personality type theory all too easily lends itself is psychologism—the reduction of the Spirit to merely psychological states. This aberration largely defines the contemporary "spiritual" scene, especially New Age thought, yet this malady also afflicts modern psychology as a whole.

Psychologizing the Enneagram

The prevalence of this reductionism reflects a profane mentality that continues to dominate the present day. In particular it shows how traditional symbols, such as the Enneagram, can be usurped by a materialist psychology. The question now arises as to why it is important to unearth one's particular ennea-type. Palmer presents two reasons for this which, in themselves, are helpful in conducting our everyday life: "The reason for discovering your own type is so you can build a working relationship with yourself"[85] and "[t]he second reason to study your type is so you can understand other people as they are to themselves, rather than as you see them from your own point of view."[86] This exclusive focus on "typology" or "fixation" is a recent phenomenon, and bears no resemblance to the Enneagram's traditional use.

The problem with a desacralized interpretation of Enneagram personality types is that it lends itself to a static view of people by falsely identifying the ego with a person's true identity. This error is testimony to a psychologism that obscures the existence of a higher order:

> The Enneagram authors have made the grave mistake of making this theory into a typology of nine "personality types" as tools for ego aggrandizement, instead of a method of ego-reduction and final transcendence of the lower ego that, in fact, is like a sickness that has to be cured and transformed, in order to become completely developed human beings in a state of self-liberation.[87]

The key to understanding this erosion of humanity's spiritual traditions can be found in the following statement by American psychologist Robert E. Ornstein, disciple and main representative of Idries Shah: "As the esoteric disciplines of other cultures become accessible to the [modern] West, they emerge as psychologies."[88] Ichazo also frames the Arica system in an analogous fashion so as to appeal to a modern mindset: "Protoanalysis follows the same path as the real ancient spirituality, and it is a modern presentation . . . of all human potentialities in order to become actualized."[89] Palmer also echoes this process: "The [Enneagram of personality types] system was being developed as an esoteric psychological tool."[90] It is apt to recall that an early teacher of Tibetan Buddhism in the West, Chögyam Trungpa, predicted this tendency in religion, stating in 1975: "Buddhism will come to the West as a psychology."[91]

While Sufi psychology, just like its Buddhist equivalent, has increased in popularity, both have suffered attempts to extract them from their traditional contexts. With Sufism, this has led to a distortion of its central message, which cannot be cut off from Islam as a whole, since all Sufi orders are linked through an unbroken "chain" (*silsilah*) stretching back to the Prophet himself. In Buddhism, some of the most advanced teachings and practices are often offered to Western aspirants with little or no commitment, or without any assessment of their qualifications.

This development has been rather nuanced, so the utmost vigilance is required to thwart a burgeoning reductionism at the heart of mainstream psychology. Ornstein writes: "My intention is not to 'reduce' totally the phenomena of the esoteric disciplines to psychological terms, but simply to begin the process of considering these aspects of the traditions which fall within the realm of a modern psychological analysis."[92] And what do we say about that which does not lend itself to verification through the five senses? The Spirit lies outside the empirical order. Does this mean that spiritual traditions that do not readily conform to the prejudices of modern psychology are likely to be ignored? There are many unfortunate implications to this trend which affect how we understand the intermediary realm of the human psyche and what lies beyond it.

While psychology today—as an autonomous science separate from religion and philosophy—began with the emergence of modernism, it is erroneous to suppose that traditional religions did not possess their own integral psychologies, even if they did not explicitly use that term. Ouspensky indicated that "it is necessary to realize that psychology except in modern times has never existed under its own name."[93] In the premodern world, the human psyche was always viewed through the lens of metaphysics, in stark contrast to the materialist tenor of modern science, which no longer recognizes the human "soul," having replaced it with the more scientifically acceptable term "mind."

"Psychology is sometimes called a new science. This is quite wrong. Psychology is, perhaps, the *oldest science*, and, unfortunately, in its most essential features a *forgotten science*."[94] The notion that modern psychology offers something "new" or "superior" to the sacred psychology of traditional peoples is related to a deficient grasp of what it means to be fully human, which is a direct consequence of authentic spirituality having become, in large measure, eclipsed in the contemporary world. Ouspensky continues:

> [P]ractically never in history has psychology stood at so *low a level* as at the present time. It has lost all touch with its *origin* and its *meaning* so that now it is even difficult to define the term "psychology": that is, to say what psychology is and what it studies. And this is so in spite of the fact that never in history have there been so many psychological theories and so many psychological writings.[95]

This exemplifies the thought process that mirrors what has been termed the "psychological impostor,"[96] a seduction that misunderstands the plenitude of authentic spirituality with its corresponding "science of the soul"—something that is quite evident in the modern enneagram community.

All spiritual traditions teach their own version of the famous inscription found at Delphi—"Know thyself" (*Gnóthi seautón*)—which did not emerge with Sigmund Freud, or modern psychology for that matter, but can be seen as a timeless truth that has been taught since time immemorial in all cultures. Rather than approaching the human psyche through the sole lens of modern science, we would be better off paying close attention to what Richard of Saint Victor had to say: "If the mind would fain ascend to the height of science, let its first and principal study be to know itself."[97] Although each religion possesses a corresponding psychology, its insights can only be fully efficacious when realized within the nurturing and protective environs of an authentic spiritual tradition.

The following passage provides a good example of how a profound spiritual symbol can be flattened to a more restricted psychological level: "The [Enneagram of personality types] teaching can help us to recognize our own type and how to cope with our issues, understand our work associates, lovers, friends, and to appreciate the predisposition that each type has for higher human capacities such as empathy, omniscience, and love."[98]

Just as the human microcosm is tripartite in nature so too is the universe—as macrocosm—mirrored by way of the formless, subtle, and gross planes of existence. We must therefore be cautious when statements are made that emphasize the importance of psychological inquiry over spiritual practice, for it is the latter alone that effects a metaphysical integration of the human psyche, and not vice versa, as we read here: "The way we get to our essential nature is not primarily through spiritual exercises but through psychological work to penetrate parts of the personality that are connected to underlying essential aspects of ourselves. Psychological inquiry leads to spiritual realization. Meditation supports this inquiry and sharpens it, but the psychological work is inseparable from the spiritual practice."[99]

While many contemporary approaches appear to embrace the psychology found at the heart of all spiritualties, they operate on several false assumptions that, when viewed more rigorously, are found to be antagonistic to the very mystical dimensions with which they seek to align themselves. The inner (or esoteric) aspect cannot exist without the outer (or exoteric); to only acknowledge the former is erroneous, and that is precisely what New Age pseudo-spirituality seeks to do—to strip religions of religion itself—so that it can then declare as true whatever conforms to its biases. Hujwīrī explains the complementary facets of the inner (*bāṭin*) and outer (*ẓāhir*) dimensions of the Islamic tradition (in a manner applicable to all religions) as follows: "The exoteric aspect of Truth without the esoteric is hypocrisy, and the esoteric without the exoteric is heresy. So, with regard to the Law, mere formality is defective, while mere spirituality is vain."[100]

Furthermore, to say that the esoteric presents itself as a spectrum of "psychologies" is very misleading, because the spiritual domain surpasses that of psychology. This is to commit the same error made by Carl Jung, when he reduced spirituality in this way—which is the very hallmark of psychologism.[101] So-called "traditional esoteric psychologies"[102] are none other than New Age aberrations. They are neither "traditional" nor "esoteric," but rather attempts to "spiritualize" a profane psychology in a way that undermines bona fide spiritual paths.

The fact that many in the humanistic and transpersonal psychology movement attribute a valid form of Sufism to a deeply problematic figure such as Idries Shah speaks volumes in itself. While Shah popularized Sufism in the West, he is not considered a valid source of traditional Sufism by respected authorities.[103] We can see here how Shah cannibalizes authentic Sufi insights to cater to a secular mindset. No matter how subtle his approach may appear at first, the end result is always the same: undermining the integrity of a genuine tradition in order to satisfy New Age inclinations.

The Horizontal and Vertical Dimensions of Personality

Modern psychology is also confused as to what comprises our real personality. Because of the difficulty it has in discerning levels of reality—and its corresponding modes of knowing—it tends to view the conditioned personality or empirical ego as a fixed form of ultimate identity, rather than acknowledging the true source of our personality in the Divine. This disorientation can be summarized as follows: confusion of the Absolute with the relative, the vertical with the horizontal, the Spirit with the psychic, the Intellect with reason, the Self with ego, and personality with individuality. The sacred psychology informed by the spiritual traditions of humanity recognizes two forms of human identity—one relative and one Absolute—without ever blurring this distinction.

Most (if not all) approaches to contemporary understandings of the Enneagram fail to delineate the distinction between personality and Essence (*dhāt*). In singling out only the relative dimension of personality, its transcendent archetype is ignored. In addressing solely the Absolute dimension of Essence, the relative aspect of an individual essence is neglected. Although this might appear as semantic nitpicking, the precise meaning of these terms as understood in their traditional context is of the utmost importance. Modern psychology is largely confined to the relative order of reality, as its understanding of identity is entirely confined to the psychic realm: "[I] dentity comes about through the projection of an unconscious association by analogy with the object."[104] By contrast, we recall the following, which speaks to the fullness of human identity: "'Inwardly' every religion is the doctrine of the one Self and its earthly manifestation, as also the way leading to the abolition of the false self, or the way of the mysterious reintegration of our 'personality' in the celestial Prototype."[105]

There cannot be an effective *Diagnostic and Statistical Manual of Mental Disorders* (*DSM*) without taking the relative and absolute criteria of human identity into consideration. That is why the *DSM*—now in its fifth edition (published by the American Psychiatric Association)—remains a caricature of itself. The same could be said for the *International Statistical Classification of Diseases and Related Health Problems* (*ICD*) published by the World Health Organization. The psychological interpretation of the Enneagram, like the *DSM*, is a categorical classification that divides personality characteristics into types consisting of defining features. As what is higher than the human psyche can alone ensure integral individuality, it may not be surprising that the *DSM* concerns itself with human pathology alone, which is apparent in the following definition: "*Personality traits* are enduring patterns of perceiving, relating to, and thinking about the environment and oneself that are exhibited in a wide range of social and personal contexts. Only when personality traits are inflexible and maladaptive and cause significant functional impairment or subjective distress do they constitute personality disorders."[106]

Analogously, the Enneagram has come to occupy a function similar to the Myers-Briggs Type Indicator (MBTI) created by Katharine Cook Briggs and her daughter, Isabel Briggs Myers. Carl Jung was the key catalyst in the promotion of MBTI, as Katharine Cook Briggs came across Jung's book *Psychological Types* in 1923, when it was first published in English. She subsequently commenced a correspondence with Jung and met him personally during his visit to the United States. Those who use the MBTI forget that Jung's contribution to psychology, while appearing to be more inclusive than his onetime master Sigmund Freud, with whom he parted ways, took the reductionistic trajectory of Freud to new heights by psychologizing religion itself.

Zero as the Supreme Identity

Throughout diverse cultures and epochs, traditional peoples have held to two presiding ideas: that of Center and Origin. The first connects everything to a sacred presence at the heart of reality—where Spirit touches the earth—and the second brings all things back to their divine origin: the timeless moment when the numinous was perceived as being nearer and all-pervasive. According to the *Tao Te Ching*: "All things come into being, and . . . thereby . . . return."[107] By truly apprehending this Center and Origin, a "science of the soul" can be found whereby "[e]verything in the behavior of ancient and traditional peoples can be explained, directly or indirectly, by reference to these two ideas."[108]

When situated in the Absolute, personality in its full plenitude is a theophany. Attributing a particular "ennea-type" to someone is to focus on their conditioned personality, which is not the same as our true identity. Regardless of how we are characterized on the nine-pointed Enneagram, none of the points on its circumference represent who we are in essence. This is the center point of the Enneagram—or "the Zero"—that is both transcendent and immanent. "[T]he number zero . . . in the numerical domain, is an image of ultimate, highest, pure Reality, of the completely undeterminable Divine."[109] What is most important is that it radiates out to the periphery, making each of the nine points what they are. The purpose of the Enneagram is to become—from a strictly human point of view—a metaphysical cipher, which occurs when the empirical ego dissolves into the Supreme Identity, known as our True Self.

The Zero point of the Enneagram circle is an abode of light, unity, and oneness. The circumference is the realm of darkness, multiplicity, and nescience. The wayfarer on the path must make their way from the periphery to the sacred center. Again, we must not forget that "the ego is error: it is a principle of illusion."[110] It is only through a spiritual practice, grounded in a divinely revealed tradition, that the Enneagram can be liberated from the throes of psychological reductionism. The higher includes the lower, and this is why only that which transcends the human psyche can situate the latter in its rightful place.

This Zero can therefore be seen as encompassing both Being and Non-Being. Rūmī affirms: "Return from existence to nonexistence! You are seeking the Lord and you belong to Him!"[111] As anyone can move through any of the points of the Enneagram numerous times in any given moment, to fixate on one's "ennea-type" is problematic for it reduces a sacred psychology to a one-dimensional level devoid of transcendence. Indeed, Gurdjieff himself cautioned against becoming fixed in a single personality type: "A motionless enneagram is a dead symbol; the living symbol is in motion."[112]

To return to the heart of the Enneagram is to reclaim our innermost identity, our sacred center. Plotinus explains a center "is an independent unity; everything within the circle has its term at the centre; and to the centre the radii bring each their own. Within our nature is such a centre by which we grasp and are linked and held; and those of us are firmly in the Supreme whose being is concentrated There."[113] Thus, it is through a metaphysical discernment that we may understand the insightful words of the French monk, theologian, and poet Alan of Lille regarding ultimate reality, which "is an intelligible sphere whose center is everywhere and whose circumference is nowhere."[114]

The following is taken from a conversation between Bakhtiar and a revered representative of the Naqshbandī Sufi order: "One day Shaykh Hisham said that he would tell me a secret about the Sufi Enneagram: The zero point in the center symbolizes the egoless person."[115] This insight reveals that the traditional Enneagram works on a transpersonal level and is not confined to the cul-de-sac of the empirical ego.

For this reason, we require a traditional vision of ultimate reality that is fully integrated, not the pseudo-metaphysics of modernity that we find in Jung: "'Metaphysical' has for us the psychological connotation 'unconscious.'"[116] This is a perspective informed by *gnosis*, considered as a transcendent knowledge of the deeper implications of Zero: "[P]rimordial unity is nothing other than Zero affirmed"[117] or "Non-Being is metaphysical Zero."[118] It is our annihilation and subsistence in the Divine, which is the "Zero" identified with our prototypical existence, known as the "Universal Man" (Arabic: *al-Insān al-Kāmil*; Hebrew: *Adam Kadmon*; Chinese: *Chün-Jēn*.) This realization not only identifies us with our sacred center, but integrates all states of being, including its horizontal and vertical dimensions. In other words, a properly human quest seeks to restore our primordial nature (*fiṭrah*), the "image of God" (*imago Dei*), Buddha-nature (*Buddha-dhātu*) or the Self (*Ātmā*)—that is, our true identity *in divinis*. This ontological correspondence is also to be found in Taoism: "Reveal thy simple self, / Embrace thy original nature."[119]

The Zero at the center of the Enneagram reconciles all polarities: "At the central point, all oppositions inherent in more external points of view are transcended; all oppositions have disappeared and are resolved in a perfect equilibrium."[120] This is why none of the personality types located on the nine-pointed symbol possess any enduring reality; neither can they awaken us to our true identity. It is only through abiding in the sacred Center—the Zero of the Enneagram—that we can find true rest, in which our spiritual travails finally come to an end.

The Enneagram and Spiritual Practice

A way of overcoming our lower impulses has been known to traditional peoples since time immemorial: namely, spiritual combat against the ego and a life sanctified by prayer and remembrance of the Divine. Ultimately, we are faced with a real conflict that is waged in the human heart and symbolized in the battlefield of terrestrial existence. For example, the Buddha himself confirms the following in the *Dhammapada*: "If a man should conquer in battle a thousand and a thousand more, and another man should conquer himself, his would be the greater victory, because the greatest of victories is the victory over oneself"[121] (8:103–106). In Christianity, this notion is conveyed by Saint Paul in his famous verse: "For we wrestle not against flesh and blood, but against principalities, against powers, against the rulers of darkness of this world, against spiritual wickedness in high places" (Ephesians 6:12). Furthermore, the Prophet Muhammad refers to both a "lesser holy war" (*al-jihād al-asghar*)—which seeks to protect the lovers of God through social or military efforts—and a second "greater holy war" (*al-jihād al-akbar*), considered as the highest form of spiritual warfare—one that takes place in ourselves. To adopt the Enneagram in a traditional context requires moral goodness (*muruwwa*), which naturally leads to a spiritual chivalry (Arabic: *futuwwa*; Persian: *jawānmardī*) that battles our pernicious identification with the false self. The following illustrates the mystical dimension of this combat in successfully traversing a spiritual path:

> During the return march to Medina after the victories of Mecca and Hunayn the Prophet said to some of his Companions: "We have returned from the Lesser Holy War to the Greater Holy War." And when one of them asked: "What is the Greater Holy War, O Messenger of God?" he answered: "The war against the soul." The soul of fallen man is divided against itself. Of its lowest aspect the Koran says: *Verily the soul commandeth unto evil*. The better part of it, that is the conscience, is named *the ever-upbraiding soul*; and it is this which

> wages the Greater Holy War, with the help of the Spirit, against the lower soul.[122]

The notion of spiritual warfare has also been used in the Shamanic or primordial religion of the First Peoples. Medicine man and Sun Dance chief Thomas Yellowtail of the Crow Tribe explained that:

> The sun dancer and the Sun Dance itself will bless all of the tribe and all creation through the inner, spiritual warfare. . . . The warrior fights an enemy who is on the outside; the sun dancer wages a war on an enemy within himself. Each of us must fight a continuing battle to keep to the spiritual values that represent our traditional heritage. If we fail to be continually alert in our prayers and our attitudes and to use good sense in all that we do, then we will fail in our interior war. In olden days, this interior warfare had the support of the whole tribe, and our life itself helped to guide us in our personal struggle. Nowadays, we must follow the Sun Dance way all the more carefully, because it contains the key to our sacred warfare.[123]

The conflict between human beings and the world is, in reality, a spiritual battle between the higher and lower nature of a person; our animality is drawn to the seductive world of sensory forms, whereas our theomorphic nature gravitates towards the Divine. The chief weapon in this combat is to "[p]ray without ceasing" (1 Thessalonians 5:17).

Accordingly, to understand the Enneagram or any other sacred psychology is to engage in spiritual practice. In particular, the universal method of invoking a Divine Name—which is capable of being practiced by all—is an especially effective antidote to the malaise of modernity. The Sufi master Shaykh ad-Darqāwī writes:

> Listen to what I am about to say to you and do not forget it, do not take it lightly or let it go unheeded. In the course of the past fifty-five years or so, I have said to many a brother: every single man has any number of needs, but in reality all men need only one thing, which is truly to practice the remembrance of God; if they have acquired that, they will not want for anything, whether they possess it or do not possess it. . . . Without fail, without fail, be constant in your remembrance

> of your Lord, as He ordained, and cling to your religion with all your strength; God will open the eyes of your intelligence and enlighten your inmost conscience.[124]

A peculiar fate has befallen all things sacred, in that they are often victims of Western consumption, and this is no less the case with the Enneagram. The nine-pointed symbol has been usurped to the point where it has become disfigured, and its contemporary uses no longer resemble its original purpose. As elusive as the Enneagram is, its proponents for the most part have stopped asking the fundamental question as to its origins; yet without knowing this, the Enneagram will forever remain veiled in mystery.

At the heart of the modern psyche lies a pervasive hunger that has been exacerbated by the spiritual vacuum created by a desacralized world. Richard Leviton laments the fate of all things of a higher order in the present day: "What was formerly hard-won esoteric knowledge is now available in mass-market paperbacks. The metaphysical world has been turned inside out and dumped into the fertile American marketplace. Mystical truths now have a price tag as if they were consumer products."[125]

With the loss of a sense of the sacred, our spiritual vision has become fragmented and disfigured. Having lost our ability to see the theophany of nature, we can no longer discern the "signs of God" (Latin: *vestigia Dei*; Arabic: *āyāt Allāh*) within the cosmos and in ourselves. We are interested here in the connection between a science of the cosmos (as informed by divine manifestation) and a science of the soul. Thus, the distinction between a science that is empirical from one that is sacred is that the former "seeks to derive principles from phenomena, the other seeks to see phenomena in the light of their metaphysical principles."[126] These signs are of a supra-individual or archetypal order; they transcend the human psyche but, at the same time, completely encompass it. As Saint Paul says: "For the invisible things of Him from the creation of the world are clearly seen, being understood by the things that are made, even His eternal power and Godhead" (Romans 1:20).

By returning to the spiritual roots of the Enneagram or the "face of God" (*wajh Allāh*)—which lie beyond the codification of personality types and the confines of what is merely psychological—we will have access to a sacred psychology that can heal our many existential maladies. The root of this crisis can be attributed to a confusion of levels, along with their corresponding modes of knowing, which simply cannot be grasped by a profane apprehension of the nine-pointed symbol. The modern Enneagram of personality types utterly fails to discern the transcendent nature of our personality as rooted in the Divine. When properly understood, the Enneagram presents itself as a universal symbol for contemporary seekers and mental health professionals, as they now have another tool with which to discover a rich "science of the soul"—available in every authentic spiritual tradition—that can lead to enduring inner well-being and transformation. Thus, the nine-pointed symbol is invaluable to those who seek answers to the most compelling of all human questions: "Who am I?" In the words of Rūmī: "Make a journey from self to Self. . . . Purify yourself from the attributes of self, so that you may see your own pure essence!"[127]

Chapter 5

Entheogens and Sacred Psychology

"For the Kaliyuga . . . only a drastic medicine . . . is effective."[1]
—Rāmakrishna

"For the same medicine is not suited for all, even when the illness is the same."[2]
—Saint Peter of Damaskos

"When your body is sick, it is sometimes necessary to take a strong drug. But when you are healthy, you don't take drugs. So this special medicine [entheogens] cures some sickness."[3]
—Seung Sahn

"[P]art of a remedy contains poison. . . . In all things there is a poison, and there is nothing without a poison. It depends only upon the dose whether a poison is poison or not."[4]
—Paracelsus

Central to any discussion of entheogens are the circumstances in which we currently find ourselves. We live in a time of extremes, many of which are visible all around us. Things not only appear to be out of place, but they are altogether abysmally wrong. To understand the psychedelic renaissance, we must consider the spiritual crisis that afflicts the modern world. As Albert Hofmann said, "The assertion that there is no truth, that everything is relative . . . is a demoralizing worldview that has had devastating consequences."[5] Without acknowledging the momentous developments that led to this eclipse of the sacred—principally scientism and materialism—it is difficult to make sense of the explosion of interest in psychedelics, and their perceived capacity to heal the maladies of our time.

The Western world is experiencing a resurgence of interest in the therapeutic potential of sacred plants with a long history of ceremonial use by the First Peoples. There is a search for more holistic forms of mental health treatment that go beyond the mere management of symptoms and, instead, pursue authentic healing and wholeness. The vacuum created by the loss of religion in the world today is often unrecognized in this discussion because of the hegemonic dominance of modern science and its empirical epistemology that rules out alternative modes of knowing reality. The wide-ranging consequence of this outlook is paramount, as Antonin Artaud asserted when he wrote: "That sense of the sacred which European consciousness has lost [is] the root of all our misfortunes."[6] For many, this void has been filled with modern psychology and science. Therefore, the psychedelic renaissance is situated at a critical juncture, in which the mental health treatments of a totalitarian modern science will either continue, or a return to the metaphysical frameworks and methodologies of sacred psychologies will allow for a pluralistic approach to healing.

Bringing the insights of humanity's spiritual traditions to the discipline of psychology will greatly enhance therapeutic outcomes from the use of entheogens. In other words, a study of psychotherapy and the human psyche is proposed according to a perspective that is both metaphysical and transcendent in its assumptions. This is consistent with how a "science of the soul" was understood by the traditional cultures of the world prior to the emergence of modernity. While phenomenology—as informed by the epistemological pluralism of the sacred—is conducive to such an undertaking, our approach to this philosophical framework will differ from conventional applications.

Some further qualifications are needed here because we must differentiate between several levels when considering the therapeutic use of entheogens in traditional cultures: general healing, religious salvation, and spiritual realization or enlightenment. If the general goal of entheogenic therapy is simply rehabilitation for the average person, this may not require adherence to a religio-spiritual framework for such treatment to be partially effective. With that said, psychedelic-assisted psychotherapy (PAT) offered in a secular context can achieve predictably controllable protocols of treatment in a relatively safe context. So while it may not be necessary to observe the strict requirements of a spiritual tradition when having recourse to such treatment, we will nonetheless present the optimal conditions under which entheogenic therapy is likely to be most efficacious.

While much can be said about entheogens, we need to be clear about the scope of this essay. Its aim is to situate PAT within the ontology and metaphysics at the heart of humanity's spiritual traditions. What it will *not* focus on are the following:

1. The idea that entheogens can produce religious-mystical experiences equivalent to those of the saints and sages of the world's spiritual traditions.[7]
2. The thesis that the nature and origin of all religions derive from entheogenic use.[8]
3. The claim that entheogens encompass the entire gamut of spiritual activity across all sacred traditions that use them in a ritual context, rather than serving as adjuncts in support of genuine religious practices.[9]

If we are going to take the highest ambitions of modern psychology seriously—for, as James Bugental insists, "A truly human psychotherapy must celebrate the uniqueness of humankind and of each human individual"[10]—we need to acknowledge that secular therapies are unable to fulfill such promises, which is why we must turn to the sacred forms of therapy rooted in humanity's spiritual patrimony. Czech-born psychiatrist and entheogenic therapy pioneer Stanislav Grof emphasized that "[p]sychedelic therapy can use the framework of different religions"[11] yet, to date, this has not been realized. It follows that entheogenic therapy must not be situated within the reductionistic and desacralized foundations of modern Western psychology. This has been pointed out for some time, yet it still holds for the plethora of novel therapies that have emerged since these words of caution from Robert Masters and Jean Houston: "[P]sychedelic[s] . . . as an 'adjunct' to old, and in some cases obsolete, therapies will not provide us with equal benefits."[12]

Many have observed that psychedelic therapy, as practiced today, lacks a fully developed theoretical basis.[13] The need for a properly integrated framework has been advocated by numerous authorities: "The fault lies not in the drugs, but in the psychotherapeutic framework in which they are used. The psychedelics are, after all, merely adjuncts to therapy, not a form of therapy per se."[14] As the wounds of our collective psyche become more apparent by the day, there is perhaps nothing more urgent than the need to recover an authentic psychology or "science of the soul" that is rooted in metaphysics, sacred science, and the *spiritual* healing of psychic illness.

In this connection, we need to stress that we are facing a global mental health calamity right now.[15] Statistics demonstrate the alarming rise in the number of people taking psychotropic medications. There is mounting research suggesting that these drugs fail to work as commonly expected—in many cases, they not only create more problems (such as unwanted side effects), but they can also cause chronic and irreversible harm. The fact that more people are being diagnosed and treated does not mean that there has been a decrease in mental health problems; on the contrary, the number of those seeking support has markedly escalated.

To escape the "countercultural" baggage of the term *psychedelic* (a Greek compound coined in 1956 meaning "mind-manifesting,")[16] the word *entheogen* ("accessing the divine within") was proposed in 1979.[17] Prior to the introduction of these terms, a common label was *hallucinogens* ("traveling in the mind") or *psychotomimetic* (also known as *psychotogenic*), which referred to the ability of these substances to mimic symptoms of psychosis, such as the alteration of perception, thoughts, and feelings.

Psychedelics in the Modern World

After nearly five decades of being underground, psychedelics have returned. Before they were banned, psychedelic research was burgeoning in the 1950s and 1960s (given the anticipated therapeutic potential), but these endeavors were hampered globally in the 1970s and 1980s despite purported evidence of enduring benefits. In the wake of the prohibition, we are now experiencing what has been widely hailed as the psychedelic renaissance, which began with the revival of research in the 1990s. Some divide this period into an initial wave of psychedelic research in the West (approximately 1950–1985), followed by a subsequent wave (2000–present). However, by many accounts, while such research was officially curbed, there were always those dedicated to this cause who continued this work in underground communities.

The war on drugs has, in large part, shaped the public's opinion on psychedelics, equating them with illegal activity and criminal behavior. These policies have disproportionately affected people of color and those struggling with mental health difficulties which, in turn, has led to mass incarcerations. This has conferred a tremendous stigma on these sacred medicines in the public mind, which is still difficult to overcome. To be sure, there were abuses of psychedelics that led to their proscription, and to scheduling that precluded clinical research from continuing, yet not everything reported was accurate.

Much was sensationalized in the mainstream media, which was focused on the detrimental effects of psychedelics. An example of this was the cover story published in the March 1966 edition of *Life* magazine entitled "LSD: The Exploding Threat of the Mind Drug That Got Out of Control,"[18] and the December 1965 editorial "LSD—A Dangerous Drug"[19] in *The New England Journal of Medicine*, a respected medical publication that ignored an entire body of research. It is therefore important to be clear about the benefits of entheogens when used under the right conditions, seeing as much fear has been instilled by poor research that has only served to thwart public access to accurate information about this phenomenon. Psychiatrist Sidney Cohen points out:

> It must be explicitly stated that some individuals should never take drugs of this category, and that one's friends are not suitable judges of who are suitable candidates. Furthermore, a secure environment is essential for the protection of the subject who takes LSD for he is vulnerable, hypersuggestible and emotionally liable. In the hands of experts these agents are relatively safe, but they are potential mind-shakers which should not be lightly or frivolously consumed.[20]

The United States government also had a large part to play in the harmful (and unethical) dehumanization of diverse peoples—especially in marginalized communities—caused by psychedelics through the MK-ULTRA and other mind-control programs of the Central Intelligence Agency (CIA), which sought to experiment with behavioral modification techniques by covert means.[21] It cannot be overlooked that the infamous cult leader Charles Manson participated in CIA-funded drug research and used psychedelics to brainwash his followers into murdering people without remorse.[22]

It can hardly escape notice that the "birth of the Psychedelic Age"[23] very much resembles the advent of the introduction of Eastern thought to the West, which figured significantly in the countercultural revolution of the 1960s. It was during this time that there was a great hunger and fascination for all things Eastern. With the weakening of faith in the dominant religions of the West (namely Judaism and Christianity), seekers sought refuge in Eastern philosophy to free themselves of the perceived baggage of the faiths they had abandoned.

The ambiance of the psychedelic movement decades later appears to be the same, albeit with more restraint and sophistication. The focus is now on the psychological health and well-being that psychedelics can offer, as evidenced by clinical trials that confirm their efficacy for use in mental health treatment. There is also recognition of the errors made in the previously widespread and indiscriminate use of these powerful substances that led to their prohibition. In order to avoid similar mistakes again, the movement has established education protocols to help shape the public narrative, to dispel myths and misinformation, and to highlight the benefits of entheogens.

As modern psychology has supplanted the role of religion in the contemporary world, people have been left alone to "find themselves," encouraged to seek relief from their travails without any recourse to the spiritual domain. Yet all valid forms of sacred psychology prior to the modern world had an ontological foundation. During the medieval period, the West shared a largely common metaphysical outlook with many of the world's spiritual traditions; it was only in the period following the Renaissance, the Scientific Revolution, and the European Enlightenment that a desacralized outlook gained ascendancy.[24]

Never before has humanity had access to these sacred medicines without having to participate in a ritual order of reality revealed by sacred tradition. Since their discovery and use in the modern world, these remedies have been employed for the first time outside a committed spiritual path. Traditional peoples have always maintained very strict formal requirements and ethical guidelines for their use. Today, anyone wishing to have the experiences they offer is free to do so with little to no constraints.

Advocacy for the use of psychedelics in isolation from a traditional spiritual context dates back to 1924, when German pharmacologist Louis Lewin documented the therapeutic potential of entheogens in his landmark study *Phantastica*:

> Not only are these [mind-changing] drugs of general interest to mankind as a whole, but they possess a high degree of scientific interest for the medical man, especially the psychologist and alienist [psychiatrist], as well as for the jurist and ethnologist.[25]

Modern psychedelic science could be said to have begun in 1938 when Hofmann synthesized lysergic acid diethylamide (LSD) at Sandoz Laboratories in Basel in Switzerland, or when he discovered the psychoactive properties of LSD when accidentally dosing himself in 1943 and taking his well-documented and life-changing bicycle ride under its influence. However, it was Richard Evans Schultes, an American biologist considered to be the "father of modern ethnobotany," who, in 1938, discovered the botanical identity of *ololiuqui* (*Turbina corymbosa*—formerly known as *Rivea corymbosa*, a species of morning glory), a psychedelic plant considered sacred to the Aztecs.[26] In 1960, Hofmann isolated lysergic acid amide from *ololiuqui* seeds, finding them analogous to LSD.[27] It is worth recalling that the earliest scientific work on psychedelics was conducted in 1897 by the German pharmacologist and chemist Arthur Heffter, who isolated mescaline from peyote (*Lophophora williamsii*).

It is important to clarify that the use of sacred medicines in the traditional world—especially for the First Peoples and their shamanic traditions—has existed for much longer than its modern Western uses. To be sure, entheogens are not new. In this context, we are reminded of the Mazatec native healer María Sabina who introduced the ceremonial use of psilocybin mushrooms to R. Gordon Wasson in June 1955, who then documented his experiences in a landmark *Life* magazine article entitled "Seeking the Magic Mushroom" (1957).[28] A week later, his wife—Russian-American pediatrician and ethnomycologist Valentina Wasson—recounted her participation in this indigenous ritual in a magazine article from *This Week* titled "I Ate the Sacred Mushrooms."[29]

One might wonder why the Wassons published their discoveries in popular magazines such as *Life* and *This Week* rather than in standard scholarly journals. Nevertheless, Wasson and his wife soon acquired a mythical status—although recent details have surfaced that undermine the narrative that has hitherto prevailed.[30] Unknown to Wasson, the funding of his 1956 expedition to Huautla de Jiménez was made by the CIA's MK-ULTRA Subproject 58, of which Sidney Gottlieb was the mastermind.[31] This reveals the CIA's role in launching the psychedelic revolution for its own nefarious covert purposes. With that noted, it was Schultes who first identified *teonanácatl* (Nahuatl for "flesh of the gods")—the sacred mushroom of the Aztecs in the late 1930s.[32]

Wasson inspired American psychologist and counterculture advocate Timothy Leary to follow in his footsteps when he traveled to Cuernavaca in Mexico during August 1960 to try psilocybin mushrooms, which changed the course of his life.[33] Leary recalls, "In four hours by the swimming pool in Cuernavaca I learned more about the mind, the brain, and its structures than I did in the preceding fifteen [years] as a diligent psychologist."[34] It was Wasson who sent specimens of the *Psilocybe mexicana* mushroom to Hofmann who, in 1958, was able to identify two psychoactive compounds for the development of a synthetic version of psilocybin. Beat writer William Burroughs traveled to the Amazon in 1953 to explore *yagé* (ayahuasca), followed by Allen Ginsberg in 1960, resulting in the popular book *The Yage Letters* (1963). Following this surge of interest, other prominent individuals emerged who ignited further interest in shamanic or indigenous entheogenic traditions, such as Carlos Castañeda[35] and Michael J. Harner. All of this attention contributed to the widespread popularization of psychedelics in the modern West, which, in turn, served to launch the 1960s counterculture and New Age movements.[36]

Shadows of the Psychedelic Renaissance

It has been said that the sacred uses of mind-altering substances are the "best kept secret"[37] in the history of humanity, referring to a hidden knowledge about the abiding use of entheogens within diverse spiritual practices worldwide. The psychedelic movement is not monolithic in nature, as it reflects varying perspectives on how entheogens should be used. The problems surrounding present-day psychedelic use are illumined by this telling comment: "[H]ow lucky those of us were who . . . approached LSD before it had either the demoniacal or the paradisiacal vibrations it has now—when it had no echoes of gurus and heroes, doctors or delinquents."[38] Given this attitude, an astute observer has remarked that "[t]he psychedelic movement is antinomian."[39] This is indeed the case, as it radically breaks with sacred tradition by not conforming to its protective wisdom and healing knowledge—preferring to be led, instead, by its own idiosyncratic inclinations.

We need to recall the infamous maxim of the English occultist Aleister Crowley:[40] "Do what thou wilt shall be the whole of the Law."[41] This is an inversion of what we find in Saint Augustine: *Dilige* [*deum*] *et quod vis fac* or "Love [God], and do what thou wilt."[42] Leary, being instrumental in launching the psychedelic revolution, was not only influenced by Crowley but thought of himself as a continuator of his legacy, dubbing himself a "high priest"[43] and writing a book called *Start Your Own Religion* (1967).[44]

The psychedelic renaissance has been marked by the problematic phenomenon known as "spiritual materialism,"[45] which is all too often unnoticed or ignored. Due to the loss of a sense of the sacred in the modern world, people are forced to find new ways to give meaning to their lives. As human beings are created for the Absolute, we cannot but yearn for it (even if unawares), but if this longing is not directed at its proper object, we will only be misled by counterfeit spiritualities such as the New Age movement, which undermines all forms of traditional wisdom. We need to be cautious about embracing a so-called spirituality based on "the religion of no religion"[46] as popularized by Frederic Spiegelberg. Within the psychedelic movement, it has been suggested that entheogens could become "the basis of a new religiosity"[47] that would replace sacred tradition altogether. What this outlook fails to recognize is that it is not enough to simply acknowledge the esoteric dimension underlying all the world's religions—what is required is to live their saving truths according to an authentic revealed tradition.

In light of this spiritual void in many modern people, we find a mentality that desperately seeks experiences and quick cures for all sorts of maladies without submitting to the discipline of a valid religion. We also witness the proliferation of psychedelic cults led by self-professed "guides" with authoritarian personalities, who lack proper initiation or traditional qualifications in taking care of the souls entrusted to them.

We are reminded to approach a spiritual path on terms determined by the Divine, not by us: "We ought to obey God rather than men" (Acts 5:29). As it has been pointed out, we should "enter houses through their proper doors" (Qur'ān 2:189). The inner, mystical dimension of religion is only accessible through its outer, formal dimension. These two aspects are complementary and inseparable from one another, since both are grounded in divine revelation. The spiritual impoverishment created by secular humanism cannot be addressed by the use of psychedelics alone; we need to come under the sway of a sacred tradition before even contemplating the use of entheogens because only conformity to a tried and tested path will ensure the safest and most beneficial outcomes. Likewise, the profane and undisciplined "expansion" of our consciousness alone will not resolve the deep-rooted crisis of modernity.

There is always a practical element to our lives, such that no matter how profound an experience we may have, there is still a need to conduct our everyday lives responsibly by attending to our work and families while navigating our perilous and ephemeral sojourn in this world. No spiritual tradition that uses sacred medicines as adjuncts does so in order to avoid reality. Rather, they are committed to preserving their sacred patrimony in order to unite their communities, and to embody this timeless wisdom in everyday life. The healing methods of First Peoples are deeply rooted in the community, as is apparent in their ritual uses of sacred medicine. While individuals may be focused on their own healing, this is always pursued in the context of the overall well-being of others. It is sacred tradition that restores and sustains wholeness for all its members.

There can be real dangers in using psychedelics. Whether one has either a "good" or "bad" trip, it needs to be remembered that any experience, even a difficult one, can also have positive outcomes that may open a door to an authentic spiritual path. We recall here Shakespeare's great insight: "Sweet are the uses of adversity / Which, like the toad, ugly and venomous, / Wears yet a precious jewel in his head."[48] We also need to be cautious about psychedelic experiences because, even when helpful, they can distract us from pursuing the Divine. Many people have been seduced by these seemingly otherworldly awakenings. For this reason, we should not concentrate on the phenomenal aspect alone, because it remains rooted in a "horizontal" dimension of existence; instead, we need to focus our hearts and minds on the noumenal, which pertains to "vertical" reality.

There is a danger in grasping for more and more psychedelic experiences. As Alan Watts is often quoted as saying: "When you get the message, hang up the phone."[49] We also recall the words of the Taoist sage Zhūangzi who remarked: "The fish trap exists because of the fish; once you've gotten the fish, you can forget the trap."[50] This idea is important, as many seekers who look for psychedelic experiences do not have any formal affiliation with an authentic spiritual tradition. For First Peoples who employ these sacred medicines ceremonially, there is no need for "hanging up the phone" because there is no "attachment" to these realms of consciousness, as entheogens have been fully integrated into their way of life and sacred traditions.

The renowned scholar of comparative religion Huston Smith offers the following perceptive observations of the shortcomings in the psychedelic mentality:

> To argue that there are things in religion that are best kept secret cuts against our democratic grain, yet tested religions do so argue. There are pearls which, cast before swine, will be damaged themselves (by trampling) or damage the swine (should the swine eat them). In the *Bhagavad Gita*, Krishna forbids imparting higher knowledge to those who are not ready for it. . . . Either (as I have said) the subject will be damaged, or the significance of the experience will be missed and the encounter trivialized. Thus either the subject is damaged, or the *dharma* is damaged, usually both. The psychedelic movement pays lip service to these dangers by advising screening and preparing subjects, but on the whole it honors the esoteric/exoteric distinction only perfunctorily.[51]

While we are loath to compare modern-day psychonauts to "swine," there are numerous pitfalls that may confront seekers when they mistake different spiritual "stations"—along the ascent of a mountain so to speak—for the summit itself. This is akin to spurious claims to enlightenment, or to ersatz spiritual realizations, which are all too prevalent in the current zeitgeist. Even within the psychedelic movement, the need to ground oneself in a spiritual practice has been asserted as imperative: "Psychedelic experience, without the accompanying daily practice, may otherwise be frittered away in an excess of narcissism and self-indulgence."[52]

Without submitting ourselves to an authentic guide, while following a proper traditional path, the ego will go down a blind alley of endless self-assertion. There have always been initiatory rites and ethical norms that governed the taking of sacred medicine. These could not be transgressed without harming the psyche, and the experience itself was mediated by means of a collective wisdom inherent to a time-tested sacred path; it was not for the ego to engage in precarious innovations. The psychedelic renaissance does away with all these protections—as do its countercultural heirs—who tend to observe a few more precautionary measures while still adhering to a fundamentally secular paradigm.

Today, many sacred medicines are being threatened with extinction because of ravenous consumerism, commodification, and a reckless extraction of these plants. The growing demand for entheogens in the West has disrupted traditional communities and their ecology; in some cases, these medicines have dwindled in number, making it difficult to access them for traditional ceremonies. The rise of psychedelic tourism has also had a significant impact on this dire situation. These developments are inseparable from modernity's spiritual malaise, along with other consequent crises such as those related to mental health and the environment.[53]

María Sabina and the Appropriation of the Sacred

The question is often asked as to which people have rights to sacred medicine. An obvious response is the indigenous peoples who have used them for millennia. Yet what remains unclear is who else might be justified in making claim to them, and what protocols ought to be observed by those who are not the traditional custodians of these remedies. The notion of "cultural appropriation" is a major hurdle to overcome. Who owns the rights to these plants, seeing as they are not always the property of one people (even if they do happen to be the traditional users)? The loss of the sacred in the modern world and the trauma of secularism that has followed in its wake should provoke a discussion regarding the destruction of cultures.[54] Because of our alienation from our primordial nature (and thus each other), we identify with culture in an absolute manner, not realizing that it enjoys only a relative status; in other words, all people are extrinsically diverse by nature, yet unified as one humanity at a more underlying level.

By contributing to the well-being of First Peoples, who have made entheogenic medicines available to the world, we can learn to fully respect their sacred epistemologies and healing modalities. Approaching diversity requires a profound sense of humility that sees culture as the outgrowth of divine revelation, which, in turn, is inseparable from spiritual tradition.

María Sabina's paternal side of the family was known to possess traditional healing knowledge. Although she came from a line of indigenous healers, she also identified with the Christian tradition and did not see any conflict in embracing both spiritual paths. María Sabina was true to the Mazatec religion while remaining committed to the Christian faith, seeking always to be close to God. The first ceremony (*velada*) she attended where mushrooms were used was when her uncle became sick and required treatment by a healer. Subsequently, María Sabina herself became very ill and it was reported that she could not move. Sacred medicinal mushrooms were then successfully administered to her, during which time María Sabina was told that she too would be able to heal people through her devotion to God. For example, her sister also became sick, and it was predicted that she would die, but María Sabina was able to cure her, and word quickly spread regarding her abilities. Notwithstanding these gifts, she had a very difficult life and suffered greatly.

Without María Sabina, Wasson's contributions to psychedelic research would not have been as influential—both as they are now and prior to the ban on these substances. However, it was because he disrespected their traditional uses that María Sabina later expressed regret for introducing Wasson to psilocybin mushrooms: Prior to his arrival on the scene, "nobody took the mushrooms only to find God. They were always taken for the sick to get well."[55] She remarked:

> Before Wasson, I felt that the *saint children* [mushrooms] elevated me. I don't feel like that anymore. The force has diminished. If Caytano [García] hadn't brought the foreigners . . . the *saint children* would have kept their power. . . . [F]rom the moment the foreigners arrived . . . the *saint children* lost their purity. They lost their force; the foreigners spoiled them. From now on they won't be any good. There's no remedy for it.[56]

This statement is very disheartening and casts a negative light on the modern uses of these substances outside of a traditional context.

It is worth documenting Wasson's response to these reflections. Although appearing apologetic, he did not regret his cultural appropriation, suggesting that this knowledge would have been lost had he not saved it from its inevitable fate. In 1976, Wasson wrote:

> These words make me wince: I, Gordon Wasson, am held responsible for the end of a religious practice in Mesoamerica that goes back far, for . . . millenia [*sic*]. I fear she spoke the truth. . . . At the time of my first velada with María Sabina, in 1955, I had to make a choice: suppress my experience or resolve to present it worthily to the world. There was never a doubt in my mind. The sacred mushrooms and the religious feeling concentrated in them through the Sierras of Southern Mexico had to be made known to the world, and worthily so, at whatever cost to me personally. If I did not do this, "consulting the mushroom" would go on for a few years longer, but its extinction was and is inevitable.[57]

He went so far as to say that what he did was necessary in order that the sacred mushroom rite "could be preserved by us, for posterity."[58] He did not believe that the Mazatec were able to preserve their sacred heritage and felt that only he and his affiliates were qualified to become its proper custodians.

Wasson's lack of remorse for what happened to the Mazatec people and their sacred tradition confirms the rank antinomianism behind the modern psychedelic movement: "I was merely the precursor of the New Day. I arrived in the same decade with the highway, the airplane, the alphabet. The Old Order was in danger of passing with no one to record its passing. The wisdom of the *Sabia*, genuine though it was, has nothing to give to the world of tomorrow."[59] Wasson could not have been more mistaken about traditional wisdom and its relevance for us today. We have much to learn from María Sabina, along with other traditional healers, to whom we ought to be tremendously grateful for our knowledge of these sacred medicines. Wasson's own pernicious appropriation mirrors precisely how many approach the use of sacred plants in the psychedelic renaissance movement.

Divulging the mysteries of sacred mushrooms to the outside world had deleterious consequences, not only to María Sabina but to the Mazatec people and their lands. Commercialization desecrated what was most sacred to them. Wasson claims that if he had not brought the world's attention to these mushrooms, knowledge of them would have been forever lost. However, this was not his decision to make. From the Mazatec perspective, the mushrooms became corrupted, which meant that they had largely lost their spiritual potency.

It is difficult to accept that psilocybin was first introduced into the modern West by Wasson—vice-president of public relations at J. P. Morgan & Company—and Henry Luce, the owner of *Life* magazine; two less likely representatives of the counterculture could hardly be imagined! Upon Wasson's return from Mexico, it is reported that he conducted ad hoc mushroom ceremonies in his Manhattan apartment.

In Search of Integrative Mental Health

The current mental health crisis has cast light on the fact that mainstream therapy does not support a wide group of people in their quest for improved mental health and deeper self-integration. Entheogenic treatments (under the umbrella of PAT) are poised between a conventional Western medical model and secular psychotherapy—these have clear shortcomings, because they cannot honor the fullness of what it means to be human in connection to Spirit, soul, and body. In the same way that modern science has its biases, we need to ensure that psychedelic research and therapy does not also limit itself to this same truncated framework. It must transcend "those fashionable ruts of thinking that we dignify by calling them logic and reason."[60]

Although we see mental health services, including medication management, being made available to more people than ever before, critical cases have not declined as might be expected. If these approaches were as effective as they are widely touted to be, numbers ought to have decreased (or at least plateaued) rather than dramatically spiked as they have done. Furthermore, there are not enough therapists to support this massive upsurge (which is likely the case), but this does not disprove the lack of remedial efficacy in mainstream psychotherapy and psychiatry. Trauma has been identified as key to many mental health diagnoses, so it is unsettling that—after over one hundred years of modern therapies—"there is no established single drug or psychotherapy treatment that gets to the root cause of trauma."[61]

The modern Western "medical model" fails to support mental health treatment that is fully integrated spiritually. This is because it remains plagued by Cartesian bifurcation, which perpetuates the separation of mind and body by neglecting both what transcends and unites them. Another blind spot is its erroneous foundation in behaviorism and psychoanalysis, with all subsequent therapeutic modalities grounded on this desacralized bedrock.[62]

Swiss psychiatrist Ludwig Binswanger made some pointed criticism of the fragmented mentality that undergirds modern Western psychology, observing that the chief culprit was a doctrinal "cancer" inherent in a "subject-object cleavage of the world."[63] A key figure responsible for this pervasive dichotomy in modern science was René Descartes, who advocated a form of mind-body dualism that continues to have an enduring influence on the development of modernity's *Weltanschauung*.

Descartes appeared to have foreseen the future of modern science, including its psychology, seeing as current mental health practices push, for the most part, treatments that are solely confined to empirically validated techniques. The Cartesian divide between *res extensa* (extended entities) and *res cogitans* (thinking entities) makes no allowance for overcoming this partition, thus reducing all human experience to a private, subjective realm bereft of objective reality.

This corrosive dualism lives on in modern science, especially in the fields of psychology and psychiatry, where its persistent influence is deeply embedded in their epistemological frameworks. It is especially to be found in the clinical diagnosis and treatment of mental illness, which severs the psychological (*psyche*) from the biological (*soma*). R. D. Laing acknowledged how widespread this medical model is, calling it the "set of procedures in which all doctors are trained."[64] It thus remains the dominant schema within these disciplines. Its thoroughly reductionist outlook views mental disorders as solely the product of physiological factors ("brain chemistry") and treats them, accordingly, as physical diseases; it generally divorces itself from broader psychological and transpersonal realities, instead becoming wholly fixed on a disease's etiology.[65]

Grof speaks to the wholescale overhaul that is needed in order to break the spell of narrow-minded scientistic beliefs:

> Scientific thinking in contemporary medicine, psychiatry, psychology, and anthropology represents a direct expression of the seventeenth century Newtonian-Cartesian model of the universe. Since all the basic assumptions of this way of viewing reality have been [seriously undermined and discredited], it seems only natural to expect profound changes sooner or later in all the disciplines that are its direct derivatives.[66]

This is not a "gap" in our knowledge about these matters, but rather a hegemonic conceptual dominance within the discipline that has determined how mental health treatment in the West is understood.

In response to concerns with this exceedingly narrow outlook, the biopsychosocial model emerged to encompass more dimensions of human reality, such as the social and cultural, with a view to gaining a fuller understanding of illness and health. It was George L. Engel who popularized this approach after having observed a crisis that he attributed to an "adherence to a model of disease no longer adequate for the scientific tasks and social responsibilities of either medicine or psychiatry."[67] In this attempt to overcome mind-body dualism, he asserted that the following levels all need to be taken into account: "the social, psychological, and biological."[68] The pioneering work of influential psychiatrist Adolf Meyer and of American psychiatrist and neurologist Roy R. Grinker Sr. contributed to the further development of the biopsychosocial model first established by Engel.

With the limitations of the medical model having been recognized, the biopsychosocial standard was soon found to have its own limitations because it could not adequately explain the various factors that determine psychopathology.[69] Even though it was more inclusive than its predecessor, it still fell short in failing to situate the spiritual dimension at the heart of the human condition. Some have advocated for a biopsychosocial model that embraces spirituality and, while this is certainly more satisfactory, its assumptions are still ad hoc and not properly integrated into a "vertical" dimension. What is not acknowledged here is that the spiritual domain transcends (while fully embracing) brain functioning, psychological dispositions, and social influences, among other factors. This corresponds to the tripartite structure of the human being, although Spirit alone can fully bring into balance and harmonize all these aspects of our human nature.

It should be noted that entheogenic therapy is not immune to scientific reductionism when situated on the erroneous foundations of modern Western psychology. Pioneers within psychedelic research have discussed the limitations found in contemporary psychotherapy models:

> Our preoccupation with behavior, because it is measurable, has led us to assume that what can be measured must be valuable and vice versa. . . . An emphasis on the measurable and the reductive has resulted in

> the limitation of interest by psychiatrists and psychologists to aspects of experience that fit in with this concept.[70]

With this observed, these pioneers have not been able to provide a better-integrated model due to the desacralized roots of modern psychotherapy and its mental health treatments. By contrast, the use of entheogenic remedies within long-established spiritual traditions has roots in metaphysics, which does not depend on the scientific method for its insights. Healing and growth, rather than treatment, is something that psychedelic therapy—under the right circumstances—could offer. To achieve more effective forms of treatment, we need to acknowledge "that where there is no therapeutic intent, there is no therapeutic result."[71]

Differentiating Psychic from Spiritual Realities

It is often overlooked that it is the traditional culture *itself*—in which entheogens are used—that supports the efficacy of healing with such medicines. Being born and raised in the ambiance of a sacred cosmology allows for supra-individual influences and time-tested shamanic practices to properly guide the use of entheogens while also affording a certain measure of psycho-spiritual protection. Notwithstanding these advantages, people in such cultures can still become ill, just like anyone else, and thus require intervention that restores wholeness. Once healing has been completed, a person returns to a sacralized life with its rites and ceremonies so as to maintain their human equilibrium; something that we do not find in modern Western psychology.

Whitall N. Perry illustrates why psychic phenomena are so seductive and difficult to discern: "The confusion is between the psychic and spiritual planes of reality, where the unfamiliar, the strange, and the bizarre are mistaken for the transcendent, simply by the fact that they lie outside the ordinary modes of consciousness."[72] This recognition appears to be missing from the standard professional literature, and in any of the discussions related to psychedelic science and the hopes invested in it. René Guénon elaborates on these dangers:

> It is impossible to be too mistrustful of every appeal to the "subconscious" . . . in a sort of "cosmic consciousness" that shuts out all

> "transcendence" and so also shuts out all effective spirituality . . . but what is to be said of someone who flings himself into the ocean and has no aspiration but to drown himself in it? This is very precisely the significance of a so-called "fusion" with a "cosmic consciousness" that is really nothing but the confused and indistinct assemblage of all the psychic influences . . . these influences have absolutely nothing in common with spiritual influences. . . . Those who make this fatal mistake either forget about or are unaware of the distinction between the "upper waters" and the "lower waters"; instead of raising themselves toward the "ocean above," they plunge into the abyss of the "ocean below"; instead of concentrating all their powers so as to direct them toward the formless world, which alone can be called "spiritual," they disperse them in the endlessly changeable and fugitive diversity of the forms of subtle manifestation . . . with no suspicion that they are mistaking for a fullness of "life" something that is in truth the realm of death and of a dissolution without hope of return.[73]

Although not adequately addressed within the psychedelic renaissance, the notion of "consciousness expansion" for its own sake can be spiritually dangerous. Lama Anagarika Govinda writes:

> [T]he mere expansion of a muddled consciousness, in which the faculties of discrimination, mental balance and understanding have not yet been developed, does not constitute an improvement and will not lead to the attainment or the realization of a higher dimension of consciousness, but only to a worse confusion, to an expansion of ignorance and an indiscriminate involvement in irrelevant impressions and emotions.[74]

He goes on to add, "Those who descend into the depth of this universal consciousness, without having found their inner centre, will be swallowed by it or will be swept away to their doom, like a rudderless ship that is lost in the immensity of the ocean."[75] Through traversing a spiritual path, we can learn to clearly recognize these realms. The Tibetan teacher Chögyam Trungpa referred to psychedelic experiences as a "double illusion" or "super samsara"[76] which could, nevertheless, be helpful in better understanding the unillumined dimension of our consciousness.

A traditional healer or shaman can "leave his body and ascend to the sky or descend to the underworld."[77] However, secular approaches cannot access these transcendent realms of consciousness and their corresponding healing modalities. Secular psychotherapy, as offered through conventional forms of mental health treatment, can only discern the lowest aspects of the psyche.

The religion of the First Peoples present us with a sacred symbolism that sustains entheogenic therapy—"the purpose of taking *yagé* is to return to the uterus, to the *fons et origo* of all things, where the individual 'sees' the tribal divinities, the creation of the universe and humanity, the first human couple, the creation of the animals, and the establishment of the social order."[78] According to the First Peoples of Africa who belong to the Bwiti religion (which also uses entheogens): "Joy, joy the ancestors give joyful welcome and hear the news. The troubled life of the born ones is finished. . . . All the misfortunes are shorn away! They leave. . . . Everything clean. . . . All is new. . . . All is bright. . . . I have seen the dead and I do not fear."[79] According to the Hindu tradition, "We have drunk Soma and become immortal; we have attained the light, the gods discovered"[80] (Ṛgveda 8:48:3). Patañjali points out that "the psychic powers may be obtained either by birth, or by means of drugs, or by the power of words, or by the practice of austerities, or by concentration."[81]

When it comes to the study of extraordinary states of consciousness, modern psychology has scant insights to offer.[82] The myopic outlook of the post-Enlightenment is still trapped within the confines of "consensus reality"[83] and struggles to see beyond its truncated foundations; however, "anomalous phenomena"[84] within consciousness studies are gradually calling into question the validity of modern science's premises.

There is a widely cited passage within the psychedelic literature from Andrew Weil: "[T]he desire to alter consciousness periodically is an innate, normal drive analogous to hunger or the sexual drive."[85] Through metaphysics, we can make sense of the compulsion to transcend ordinary consciousness. This is not about attaining exalted states per se, but rather reclaiming who we really are: namely, human beings who are inseparable from the Absolute.

Leary once wrote about the lack of understanding of non-ordinary states of consciousness within present-day mental health treatment: "We were on our own. Western psychological literature had almost no guides, no maps, no texts that even recognized the existence of altered states."[86] Hence, it was declared that "[c]onsciousness eludes any scientific explanation"[87] and that thus far "there is no good theory of consciousness. There is not even agreement about what a theory of consciousness would be like."[88]

Beyond the corporeal and psychic realms, traditional forms of wisdom maintain that human beings are able to occupy multiple states of consciousness. Buddhist writer Marco Pallis explains that "[m]an is but one of an indefinite number of states of the being."[89] William James appears to concur:

> [O]ur normal waking consciousness . . . is but one special type of consciousness, whilst all about it, parted from it by the filmiest of screens, there lie potential forms of consciousness entirely different. We may go through life without suspecting their existence; but apply the requisite stimulus, and at a touch they are there in all their completeness. . . . No account of the universe in its totality can be final which leaves these other forms of consciousness quite disregarded. How to regard them is the question. . . . At any rate, they forbid a premature closing of our accounts with reality.[90]

The sacred psychologies of humanity's diverse cultures provide us with a key for understanding these other states of mind. Due to their limited scope, empirical epistemologies fail to grasp them, as they can only take into account "horizontal" dimensions of reality. Perhaps the closest that modern psychology comes to acknowledging unconventional states of consciousness is through the notion of "unhabitual perception."[91]

Psychotherapists need an adequate metaphysical-spiritual framework in which to situate the myriad phenomena that arise when dealing with psychic forces; however, this possibility cannot be admitted by mainstream psychology, as the discipline has renounced any connection to higher orders of being. It simply will not acknowledge any realities that cannot be quantified within the narrow confines of its reductionist scientific framework.

The Transpersonal Dimension of Healing

Traditional cultures recognize the human body's innate wisdom and capacity to heal, along with the spiritual dimension that supports this transformation. If psychology does not return to its sacred roots, it will fail to see the tripartite division of human beings into Spirit, soul, and body—this is critical to appreciating each person's innate healing modalities.[92] As traditional healers affirm, "There is no sickness without a cause,"[93] yet it is incumbent on therapists to discern the interplay of these dimensions of a person, and to work with them in a wise and skillful manner.

True wholeness flows from the transpersonal order, yet only the outer self requires therapy, as the inner self always remains intrinsically whole. The "science of the soul," as informed by the world's spiritual traditions, is able to support the human psyche in becoming fully integrated into all its modes of knowing and corresponding ways of healing: "The soul's apprehension of the nature of things changes in accordance with its own inner state."[94] In the same way that sages have taught the existence of an inner teacher—"the Guru is always within you"[95]—there is also an inner therapist, along with the required remedy to heal us from within. But this first requires the spiritual guidance of a valid tradition to help prevent us from going astray and becoming lost in our turbid subjectivity.

A true sacred psychology ensures that the assessment, treatment, and healing of a person is informed by a transpersonal dimension—this is confirmed when we discern the intrinsic wisdom reflected in the human body.[96] Therefore, becoming a wayfarer on a spiritual path is indispensable. Paracelsus speaks of the "inner physician" hidden within each person and says that "[e]ach . . . disease bears its own remedy within itself."[97] Rūmī states something similar: "The physician comes to the sick man and questions the inward physician; for within you there is a physician."[98] Saint John Cassian writes: "The Doctor of our souls has also placed the remedy in the hidden regions of the soul."[99] According to 'Alī ibn Abī Ṭālib: "Your cure is within you, but you do not know."[100] Traditional healers and shamans allow the immanent "doctor within"[101] each person to support their healing process.

It is through traditional forms of the "science of the soul"—grounded in metaphysics and cosmology—that we can understand the complexities of the human psyche and avert potential harm. Guénon provides the following example:

> [S]omeone who, hoping to secure his health . . . more effectively, makes use at one and the same time of many different medicines the effects of which neutralize and destroy each other and sometimes even provoke unforeseen reactions harmful to his organism. There

> are things that are efficacious when used separately but that are nonetheless radically incompatible.[102]

Similarly, psychedelic researchers and practitioners have suggested the concept of an "inner healer" or "inner healing intelligence."[103] This certainly makes sense in a sacred context, whereas secular psychotherapy struggles with such notions, given it lacks a framework informed by divine transcendence and immanence. This confusion partly stems from erroneously assuming that "The psyche is a self-regulating system."[104] This misconception captures the very predicament that afflicts modern psychology: namely, seeing the human psyche on a purely profane level, cut off from its "vertical" dimension—which alone can resolve the debilitating impasse that this discipline has brought on itself.

Set and Setting

The "set" (the mindset or expectation that one brings) and "setting" (the environment in which it takes place) of the entheogenic experience are crucial—something that traditional healers always understood. Researchers and mental health professionals are trying to deviate from using spaces that look like generic hospital rooms for the administration of these compounds, which is a step in the right direction towards ideal forms of treatment, but traditional approaches offer much more than just atmosphere. Sacred uses of this medicine presuppose a profound ecological knowledge rooted in metaphysics and spiritual principles that supported a person's connection to all sentient beings in the web of life. No hospital or outpatient clinic can deliver this, even if the treatment were to be offered in a natural ambiance.

A pioneering effort to account for set and setting within psychedelic research is as follows: "Of course, the drug dose does not produce the transcendent experience. It merely acts as a chemical key—it opens the mind, frees the nervous system of its ordinary patterns and structures. The nature of the experience depends almost entirely on set and setting."[105] Elsewhere, this has been described in the following way: "Some of the more important variables are the personality of the individual, his current life situation, the attitude of those in contact with him during the experience, the setting and the reasons why the drug was taken and given."[106] Other "extrapharmacological factors"[107]—such as non-drug variables—include inadequate preparation, negative expectations, poorly facilitated sessions, personalities of both the subject and therapist (including their relationships), along with all the complex factors related to set and setting in the psychedelic therapy session.

Outside of a sacred tradition, we cannot ensure optimal set and setting. Traditional cultures provide a more appropriate environment for a shared experience, in keeping with the spiritual expectations of such an occasion. This is why, even in the most ideal conditions, there will always be something lacking in modern secular approaches to PAT.

Psychedelic research has also noted the importance of aesthetics and the need to adopt the use of entheogens in a "beautiful natural setting."[108] Although considerations of beauty are largely overlooked in the present day, this dimension is essential for the flourishing of human beings and can hardly be thought of as an expendable luxury.

From the metaphysical perspective, every form influences the human psyche. In fact, no form is neutral. This is clearly understood in traditional varieties of entheogenic therapy, yet it needs to be better appreciated by PAT. Beauty offers great sustenance to both our inner and outer lives, and is thus essential to our human flourishing. The loss of a sense of the sacred in the modern world has also led to a degradation in our apprehension of beauty, an affliction that continues to wound the human psyche in incalculable ways.

Music—in the form of song and chanting—has been an integral part of humanity's religious traditions and is employed widely within entheogenic therapy, both in a sacred and secular setting. It has been shown to support long-term positive mental health outcomes. Music can aid in the cultivation of useful emotions, positive mental imagery, and a sense of therapeutic safety. Properly utilized in a sacred context, its therapeutic benefits can be linked to metaphysical roots, insofar as music arises out of a silence that is prior to all sound. While each person responds differently in its presence, they are all nevertheless connected to the sacred when listening or playing music. So, even though PAT certainly makes use of music, its transcendent dimension appears to be altogether ignored.

Outside the proper supports of set and setting, there remain certain dangers to entheogenic therapy. This requires a great sense of responsibility on the part of its practitioners, yet what does this mean in a secular framework? As Cohen writes:

> Neither the person himself nor those around him may be aware that he is a high-risk candidate for [entheogens]. It is, therefore, no slight responsibility to turn another person on. Furthermore, the drug is all too frequently taken without the safeguards of a responsible, skilled, sober person to take care of the[m].[109]

Entheogenic Therapy

Although the therapeutic uses of entheogens were recognized before their prohibition, one of the key features of the psychedelic renaissance is their use for supporting mental health and well-being. Many are enthusiastic at the prospect that entheogens may "serve as a new tool for shortening psychotherapy."[110] Masters and Houston asserted in 1966 that psychedelics "afford the best access yet to the contents and processes of the human mind."[111] While there are always risks, if entheogens are used responsibly and within a proper set and setting, they have tremendous potential to benefit those suffering from mental health difficulties: "If properly used, it could become something like the microscope or the telescope of psychiatry."[112]

The early researchers of psychedelic science never suggested that entheogens were a panacea: "[LSD] does not construct character, educate the emotions or improve intelligence. It is not a spiritual labor-saving device, salvation, instant wisdom, or a short cut to maturity. However, it can be an opportunity to experience oneself and the world in a new way—and to learn from it."[113] However, even with these cautions in mind, we need to be clear about what entheogens are and are not. As has long been pointed out, "Every therapy has contraindications. Psychedelic therapy is no exception."[114] What is missing in mental health practice today is an acknowledgement that proper healing is grounded in a knowledge of reality that is fundamentally metaphysical.

Many within the psychedelic movement refer to Aldous Huxley's use of the hypothesis known as the "reducing valve."[115] Originally conceived by Henri Bergson,[116] it suggests that the brain and nervous system act as a filter that keeps biological survival possible by restricting access to our consciousness. English philosopher Charlie D. Broad describes this process and why it exists:

> Each person is at each moment . . . capable of remembering all that has ever happened to him and of perceiving everything that is happening anywhere in the universe. The function of the brain and nervous system is to protect us from being overwhelmed and confused by this mass of largely useless and irrelevant knowledge, by shutting out most of what we should otherwise perceive or remember at any moment, and leaving only that very small and special selection which is likely to be practically useful.[117]

The notion that entheogens offer a quick and easy shortcut to wholeness is mistaken. People are cautioned that "everyone who pursues the use of psychedelics for personal growth must be prepared for the 'dark night of the soul' experiences."[118] It seems that entheogenic therapy provokes a disturbing confrontation between our nescient egoic self and our True Self, which has fully integrated the human psyche into the Spirit.

Although the full benefit of entheogens can only be gained within their sacred traditions, they have some therapeutic value even when used in conjunction with secular psychotherapy. It has been shown that psychedelics can aid the ego in getting out of its own way in service of its healing: "For the moment that interfering neurotic who, in waking hours, tries to run the show, was blessedly out of the way."[119] Entheogens have reportedly "reduced defensiveness and fear of emotional injury, therapy facilitating more direct expression of feelings and opinions, and enabling people to receive both praise and criticism with more acceptance than usual."[120]

The entheogenic therapist asks the person to reflect on themselves openly and without fear. Psychedelic researcher Myron Stolaroff exhorts the people he worked with as follows: "Look at what you're afraid of, just look at what you're afraid of. All you have to do is just look at it; don't do anything about it, just look at it. Just keep on looking at it and just tell me what you experience when you're looking at it."[121] Another modality of therapy observes that "[t]he psychological problem solving that occurs is . . . most frequently a shift in perspective, a reframing of a belief that may also be healing."[122] There is also potential for repairing family ruptures: "A characteristic of such transcendental experiences is that family relationships, in the nexus of which personality is formed, become present to one with intense vividness."[123]

Huxley, in correspondence with British psychiatrist Humphry Osmond, noted: "People will think they are going mad, when in fact they are beginning, when they take it, to go sane."[124] Entheogens could also be a valuable teacher for understanding psychosis as they allow the therapist to "enter the illness and see with a madman's eyes, hear with his ears, and feel with his skin."[125]

It has often been stressed that a central factor in therapy is the experience rather than the chemical. This is something that Sidney Cohen recognized in an article published in 1965 when he coined the expression "therapy by self-transcendence."[126] It is with a more expansive sense of identity informed by humanity's spiritual traditions that we can understand entheogens:

> The individual's conviction that he is, in essence, an imperishable self rather than a destructible ego, brings about the most profound reorientation at the deeper levels of personality. He perceives illimitable worth in this essential self, and it becomes easier to accept the previously known self as an imperfect reflection of this. The many conflicts which are rooted in lack of self-acceptance are cut off at the source, and the associated neurotic behavior patterns die away.[127]

With an expanded understanding of ourselves, we can be more aware of our dualistic identity that separates us from ourselves, others, and the natural world.

The terms "ego" and "self" are interchangeable as they represent the horizontal order of our personal reality. Sigmund Freud supports this view: "The ego represents what may be called reason and common sense"[128] and, likewise, "there is nothing of which we are more certain than the feeling of our self, of our own ego."[129] At the same time, he observes that "the Ego is not master in its own house."[130] In psychedelic therapy, one often reports the experience of the ego's "dissolution" or "death," yet undergoing such a radical transformation is dangerous outside the protective measures afforded by a sacred tradition. It is the transpersonal order that provides a safe enclosure in which a therapist may safely work.

Entheogens function as an impetus, even as "gnostic catalysts,"[131] to support us in working through our mental health struggles, and to see who we really are beyond our psychological challenges. They are also referred to as a powerful "unspecific amplifier"[132] of mental processes—so that when we experience something difficult, it may feel intensely sad, alarmed, or enraged. Equally, something experienced as pleasant can become associated with intense joy.

One of the therapeutic outcomes of entheogenic therapy is the adoption of a more flexible mindset that is less defensive and reactive. According to a sage from the Chinese tradition: "To set up what you like against what you dislike—That is the disease of the mind."[133] Entheogenic therapy allows for a "passage to the mind's antipodes"[134] and fosters "an exteriorization and magnification of the conflicts intrinsic to human nature."[135] It is in this expansive state that we can navigate difficult thoughts and emotions, so that we may see our lives in light of a greater plenitude. In this way, psychedelics can provide a unique opportunity to exercise a greater range of cognitive flexibility.

Once a person has completed entheogenic therapy, a sense of fear can sometimes arise concerning the loss of what one has learned during the treatment. Within sacred psychology, it is understood that the spiritual gifts that come to us from above cannot be claimed as ours. A large component of any spiritual practice is the requirement to remember what we are continually prone to forget in our earthly sojourn. This is another reason why entheogenic therapy needs to be rooted in sacred soil.

Grof writes, "Probably the single most important element determining the nature of an LSD experience is the feeling of safety and trust on the part of the experient."[136] When understood metaphysically, this notion becomes more complicated. The question of invulnerability cannot be answered merely on a physiological or psychological level. Like all forms of healing, the spiritual dimension needs to be recognized. The mantra "I am here, you are here—you are safe in a therapeutic context" does offer the protections afforded in traditional forms of healing with entheogens, because there are always spiritual forces at play when this process is undertaken properly that cannot be controlled by the "therapeutic context."

Trauma, Entheogens, and the Self

A desacralized world is a formidable impediment to knowing ourselves and the world around us. It is the immanent Spirit within each of us that can guide and heal humanity. This has been acknowledged by some authorities on the subject: "[T]he God within them knows what's wrong with them and provides them with whatever they need which I don't know anything about and *they* don't even know anything about. They don't know what their real needs are. All they know is what their wants are."[137]

Entheogen therapy can help us see through the separating veils imposed by our benighted self. As Cohen explains:

> A new awareness of one's relatedness to others and to the universe is strengthened because the reality of these feelings is totally accepted. One's concept of self is drastically altered. The hopeless, sinful derelict is now an identity with meaning and worth. . . . A break is made between the miserable past and the hopeful future.[138]

When researching trauma, it becomes apparent that "your wound is the darkness of your [spiritual] states"[139] and—while healing ultimately comes from within—its source is transcendent and Divine: "Recognise that . . . [healing of the wound] proceeds from the ray: do not regard it as [proceeding] from your own constitution."[140] Trauma can consume a vast portion of our soul, but it can never completely obscure our integral connection to the Spirit that is our primordial nature. The ability of entheogenic therapy to aid in the clear examination of our anguish is described by William V. Caldwell:

> Much of the problem of psychedelic therapy is the healing of the deepest psychic fissures which drain off so much of our psychic energy. Once a patient has healed one, he feels an immediate, dramatic relief. He does not come in a week later saying he feels generally better; the moment it happens his face relaxes, his whole mind seems suddenly to unfold in ebullient joy. Some of the happiest experiences of therapy come from the resurgence felt when these scars of the mind are healed.[141]

The importance of paying attention to the somatic manifestations of trauma in the body is key to any mental health treatment, especially entheogenic therapy. Grof elaborates on how this can benefit the person undergoing treatment:

> At the time when the effect of the drug is decreasing it is important to engage in verbal exchange with the subject, to get detailed feedback

> on his or her emotional and psychosomatic condition. If at this time he or she is experiencing discomfort, such as depression, anxiety, blocked aggression, feelings of guilt, circular thinking, headaches, nausea, muscular pains, intestinal cramps, or difficulties in breathing, this is the time to suggest active intervention. The possibility of this happening should have been discussed during the preparation period. The first step is to find out exactly what type of experience is involved. . . . It is also important to encourage the subject to scan his or her body for signs of physical pain, tension, or other forms of distress indicating energy blockage. There is, in general, no emotional distress or disturbing and incomplete psychological gestalt that does not show specific somatic manifestations. These concomitant psychosomatic symptoms then become the entry points for . . . intervention.[142]

Given that we observe a high incidence of entheogens not only decreasing symptoms, but in many cases removing them altogether, some important questions remain. When healing has been successful, what happens to a person's identification with a trauma that they have hitherto long lived with—sometimes for an entire lifetime? What happens if this trauma, following its cure, exposes a deep vulnerability that was previously suppressed? These queries have not been adequately tackled. A person may well be "healed," but they might continue to be troubled by the perennial quandary of: "Who am I?" "The self disappears, but no other self appears to occupy the empty space it has left."[143]

So much of a person's time and energy can be expended on an all-consuming trauma that once it subsides with any functional impairments having been restored, they are essentially lost without an abiding sense of self. In traditional healing, this was never a problem, as identity was embedded in the sacred use of entheogens which lent the experience a transcendent purpose. It has been affirmed that entheogens can "lead the self back to its true source"[144]—our true identity prior to our fallen or *saṃsāric* state. In a desacralized cosmos, however, this is not possible; our grasp of who we are is largely forged in a profane ambiance that rejects the possibility of an enduring self beyond the confines of the ego.

The Therapeutic Posture

What is most urgently required right now are fully integrated models informed by sacred psychology that facilitate epistemological pluralism and multidimensional perspectives. In this regard, it has been asserted: "Unless you have an experienced guide . . . it would be extremely reckless"[145] to experiment with entheogens. Given the dominance of secular approaches to mental health, we need to be aware of the great obstacles faced by traditional healers who seek to facilitate entheogenic therapy, which radically differs from the "Western medical model." Austrian anthropologist Gerardo Reichel-Dolmatoff provides us with the following account of the tremendous demands of this calling:

> In order to become a payé [shaman] an individual must have demonstrated since childhood a profound interest in the religious traditions of his culture besides having a good knowledge of myths, genealogies, and invocations. He must know how "to sit on his bench" and reflect; he must practice sexual abstinence, and he must also be a good drinker of chicha, a good dancer and singer, and he must be able to give sound advice to others. He should not be too fond of women, and he must channel his sexual energy toward other goals; however, he should be a family man. The most necessary quality is that he have the capacity to achieve well-defined hallucinations when he takes a concoction, and to be able to interpret them. Also, in the learning of myths and traditions what is involved is not so much a good memory but a capacity for interpreting their symbolism, and of "hearing the echo" of the tales told by tradition.[146]

The above description of a traditional healer's role suggests a discipline that lies well beyond anything that secular mental health practitioners are trained in. From the perspective of modern medical and therapeutic models, the path taken by a traditional shaman in becoming an effective healer must seem altogether unintelligible.

The shortcomings of modern Western education as a suitable PAT have already been identified within the psychedelic movement:

> A medical degree doesn't equip one to pilot a jet plane or to understand the incredible complexities of consciousness. The LSD experience is so novel and so powerful that the more you think you know about the mind, the more astounded and even frightened you'll be when your consciousness starts to flip you out of your mind. A new profession of psychedelic guides will inevitably develop to supervise these experiences. The training for this new profession will aim at producing the patience of a first-grade teacher, the humility and wisdom of a Hindu guru, the loving dedication of a minister-priest, the sensitivity of a poet, and the imagination of a science fiction writer.[147]

To start with, there can be no confidence in a therapist who has not attained a certain level of experience and understanding of the sacred medicines, such as to be thoroughly familiar with the various realms of consciousness, and to know how to help others navigate their perilous waters: "It scarcely needs to be stated that no one can be a proper guide without having experienced psychedelics himself or herself."[148]

The presence of the therapist in all forms of sacred psychology is invariably more important than the words spoken or even the actions taken. From Lao Tzu we hear: "He who knows does not speak. He who speaks does not know."[149] Becoming attuned to this posture requires us to embrace the Taoist attitude of "non-action" (*wu wei*), which is not idleness but the supreme activity because the person is then fully present and detached from all outward commotion wherein there are no oppositions. This awareness makes possible an entirely different reality, as Shunryū Suzuki points out: "In the beginner's mind there are many possibilities; in the expert's mind there are few."[150]

True non-directive forms of therapy make more sense when understood from this traditional perspective. Embracing true silence and equanimity in the "eternal now" is the most effective way to consummate the healing process. The following observation by Seng-ts'an, the Third Patriarch of Zen, is also useful here: "The Great Way is not difficult for those who have no preferences. When love and hate are both absent, everything becomes clear and undisguised."[151]

Although the traditional healer may not appear to be "doing" anything when conducting a healing ritual, their immersion into the spiritual world—while abiding in a posture of ceaseless prayer—provides great protection for the person being treated. We are told that "healers have a metaphysical system available to them and protective supernatural entities . . . beliefs which they share to one degree or another with their clients."[152] What secular psychotherapy cannot provide, by way of real safety and recovery, is something that a traditional shaman alone can offer an ailing patient; namely, "protection from . . . evil."[153]

Now that we have explored the uses of sacred psychology alongside entheogens, how does this differ from modernist approaches? The role of the secular psychedelic-assisted psychotherapist has been described as follows: "The task of the sitters is to give support and protection to the subjects, take care of their various psychological and physiological needs, facilitate the full unfolding of the experience, and deal with various forms of resistance as they occur during the session."[154] What is overlooked here—other than the complete exclusion of spiritual considerations from this therapy—is that treatment from a secular perspective itself implies an unacknowledged metaphysical worldview. With that said, it is not possible to provide true healing without taking into account the triad of Spirit, soul, and body that comprises a complete human being. Treatment on any other basis can only fall short of achieving its objective.

The metaphysical and ontological roots of sacred psychology not only ensure the efficacy of its practice, but also provide protection for both the healer and patient. "While many therapists and physicians in industrialized society suffer a burn-out syndrome," the energies of traditional shamans "are not drained by the onslaught of patients"[155] because their healing strength draws from a wellspring greater than themselves.

Early pioneers within the psychedelic movement found that entheogens permit "you to see more clearly than our perishing mortal eye can see."[156] For this reason, they often referred to the English poet William Blake, who famously spoke of the "cleansed doors of perception."[157] What is often missing from this outlook is that, unless we ourselves have first become pure, our spiritual vision will remain obstructed. As Eckhart says: "However small a thing it is which sticks to the soul, we shall not see God."[158]

The call to go beyond Cartesian bifurcation in psychotherapy or mental health treatment is not as simple as it might appear, seeing as what constitutes a relationship is a much more complex and nuanced question. Furthermore, there are inherent obstacles implicit in the therapeutic relationship that cannot be ignored. It is that the phenomena of "transference" and "countertransference"—comprising a two-way, transactional process—are in fact unavoidable as these are challenges implicit in the horizontal realm of the human psyche that cannot be transcended or integrated without the presence of a vertical dimension. It needs to be emphasized that a true seeing of another person cannot be facilitated through either "transference" or "countertransference" or any horizontal modality for that matter.

Relationship encompasses an indefinite number of realms of consciousness and levels of reality—constituting a sacred unity both within the created order and of what lies beyond it. The Lakota proclaim: *Mitakuye oyasin* or "We are all related" (literally, "All my relatives"); similarly, the Christian tradition tells us: "We are [all] members one of another" (Ephesians 4:25). The Hindu tradition has what is known as *satsang*, or an association with truth or reality, which consists of being in the company of saints and sages; however, it also signifies our ultimate encounter with the Self or the Supreme Identity. This is never truly the human confronting the human, but the Divine encountering the Divine; it only appears as the former from a relative point of view. However, from the aspect of Ultimate Reality or the Absolute there is none other than the Divine Itself. In other words, the pure Subject as the Self realizes the object within itself and its inherent oneness.

It is through the sacred psychology informed by the spiritual traditions that we can access what in Hinduism is referred to as "distinction without difference" (*bheda-bheda*) or Eckhart's expression "fused but not confused." An awareness of what the Hindu tradition refers to as *neti-neti* (not this, not that) or what Eckhart terms "neither this nor that"[159] helps us to dis-identify from the phenomena that arise in our consciousness; yet this does not mean that we become sundered from the psychophysical order, because we are still required to be fully aware of our tripartite nature as Spirit, soul, and body. In other words, we need to be aware of the Highest Divinity, and while being attuned to this reality, be aware of what is arising moment by moment. Through abiding in *neti-neti*—not this, not that—we can remain open to the fullness of reality and be present with another person's experience and healing process.

Ultimate Reality is ineffable, transcending linguistic limitations and the rational mind's definitions and conceptualizations; it is beyond all categorization. The cataphatic way, also known as affirmative theology (*via affirmativa*), concerns what can be articulated about the Divine or God. By contrast, the apophatic approach, also known as negative theology (*via negativa*), pertains to the unknowable nature of the Divine Essence or Godhead. These are both valid ways of approaching spiritual reality.

To overcome these impediments, the discipline of psychology needs to recover the "eye of the heart" (or the transpersonal Intellect).[160] The practice of sacred psychology requires that thought, being, and reality be brought together in a unified mode of knowing: "Knower, Known, and Knowledge are truly one only."[161] Medieval epistemology defined knowledge as "*adaequatio rei et intellectus*—the understanding of the knower must be *adequate* to the thing to be known."[162] Parmenides emphasized something similar: "To be and to know are one and the same."[163] This is to say that, in the premodern world, there were degrees of knowledge—with their corresponding levels of reality—by which one could realize the Supreme Identity. According to this understanding, a distinction is always made between relative orders of reality and the Absolute.

The Meaning of Integration

Entheogenic researchers and practitioners have emphasized the importance of integration but, until recently, little direction has been provided on how to achieve this. A succinct account of what is meant by integration is "a process in which the patient integrates the insights of their experience into their life."[164] Moreover,

> The integrative experience should be described further because it has not been a matter for scientific scrutiny and the semantic difficulties are considerable. There is usually a perceptual component which consists of looking upon beauty and light. Affectually, there is a feeling of great relaxation and hyperphoria. The patients describe an insightfulness into themselves, an awareness of their place in the environment, and a sense of order in life. These are all fused into a very meaningful episode, and it is believed that this can be significantly therapeutic.[165]

Other definitions include references to revisiting and working through what occurs during a therapeutic session: "Different aspects of a process that includes making sense out of the experience, filtering the content, assimilating and accommodating the experience psychologically, and implementing insights into lasting changes."[166] Again, the general idea here is that "[i] ntegration is the process of bringing separate elements together into a whole . . . and anchoring them into our lives."[167] Another way of thinking about the "integrative experience" is "a state wherein the patient accepts himself as he is, and a massive reduction in self-conflict occurs."[168] An attempt to synthesize a number of existing definitions has led to the following:

> Integration is a process in which a person revisits and actively engages in making sense of, working through, translating, and processing the content of their psychedelic experience. Through intentional effort and supportive practices, this process allows one to gradually capture and incorporate the emergent lessons and insights into their lives, thus moving toward greater balance and wholeness, both internally (mind, body, and spirit) and externally (lifestyle, social relations, and the natural world).[169]

As thorough and useful as this definition may sound, its inclusion of the spiritual dimension cannot readily be accommodated within current models of modern Western psychology, seeing as their ontological foundations are bereft of a transcendent perspective that validates sacred forms of therapy and healing. Without access to the spiritual dimension, the full potential inherent in the psychic and corporeal realms will not be fulfilled, thus limiting the mental health treatment possibilities available to us.

The First Peoples use entheogens in a ritual context so as to infuse spiritual norms into the cultural fabric of daily life. A steadfast focus on the sacred radiates through each individual into the collectivity as a whole. In effect, such integration is self-sufficient and does not require anything outside itself in order to render traditional communities complete.

Key to understanding the integration offered by entheogenic therapy are the perspectives of complementariness and the union of polarities. Through a metaphysical lens, we may discern the existence of binaries at one level of our experience; yet, from another angle, we might not perceive them in the same way. The existence of complementarity is not only important to understanding our own mental health challenges, but is also significant in the context of both female and male therapists working together to enhance the healing process: "[G]rowth happens best in the presence of yang and yin"[170] consisting of "two sitters, a male-female therapeutic dyad."[171]

Joseph Epes Brown, renowned scholar of Native American traditions and world religions, outlined the following transformative process which appears to be universal:

> All true spiritual progress involves three stages, which are not successfully experienced and left behind, but rather each in turn is realized and then integrated within the next stage, so that ultimately they become one in the individual who attains the ultimate goal. Different terms may be used for these stages, but essentially they constitute purification, perfection or expansion, and union.[172]

Across the diverse religious traditions of the world, these stages are present in sundry forms: "Despite the many differences of technique and approach in various paths of spiritual realization, there is in every process of realization the three grand stages of purification, expansion, and union. Something in man must die, something must expand, and only then the essence of man is able to achieve that union."[173] If this is the final goal of all spiritual disciplines, then the impure must not be conjoined with the pure. For this reason, a purgative process is necessary.

A prominent teaching in the world's religions is the injunction to "die before you die" (*mūtū qabla an tamūtū* in the words of the Prophet of Islam)—an exhortation to seek a "spiritual death" in this life. As Eckhart made clear, "a truly perfect man should be accustomed to regard himself as dead"[174]; or, as found in the Jewish tradition, one should aspire to the "cessation or annihilation of existence" (*bittul ha-yesh*)[175]—by implication in the ultimate reality. In the First Peoples and shamanic traditions, we hear of "the death and mystical resurrection of the candidate by means of a descent to the underworld and an ascent to the sky."[176]

Hofmann also speaks to this: "The danger exists that what one has experienced cannot be integrated into normal consciousness in a meaningful way."[177] Cohen speaks of the perils inherent to entheogenic use in the absence of an integrated psychotherapy:

> There are hazards. If a person has seen the glory and goodness of life via psychedelics and then backslides, the guilt of failure is added to the hopelessness of his situation. The depression may be deeper than before the treatment. Others who have been touched by the Light may

> develop so unrealistic a view of themselves and the world that they become most difficult to live with. These hazards demonstrate the need for counseling even when the psychedelic technique is employed.[178]

Psychedelics are not like psychotropics—they require preparation, integration, and ongoing inner work. Psychiatric drugs often suppress symptoms, which can sometimes be helpful. While psychedelic therapy can catalyze the therapy and address the underlying cause, symptoms may well become more pronounced before they improve.

When thinking about models of integration, we ought to be mindful of the wise adage: "[B]y their fruits you shall know them" (Matthew 7:16). This is evidenced by someone who knows the psychedelic movement well: "Look at what the whole psychedelic culture has produced, and not produced. Has it brought forth a Buddha or Ramana Maharshi? . . . All I have seen through . . . meeting many of the psychedelic leaders is, at best, openings or illuminations that have led people to an ongoing path."[179]

Our isolated selves rely on the transpersonal to guide them toward wholeness. This is why we need to carefully observe what arises in our consciousness, so that we are not seduced into thinking that everything we encounter therein is true. Recourse to a dimension beyond the ego is essential if we are to discriminate correctly and to properly integrate our shadow side. Many people taking these substances are still dominated by their egos, so what they get exposed to becomes just another profane experience. Even if these are profound in nature, the loss of the sacred in our lives makes us want to repeat such experiences over and over again in a desperate attempt to fill the abyssal void within us.

One of the most important things to keep in mind regarding entheogenic therapy is that "the goal is not altered states but altered traits."[180] Transformative experiences can sometimes bring forth enduring change, but they tend to fade unless stabilized by ongoing spiritual practice. This is why the great saints and sages of humanity, even following their spiritual awakening, always continued to live in accordance with the prescriptions of their faith, never abandoning their traditional practices.

The Dangers (and Potential) of Secular Approaches

At the outset, we stated that the focus of this article would be to situate entheogens in their proper metaphysical context, particularly with regard to mental health treatment. With that said, most forms of entheogenic therapy will likely take place in a secular space, so it is worth making a few observations about this. It has been widely recognized that "no psychedelic substance is a 'magic bullet' that will permanently cure any condition."[181] This is why it is critical to ensure that entheogenic therapy is buttressed by the abundant valuable resources found in all valid spiritual traditions.

It has been noted that "[n]ot infrequently, the more troubled the patient the better the prognosis since impetus to change may be greater."[182] Success was also observed with "unhappy and floundering individuals who had lost the ability to believe in anything or to identify with any concept larger than themselves."[183] In many cases, it has been found that entheogens seem "to do for each person what the person needs."[184]

Clinical studies demonstrate the utility of PAT in supporting those struggling with mental health challenges. Yet it remains unclear as to whether those who do not adhere to a spiritual tradition can benefit—to the same degree—from these sacred medicines as those who do, even under optimal conditions. It is also not known whether the positive gains conferred by entheogenic therapy diminish over time outside a metaphysical context.

Psychiatrist and psychedelic researcher Rick Strassman notes that "spiritual practice will have made us familiar with the skeletons in our closets and will have better equipped us to contend with them if and when they emerge."[185] Beyond the safeguards afforded by sacred tradition, there are no effective means to offset the possible harm caused by secular uses of entheogens. Leary readily admitted that the "cortex . . . washed clean of . . . rituals" may be susceptible to "psychedelic brainwashing."[186]

The cultivation of spiritual virtue is a direct participation in the Divine nature. Therefore, this may prove an indispensable complement to a lasting cure for those suffering mental illness. Many afflicted people who embark on a life of virtue often recover in an inexplicable manner. Yet virtue, on its own, may not always assist someone who has been so deeply traumatized as to prevent them from knowing how to become virtuous in the first place. In such cases, an entheogen may provide a liberating release as a preliminary step toward a more enduring recovery.

Entheogens do appear to harbor a spiritual power that can serve to undermine the stranglehold that materialism and scientism have over many people today. In other words, treatment of this kind may be the antidote to a disenchanted worldview by restoring a "sacramental vision of reality"[187] that recalls to us the "divine source of all existence."[188] Under the right conditions, entheogenic therapy "can bring a sudden liberation from ignorance or illusion, enlarge the spiritual horizon and give new meaning to life."[189] Furthermore, "it may lead to a lessening of alienation, to a rediscovery of the self, to a new set of values, to the finding of new potential for growth and development and to a new beginning."[190] In some cases, entheogens have led people to "a new faith in God."[191]

Owing to the spiritually compromised nature of modern people, psychedelics may be made available to not only heal worldly afflictions, but to bring us closer to our true selves. It is from this metaphysical standpoint that we may justify the need to make available, to all people, powerful medicines for mental health purposes—a use that was hitherto forbidden outside of a sacred environment. The highly anomalous times in which we live today appear to call for a corresponding response that is also irregular and unconventional, but with a view to a greater good that serves to give relief to those who need it most.

Pitfalls of a Chemical Utopia

The modernist mindset is distinguished by a debased notion of permanence, sometimes referred to as the "immanentization of the eschaton"[192] or the "counterfeit of Eternity."[193] From a metaphysical perspective, everything in our transient world comprises causes and conditions that will inevitably exhaust themselves; yet the Real is timeless and cannot perish.

The secular ideologies that sustain the psychedelic movement are undoubtedly powerful and seductive. They should not be dismissed as the opinions of a minority, especially as the world becomes increasingly dystopian. Nevertheless, given the conditions of our flawed and ephemeral existence in *saṃsāra*—this "burning house," as the Buddha described it—there is no possibility of creating an earthly paradise, as much as many are tempted to do so (having given up any notion of a transcendental mode of perfection). Huxley writes:

> If we could sniff or swallow something that would, for five or six hours each day, abolish our solitude as individuals, atone us with our fellows in a glowing exaltation of affection and make life in all its aspects seem not only worth living, but divinely beautiful and significant . . . then, it seems to me, all our problems . . . would be wholly solved and earth would become paradise.[194]

Propaganda and pharmacology were themes also explored by Huxley in his 1936 essay "Writers and Readers," underscoring how mind-control drugs would influence future society.[195] This question is addressed in his utopian manifesto *Island* (1962), where he brings together his final reflections on education, psychology, metaphysics, and the role of entheogens in exploring human potential.[196] In this work, he invented a new mind drug called *moksha*-medicine, "the reality-revealer, the truth-and-beauty pill."[197] It is as if the universal and timeless wisdom of the world's spiritual traditions is distilled into a pharmacological solution. Accordingly, "for a little while, thanks to the *moksha*-medicine, you will know what it's like to be . . . what in fact you always have been."[198]

> But, like everything else . . . it will pass. And when it has passed, what will you do with this experience? What will you do with all the other similar experiences that the *moksha*-medicine will bring you in the years to come? Will you merely enjoy them as you would enjoy an evening at the puppet show, and then go back to business as usual, back to behaving like the silly delinquents you imagine yourselves to be? Or, having glimpsed, will you devote your lives to the business, not at all as usual, of being what you are in fact. . . . And all that the moksha-medicine can do is to give you a succession of beatific glimpses, an hour or two, every now and then, of enlightening and liberating grace.[199]

In his earlier novel *Brave New World* (1932), a medicine known as "soma" is used to control people by making them happy and complacent within a dystopian status quo.

Prior to his death, Hofmann expressed his entheogenic idealism as follows: "It is my wish that a modern Eleusis will emerge, in which seeking humans can learn to have transcendent experiences with sacred substances in a safe setting."[200] Dare we conclude that this utopian wish is being fulfilled through the emergence of PAT? According to Grof, "[P]sychedelic therapy . . . represent[s] a twentieth-century version of a process that has been practiced through millennia in various temple mysteries, rites of passage, secret initiations, and religious meetings of ecstatic sects."[201] Despite this outlook articulated, the psychedelic renaissance could benefit from recalling the cautionary words of its earlier pioneers about the search for a chemical utopia—"a naïve belief that the keys to Utopia have finally been placed into the hands of man."[202]

A chemical utopia is characterized by the coming together of psychedelic research, the nascency of Silicon Valley, the rise of artificial intelligence (AI), and a burgeoning transhumanism.[203] Utopian discourse may give the impression that global tech elites are planning, through such means, to save the world by ending poverty, curing all disease, solving the ecological crisis, and establishing idyllic working conditions—with the ultimate aim of achieving immortality through a grotesque fusion of humanity and technology that promises to liberate us from the constraints of the flesh. Despite this techno-optimism, the contrary appears to be the case in that the fruits of these dystopic measures will not in fact deliver increased material prosperity, comfort, and leisure, but rather unimaginable forms of bondage. It is here that we can discern the true goal of the post-Enlightenment movement, which is none other than to radically redefine human beings as the monstrous creation of a depraved subversion of spirituality—the very antithesis of the Divine image that we really are.[204]

Entheogens and PAT defy all simplistic constructs and cannot fit into a Procrustean bed. To do so only serves to reinforce the pernicious supremacy of the Western medical model and its myopic approaches to mental health. Some might suggest that having recourse to psychedelics in a world that is in such disarray could be seen as *upāya*—or "skillful means," as the Buddhists would say—precisely because they offer some kind of psychological salve for the abnormal conditions spawned by our desacralized environment. Entheogens can be useful if we understand them in the way indicated by the Buddha; namely, as a finger pointing at the moon. They provoke an experience larger than ourselves to support healing and wholeness, but they are not the liberating reality itself. In other words, entheogens can undoubtedly be used to restore a basic level of equilibrium in certain people. While certainly helpful, this is not an end in itself, for what is called for is a further dimension of healing that involves the spirit and its rehabilitation.

Perhaps as a saving mercy in these end times, psychedelic medicine may now prove beneficial—not only to the religiously faithful, but also to secular society at large; in other words, the traditional restraints on the use of these substances may, providentially, be set aside in extremis, so to speak. With that in mind, we recall the following saying (*ḥadīth*) of the Prophet Mohammed: "At the beginning he who omits one-tenth of the law is condemned; but at the end he who accomplishes one-tenth of the law is saved."[205]

Whether the psychedelic experience is comparable to the spiritual realization promised in the world's religions is not really the issue here. What is central is living in accordance with a revealed tradition and doing so with steadfast commitment and sincerity. A wholehearted reliance on what transcends the human condition as a way to secure lasting health and well-being is confirmed across the sapiential traditions: "Man shall not live by bread alone" (Matthew 4:4); this counsel also extends to entheogens.

At its best, entheogenic therapy undertaken with the right set and setting can facilitate an opening to a realm beyond our fleeting world that affords a passing glimpse of Reality. Some might compare this to the vision of English poet and theologian Thomas Traherne:

> You never enjoy the world aright, till the Sea itself floweth in your veins, till you are clothed with the heavens, and crowned with the stars: and perceive yourself to be the sole heir of the whole world, and more than so, because men are in it who are every one sole heirs as well as you.[206]

In this context, we may turn to the following prayer dedicated to the use of sacred medicines: "We humbly ask Our Heavenly Mother the Virgin Mary, help of all who call upon Her, to aid us to know and understand the true qualities of these psychedelics, the full capacities of man's noblest faculties, and according to God's laws, to use them for the benefit of mankind here and in eternity."[207]

At the same time, we must not confuse this "opening" with an end in itself. Huston Smith reminds us that "the human opportunity, the religions tell us, is to transform our flashes of insight into abiding light."[208] As promising as entheogenic therapy appears to be, we need to keep in mind that psychedelics are simply catalysts; they are not enlightenment itself, and certainly far from the panacea they are made out to be. Likewise, we cannot forget that what is safe in one situation may not be so in another, and that serious abuses do occur: "It is true that uninformed or misdirected use of psychedelics can be harmful."[209] If we are serious about entheogenic therapy, we need to set aside all the hype and abandon our belief in quick fixes.

The commodification and commercialization of sacred medicines in our era is of growing concern. The present day presents much suffering that can be alleviated when entheogens are used wisely in a safe context, but they are no substitute for the sacred, for which many in the modern world acutely hunger. Today's mental health crisis makes clear that what we need now are true forms of healing, and that we should avoid the temptation to overmedicalize entheogenic therapy.

We already have at our disposal the vast knowledge and healing modalities of humanity's treasury of traditional wisdom. As Saint Teresa of Ávila affirms: "Clearly, many remedies are necessary to cure us"[210] and as Mou-Tzu, the second-century Buddhist and Taoist philosopher writes: "What accords with principle is to be followed, what heals the sick is good."[211] Likewise, we can apply the straightforward principle: "Whatever helps, I call good medicine."[212] The differences between traditional spiritual uses and those that are secular are far from negligible; they represent antithetical views of reality and ways of life, revealing a profound conflict between the diverse epistemologies grounded in sacred metaphysics and those that are secular, materialist, and reductionist in their outlook.

PAT, in the same way as modern Western psychology, is rendered anomalous when devoid of a metaphysical foundation. For psychology to be considered an authentic discipline, it will have to tend to its self-inflicted wounds in the wake of the Enlightenment project and its secularizing agenda. Attempts to heal the psyche, including by means of entheogenic therapy, can only be thwarted without a true ontology nourished by the wellsprings of spiritual tradition.

PAT may, at times, be able to restore the loss of our sense that "everything that lives is holy."[213] Likewise, as Goethe points out, "What greater in this life can mortal gain / Then that to him God-Nature be revealed."[214] Nevertheless, there is no getting around the need to ground ourselves in one of humanity's time-tested paths to fully benefit from our innate healing potential. Due to an unfettered humanism that has lost its spiritual center, many today are not interested in finding their way back to one of humanity's spiritual traditions. Entheogenic therapy may indeed support a person's discovery of this hidden longing, but some may choose to explore their connection to the sacred through nature, for example, without seeing any necessity to embrace a traditional salvific vehicle. In such cases, the therapist will have to trust that their focus on the healing work is sufficient and that they cannot take it upon themselves to do any more than this. After all, there are mysteries that transcend our conceptualization of reality: "There are more things in heaven and earth . . . , / Than are dreamt of in your philosophy."[215]

Chapter 6

The Nature of True Well-Being

Talk of "self-care" is heard everywhere today. It has become a buzzword that has entered every facet of mainstream society, a secular mantra of the "therapeutic" ethos that has been absorbed into today's dominant culture, where we are continually called to "practice self-care." We are usually not told exactly what this entails but are simply urged to undertake whatever works for us. Indeed, we are told that we can never do this enough.

Self-care is a nebulous term, and rarely is it asked: What is the self that we are trying to look after? Self-care is no longer limited to mindfulness, walks in nature, meditative apps, yoga, or even journaling for that matter. Now anything is pretty much considered self-care: healthy or self-indulgent eating, being alone or socializing, exercising or resting ("me time"), shopping, or simplifying—everything finds a place under this all-encompassing rubric. American psychotherapist Virginia Satir writes:

> All of us in some part of ourselves know that caring for ourselves is an essential part of our lives. It is a cliché to say that even though we know about it, we somehow do not do much about it . . . two reasons why this is so: one is that even if we know it is important, we do not believe it; the second may be even more significant and that is that many of us who believe it may not know how to do it.[1]

It is not difficult to identify certain resemblances to earlier forms of the New Age movement and self-help.[2] The current obsession with self-care appears to be a crafty rebranding of the older term, which seemed to indicate a deficiency. Self-care, by contrast, gives the impression that everything is already fine just the way it is. This stance is evidenced by an inordinate focus on the self, and a complete reliance on its capacity to help realize our human potential, as though this was the true meaning of our existence. Yet, to rely fully on the self is to forget that such potential is "on loan," so to speak, in that it belongs not to us but to the Divine. An essential distinction thus needs to be made between true self-care and its spurious modern replacements.

In the absence of a sacred orientation in people's lives, self-care has become a secular substitute for traditional forms of spiritual practice. Instead of practicing traditional virtues that help us conform to Divine reality, we are taught techniques—both arbitrary and individualistic—to manage our responses to the increasingly chaotic conditions of modern life. This inversion of traditional norms has contributed to the rise of "therapeutic" culture and to human beings in modernity being defined exclusively in "psychological" terms—these are signs, in themselves, of the decline that has brought on the current spiritual crisis in our midst. Huston Smith makes a key point about the challenges of achieving well-being, given the relentless momentum of today's spiritual crisis: "[A] meaningful life is not finally possible in a meaningless world."[3]

No one will dispute that caring for ourselves is essential, but this cannot be done properly unless we focus on the whole self—comprising Spirit, soul, and body—and reconnect with our spiritual dimension. Any attempt to improve ourselves will fall short if we neglect our transcendent needs. Some distinctions must be made between true self-care and self-indulgence, the former being that which supports our well-being, in contrast to simply surrendering to one's desires without regard to consequences.

In light of the escalating mental health crisis today, we see the reduction of human reality to psychological phenomena alone, and an excessive pathologizing that views symptoms as signs of disorder. Yet not every dilemma needs to be diagnosed as a psychological disorder, and not all issues require mental health interventions. With the growing focus on personal strengths as opposed to pathology-driven ones, we can see that self-care options are a way of safeguarding ourselves from the trappings of a world that is preoccupied with illness and has lost its equilibrium.

Without the arising of wisdom, we will readily become confused and thus fail to discern who we really are, because the degradation of our spiritual energy merely serves to feed the egoic self. Secular approaches to self-care (akin to secular psychotherapy) can certainly have benefits such as setting boundaries in interpersonal relationships, being aware of our emotional life, engaging in meaningful activities, and regular exercise, for example. There is nothing wrong with addressing such matters in themselves, yet without knowing what it truly means to be human, everything that is intended for our good on the surface can be spiritually harmful and, therefore, serve to undermine our self-care in the end.

Self-care is often described as the cultivation of compassion for oneself. Sometimes it is also defined as the "process by and through which self-respect, self-worth, and self-liking are developed."[4] Additionally, "Self-Care includes acceptance of oneself as a human being."[5] However, we can only become truly compassionate when we cleave to the Divine through our adherence to spiritual or religious practice, for the true source of love and compassion is the highest reality itself. The secular world tries to convince us that we alone are able to provide for our own self-care; however, without grace nothing is possible, and it is through divine working that grace becomes active. Without a spiritual foundation for our lives, we are apt to confuse immanence with transcendence. We are first called to see that "[m]y kingdom is not of this world" (John 18:36) before we are able to acknowledge "[t]he kingdom of God is within you" (Luke 17:21), "I am the Self . . . seated in the heart of all beings"[6] (Bhagavad Gītā 10:20), or "We are nearer to him than the jugular vein" (Qur'ān 50:16).

A regard for all sentient beings, including ourselves and all the created order, is central to every spiritual tradition. In the Hindu and Buddhist traditions, it is envisaged as *benevolence* or *loving-kindness* (Pāli: *mettā*; Sanskrit: *maitrī*), and within Mahāyāna Buddhism, it is simply called *compassion* (Sanskrit: *karuṇā*). In the Christian tradition, it is said that "God is love" (1 John 4:16) and in Islam, love (Arabic: *'ishq*) is an attribute of the Divine, as Rūmī points out: "Love's creed is separate from all religions: The creed and denomination of lovers is God."[7] Although self-care rightly affirms the need for compassion towards ourselves, the true genesis of that compassion lies solely in the Divine. We often hear today of the need to love ourselves, yet what we really need is to love not our egoic self, but the

Divine within us and all beings, which is the true source of abiding felicity during our brief human sojourn, and beyond.

The growth of a global marketplace of self-care for mass consumption suggests that it is not for the betterment of the human condition, but rather a means of capitalizing on our distress instead of improving our well-being. To be sure, self-care is a big business, comprising a billion-dollar industry that has become a hallmark of corporate wellness programs around the globe. This problematic phenomenon is perhaps better known today by what Tibetan Buddhist teacher Chögyam Trungpa has termed "spiritual materialism." He writes: "The problem is that ego can convert anything to its own use, even spirituality."[8]

This is not to say, of course, that all mental health problems can be reduced to spiritual problems. The American clinical psychologist John Welwood coined the term "spiritual bypassing" to describe a common tendency to adopt spiritual ideas and practices so as to avoid dealing with the "unfinished business" of our lives. He admits that it is "tempting to use spirituality as a way of trying to rise above this shaky ground. In this way, spirituality becomes just another way of rejecting one's experience."[9] It goes without saying that true spirituality has nothing to do with bypassing mental health issues but is rather about encountering oneself fully in one's depths with a view to purifying the human psyche.

Due to the burgeoning mental health epidemic and the inability of its practitioners to manage this crisis effectively, self-care has been proposed as a possible solution, especially as a way for mental health professionals to avoid burnout and compassion fatigue. Given the unprecedented number of suffering individuals, many have been encouraged to take responsibility for themselves, having fallen under the spell of self-care therapies as some kind of panacea. To get to the root of this phenomenon requires dispelling the myths and confusion that plague modern psychology.

Although the self-care movement urges us to engage in healthy socialization, and acknowledges the importance of human connection, it does so on purely individualistic terms, paradoxically leaving us to manage our inner lives in isolation from others, which runs counter to the advice we find among the spiritual traditions of the world. Today, the truth that "No man is an island,"[10] and that all of existence is interconnected, is often ignored. However, the human psyche is an integral part of the web of life and its underlying cosmic order. Given the heightened levels of alienation that we experience today, it is difficult to discern any apparent wholeness. Isolated and disconnected, the human psyche remains fractured, unable to find psychological health and well-being.

Human beings are not altogether self-governing, despite the views of prominent thinkers like Michel Foucault who defined man as being "destined to care for himself."[11] Yet, no amount of self-care or prescribed "me time" will bring us to the realization of who we truly are and what we ultimately need, as these concerns cannot be addressed outside of a sacred context. Otherwise, the person that needs help is none other than the one who is expected to provide this very same care, thus perpetuating a vicious cycle. The transpersonal Self is not in need of care, for it alone can fulfill all our deeper needs. We are thus called to surrender and take refuge exclusively in the Divine, for this is the ultimate source of our well-being and wholeness. As we read in the *Bhagavad Gītā*: "Abandoning all dharmas, come to Me alone for shelter"[12] (18:66).

In the midst all of this, a "culture of narcissism" is starting to emerge, as the prominent American historian and social critic Christopher Lasch observed:

> Plagued by anxiety, depression, vague discontents, a sense of inner emptiness, the "psychological man" of the twentieth century seeks neither individual self-aggrandizement nor spiritual transcendence but peace of mind, under conditions that increasingly militate against it. . . . [I]n the struggle for composure; he [has] . . . hope[s] of achieving the modern equivalent of salvation, "mental health."[13]

There is no escaping the fact that as a civilization, we have lost a sense of the sacred and that dehumanization is rampant in the modern world. Our preoccupation with self-care would not prevail in a society that is rooted in the sacred, and thus, spiritually healthy. It needs to be asked: How is self-care possible in a desacralized ambiance? Each day passes with increasing speed, placing greater responsibilities and burdens on people, leaving very little time to do much of anything, let alone contemplate the deeper truths of existence. To do so appears to many as a luxury—something that only the affluent can afford—but this is not the case. In fact, all spiritual traditions offer teachings and practices that can be adopted wherever we may find ourselves and in whatever circumstances.

Prayer allows for a direct relationship to the Divine. When surveying the world's diverse religions, and their mystical dimensions, it becomes apparent that prayer defines the centrality of the human condition and holds an eschatological relevance. This is because human beings cannot go beyond themselves by personal effort alone; they need the support of that which transcends the empirical ego.

The prescription for all our earthly malaise has, traditionally, been the medicine of Divine Remembrance; in other words, prayer is the means by which we may become integrated into our transpersonal essence. Within the Christian tradition, we find the Jesus Prayer that is supported by the injunction: "Pray without ceasing" (1 Thessalonians 5:17). This remembrance of God (*dhikr Allāh*) in the Islamic tradition is considered therapeutic: "Verily in the remembrance of Allah do hearts find rest" (Qur'ān 13:28). In the Hindu tradition, the repetition (*japa*) of the Divine Names is a spiritual method available to all regardless of social status or spiritual aptitude. According to the 68th Jagadguru of Kanchi, this remembrance is always available: "He may think of god even on the bus or the train as he goes to his office or any other place."[14] Within the Buddhist tradition, there is the practice of *nembutsu* or invoking the name of Amida Buddha. This practice is also to be found within the religion of the First Peoples as exemplified by the Lakota *wicasa wakan*, or holy man, Black Elk: "[W]e Indians know the One true God, and . . . we pray to Him continually."[15]

There is never a moment when the Divine is absent; rather, it is we who are absent—this is our greatest obstacle. The obsession with self-care is, in fact, linked to the spiritual crisis facing humanity. When properly understood, true self-care becomes impossible for one who accepts the modern worldview regarding who we are. An excessive focus on the profane self *is* the problem, because, relying on its own resources, it cannot support psychological well-being or the quest for our true Self.

The assumption behind obsessive self-care is that we *can* in fact fully care for ourselves, but the notion that we have ultimate agency over our lives is illusory. While personal effort and perseverance are certainly necessary, taking refuge in the Divine ought to be our primary focus. We are told that true respite from the difficulties of daily life may only be found in spiritual refuge:

> Come unto me, all ye that labor and are heavy laden, and I will give you rest. Take my yoke upon you, and learn of me; for I am meek and lowly in heart: and ye shall find rest unto your souls. For my yoke is easy, and my burden is light (Matthew 11:28–30).

Likewise, the antidote to anxiety is faith and trust in the highest reality:

> Do not be anxious about anything, but in every situation, by prayer and petition, with thanksgiving, present your requests to God. And the peace of God, which transcends all understanding, will guard your hearts and your minds in Christ Jesus (Philippians 4:6–7).

It becomes apparent that before we can even discuss self-care, it is critical to establish what is meant by the very self whose care is being urged. Modern psychology for the most part is confined to a horizontal understanding of human identity and is unable to recognize the vertical dimension that pertains to our primordial nature. The founder of the "talking cure," Sigmund Freud, writes: "The ego represents what may be called reason and common sense"[16] and, likewise, "there is nothing of which we are more certain than the feeling of our self, of our own ego."[17] At the same time, even he expresses its shortcomings: "[T]he Ego is not master in its own house."[18]

To equate the self with the ego is a betrayal of the Spirit, which it seeks to subvert and overthrow. Therefore, whatever thwarts our remembrance of the Divine needs to be resisted. Many traditions assert the existence of both a lower self and one that is "transpersonal"—that is, grounded in a universal reality. However, when the lower self is entirely held captive by the ego, and sees nothing else, our human identity becomes disfigured and impervious to a higher illumination. Accordingly—and notwithstanding the proper role of personal effort up to a point—we need to be receptive to the working of divine reality in helping fuel our aspiration towards Plato's three great transcendentals: the Good, the True, and the Beautiful.

According to the Hindu tradition, it is the confused or deluded person who asserts, "I am the doer"[19] (Bhagavad Gītā 3:27), as in most cases it is the Divine alone who is the doer. Our identification with the "doer" is the problem, as Swami Ramdas observed: "The ego is the cause of soul's bondage and misery."[20] In the Taoist tradition, there is the notion of "non-action" (Chinese: *wu wei*). This does not signify inertia, but rather stems from the very source of all action in the Tao, which is not the product of individual initiative. Shin Buddhism makes the distinction between "other power" (*tariki*) and "self-power" (*jiriki*), which is to say the distinction between reliance on the Primal Vow of Amida Buddha, as opposed to our own efforts, to attain nirvana. The Christian tradition teaches us to turn away from our self-preoccupation in an act of self-naughting; we must deny ourselves (Matthew 16:24; Mark 8:34; Luke 9:23) so as to make room in our hearts for something other than the human ego. This common theme among spiritual traditions shows that an exaggerated notion of our own agency can only lead to inadequate self-care.

If we ask ourselves who is the doer that practices self-care, we will get closer to resolving this question; however; this will not make sense in the absence of an appropriate metaphysical framework. This is made evident when Saint Augustine affirms: "For Thou hast made us for Thyself and our hearts are restless till they rest in Thee."[21] All attempts to seek wholeness in anything other than the Divine are bound to fail. As Julian of Norwich rightly discerned: "Our soul may never have rest in anything which is beneath itself."[22] Mainstream psychology and the field of mental health only know of a self that is separate—not one that transcends the psychophysical order. The lower levels of our being are unable to grasp that which is higher, seeing as the latter transcend (yet include) the former. Through abiding in the Divine, we may gain access to our core identity.

A significant burden on people living in a desacralized world is that they are engaged in work that is not in conformity with their true vocation. They are simply compelled to do so by the need to secure an income, which undoubtedly contributes to widespread discontent in our era. Therefore, there is a need today for clear boundaries between one's professional and personal life, where we often find a divide between what we do for a living and what nourishes our spirit.

Now that misconceived notions of self-care have been addressed, we will consider the correct understanding of how traditional cosmology and psychology view the human body as a reflection of the cosmos. Throughout the sacred scriptures, we are reminded that our "bodies are temples of the Holy Spirit" (1 Corinthians 6:19), and in the Qur'ān's account of the creation of man, God says, "I blew into him of My spirit" (Qur'ān 15:29, 38:72). This is why we are instructed to care for the human body, but we must not do so according to our own individualistic notions, for we are given clear guidance by humanity's sapiential traditions.

Human beings are not limited to their corporeal reality; rather, we consist of a tripartite nature—Spirit, soul, and body. It is the transpersonal dimension that animates both soul and body, thus rendering them whole; without the soul, the body cannot come alive; without the body, the soul would be bereft of a suitable dwelling; and, without the Spirit, neither would exist. Therefore, any discussion of self-care must be mindful of both the science of nature, as well as that of the human soul.

The more we seek the source of self-care in our lower selves, the more fleeting it becomes. The act of self-care requires doing something in order to stay well or keep going, which implies constant maintenance. Again, it is never asked who the "doer" is; only that its activity continues. Any fixation can take us in the opposite direction to what we originally intended. In the often-cited words of Dōgen: "To learn the Buddha Way is to learn one's self. To learn one's self is to forget one's self."[23] This is reminiscent of the spiritual advice of Saint Ignatius of Loyola, the Spanish Catholic theologian: "For each one must realize that he will make progress in all spiritual matters in proportion to his flight from self-love, self-will, and self-interest."[24] Neither happiness nor fulfillment can be procured outside of the sacred. To be fully human is to recognize our fundamental relationship with the Absolute, which is to say that our true identity in the Divine is the primordial nature (*fiṭrah*), the "image of God" (*imago Dei*), Buddha-nature (*Buddha-dhātu*), or the Self (*Ātmā*).

Our true Self cannot be understood through the myopic lens of modern science, which has proven incapable of delivering itself from its erroneous theoretical foundations. The same applies to the radically limited scope of modern psychology, and its mental health treatments, which are devoid of a transpersonal dimension. As René Guénon explains:

> As for modern Western psychology, it deals only with a quite restricted portion of the human individuality, where the mental faculty is in direct relationship with the corporeal modality, and, given the methods it employs, it is incapable of going any further. In any case, the very objective which it sets before itself and which is exclusively the study of mental phenomena [the empirical ego], limits it strictly

> to the realm of the individuality, so that the state which we are now discussing [the Self (*Ātmā*)] necessarily eludes its investigations.[25]

In a sense, all true spiritual practices sanctioned by revealed traditions aid us in returning to ourselves. Even within the realm of mental health, there is often the self-care prescription of breathing slowly and deeply in order to be mindful of our breath. It is worth recalling that the term "Spirit" derives from the Latin word *spiritus*, meaning "spirit" or "breath," which stems from the verb *spirare*, "to breathe." It appears to be so simple to breathe, yet, in our fast-paced digital age, we forget to be aware of even this vital process. This sacred and automatic process confirms that human beings are inherently connected to the divine and made for the Absolute.

When the separate self is given prominence and its maintenance is supported above all else, it becomes an obstacle to the unfolding of the true Self. Many mistaken ideas are prevalent in the current zeitgeist, one of them being that this existence owes us something, or that we are free to pursue whatever we desire. Nothing could be further from the truth. We are entitled to nothing and are only given the blessing of this life—with all its trials and tribulations—for the sole purpose of encountering the Divine in ourselves, in others, and in the world around us. The universal and timeless wisdom found throughout the diverse cultures of the world teaches an essential truth: "Your natural state is one of happiness."[26]

Prioritizing our personal welfare, though understandable in light of our biological needs, often leads to a host of problems. A spiritually well human being is selfless rather than selfish, and we can attenuate the demands of our egoic self when purged of all that does not truly belong to us—in other words, when we overcome ourselves. Self-care, in the truest sense, is to rest always in an awareness of the Absolute—the more we surrender to it, the less importance we place on ourselves. To remember the "one thing needful" (Luke 10:42) is to cease being a spiritual "doer" so that we can awaken to our true Self. It cannot be forgotten that no matter how much so-called self-care we practice, we are unknowingly always searching to transcend ourselves because we can never find satisfaction within the confines of our limited lives, lived "horizontally" in a world that is similarly constricted.

Paradoxical as it may appear at first, it could be said that self-care has inadvertently become infused with the true meaning of *religion*. We recall that the etymological root of the English word "religion" is the Latin *religare*, meaning "to rebind" or "to bind back," by implication to the Divine or a transcendent reality. Recovering our primordial nature, a task thwarted by our desacralized world, is the path toward true self-care. As Whitall N. Perry points out: "The great imponderable in all spiritual work is: how to be what one is, and how to cease being what one is not."[27] In order to protect ourselves spiritually, we need to be vigilant in the face of nihilism's subversive dominance in the present day, and to never forget the contradiction that undergirds all relativism wherein "[e]verything is doubted except for doubt."[28] Yet, on a more positive note, we do well to bear in mind that "[o]ne of the fundamental conditions of happiness is to know that everything that one does has a meaning in eternity."[29]

The entirety of our existence may be described as a journey from the wilderness of our fragmented self to the true home that is our transpersonal Self. It goes without saying that were it not for the chaotic conditions of modern life—and for humanity having lost its moorings to our venerable spiritual traditions—there would be no need to discuss self-care. It is only when self-care practices are restored to their millennia-old tradition roots that they will be able to provide the lasting efficacy that we seek from them. We would do well to recall the words of the great Bard: "This above all: to thine own self be true."[30]

Afterword: The Way Forward

Where do we go from here, and how can we integrate these metaphysical perspectives into our daily work as mental health practitioners, or as individuals trying to benefit from psychotherapy? This is a key question that is asked time and time again. The first thing to bear in mind is that we need to respect the uniqueness of each person—and their spiritual life (if any)—which then allows for differences in approach to unfold naturally.

For some, this will require learning more about the faith of their family and forebears, with a view to returning to this path should they have, indeed, strayed from it—but only if, on serious reflection, it begins to speak to them. This shift in one's heart may follow an examination of sacred scriptures, participation in liturgical rites, or even dealing with the aftermath of a personal tragedy. This process will take time and should not be rushed. If we come from a completely secular background, but are still seeking something deeper in our lives, we will then need to look further afield for counsel and support. An advantage of living in a multicultural society (as many in the West are) is that many religious traditions are likely to be represented in the vicinity of where one lives. Failing that, online spiritual communities are more easily accessible now than ever before (although sound advice is always required to avoid being led astray by dubious content).

Where certain individuals have been harmed by clergy or spiritual advisors, such an undertaking will understandably be more difficult. Even the mere mention of 'religion' can be triggering in that it may evoke past traumas. While therapy can support this healing process, it is our view that such a transformation will be much more profound and enduring when sustained by a transcendent agency. It is often forgotten that psychotherapy is a diminished by-product of a society that has lost its sense of the sacred, and rejected religion altogether. Yet even our very longing for the divine can be restored through the indispensable operation of grace, leading to an encounter with it in our own lived experience (often with the compassionate guidance of qualified spiritual guides).

Many have left their native religion because it failed to satisfy their fundamental yearning for something authentic. As a result, they have turned to other paths, especially from the East, perhaps unaware that effective contemplative practices can also be found within their own traditions. Therefore, such seekers should be encouraged to explore the mystical dimensions of faiths closer to home. As changing religions can cause unsettling cultural and psychological displacement, such a decision should be given very careful consideration, and not be undertaken lightly.

Having a close-knit community is essential to our lives, as most people are unable to navigate the spiritual path alone; indeed, we are cautioned against doing this unless it is strictly necessary. Nevertheless, we are urged to prayerfully ask for the guidance we need, as such help is always available to those with a sincere and humble disposition. It does not matter if we do not know how to clearly conceive of the highest reality; what is important is that we communicate our sincere need with both heart and mind. When this is done wholeheartedly, we are likely to attract influences that will support us in our spiritual search. We might even begin to meet people who can share with us the teachings of a particular path, or we may come across books or video programs that appear as though they were specifically meant for us—as if everything were coming together thanks to the beneficent working of something beyond our immediate apprehension, in which we gradually come to trust with increasing certainty.

There are many ways in which we can return to our spiritual patrimonies, but what is most important here is to focus on the cultivation of virtue, humility, and discernment. Only in this way can we truly come to know who we really are, and to understand others and the world around us in all their richness and mystery. Therefore, the work of recovering our psycho-spiritual balance in the world must begin with ourselves. As the cosmos is mirrored within us, it is only through our own inner reformation that harmony in the outer world can be renewed.

It is worth noting that patience is required on this journey, for it may take time for certain questions to be answered, or for our destination to become clear. Once things fall into place, however, it is sure to feel like a true homecoming. When deeply rooted in our own spiritual tradition, we are able to draw upon its many graces in light of a sacred psychology that will nourish us in our ongoing struggle with the spiritual crisis of the modern world, and the trauma of secularism, for which the sole true remedy is the "one thing needful" (Luke 10:42).

Endnotes

Chapter 1 — Modern Psychology and the Loss of Transcendence

1 René Guénon, "The Confusion of the Psychic and the Spiritual," in *The Reign of Quantity and the Signs of the Times*, trans. Lord Northbourne (Sophia Perennis, 2004), 239.

2 Martin Lings, "The Decisive Boundary," in *Symbol and Archetype: A Study of the Meaning of Existence* (Quinta Essentia, 1991), 17.

3 Titus Burckhardt, preface to *Chartres and the Birth of the Cathedral,* trans. William Stoddart (Golgonooza Press, 1995), 9.

4 Sigmund Freud, "Chapter 10," in *The Future of an Illusion*, trans. and ed. James Strachey (W. W. Norton & Company, 1989), 71.

5 René Guénon, "The Confusion of the Psychic and the Spiritual," in *The Reign of Quantity and the Signs of the Times*, trans. Lord Northbourne (Sophia Perennis, 2004), 237.

6 Rūmī, Discourse 12, *Discourses of Rumi*, trans. A. J. Arberry (Routledge-Curzon, 2004), 68.

7 Saint Augustine, quoted in *Nicene and Post-Nicene Fathers of the Christian Church, Vol. V: Saint Augustine: Anti-Pelagian Writings*, ed. Philip Schaff (Christian Literature Company, 1887), 370.

8 Saint Thomas Aquinas, Question 75, First Article, *Summa Theologica, Part I, Third Number, QQ. LXXV–CXIX*, trans. Fathers of the English Dominican Province (R. & T. Washbourne, 1912), 2.

9 Seneca, Moral Epistles 31.11, *Ad Lucilium Epistulae Morales, Vol. 1*, trans. Richard M. Gummere (G. P. Putnam's Sons, 1917), 229.

10 Saint Augustine, quoted in *Nicene and Post-Nicene Fathers of the Christian Church, Vol. V: Saint Augustine: Anti-Pelagian Writings*, ed. Philip Schaff (Christian Literature Company, 1887), 363.

11 Ibn 'Arabī, quoted in William C. Chittick, *Ibn 'Arabi: Heir to the Prophets* (Oneworld Publications, 2005), 103.

12 Hermes Trismegistus, quoted in Titus Burckhardt, *Alchemy: Science of the Cosmos, Science of the Soul*, trans. William Stoddart (Element Books, 1986), 196.

13 Shaykh ad-Darqāwī, quoted in *Letters of a Sufi Master: The Shaykh ad-Darqāwī*, trans. Titus Burckhardt (Fons Vitae, 1998), 21.

14 Shaykh ad-Darqāwī, quoted in *Letters of a Sufi Master: The Shaykh ad-Darqāwī*, trans. Titus Burckhardt (Fons Vitae, 1998), 41.

15 Plato, Phaedo 88b, *The Collected Dialogues of Plato*, eds. Edith Hamilton and Huntington Cairns (Princeton University Press, 1980), 70.

16 Mulla Sadra, "Principle (concerning the soul as 'spiritual body')," in *The Wisdom of the Throne: An Introduction to the Philosophy of Mulla Sadra*, trans. James Winston Morris (Princeton University Press, 1981), 148.

17 Meister Eckhart, *The Complete Mystical Works of Meister Eckhart*, trans. and ed. Maurice O'C Walshe (Crossroad Publishing Company, 2009), 28.

18 Meister Eckhart, "Tractates 3: The Rank and Nature of the Soul," in *Meister Eckhart*, trans. C. De B. Evans, ed. Franz Pfeiffer (John M. Watkins, 1924), 290.

19 Plato, Phaedrus 248b–c, *The Dialogues of Plato, Vol. 1*, trans. Benjamin Jowett (Charles Scribner's Sons, 1911), 553.

20 Vedānta Sūtras, quoted in *The Essential Vedānta: A New Source Book of Advaita Vedānta,* eds. Eliot Deutsch and Rohit Dalvi (World Wisdom, 2004), 88.

21 Thomas Traherne, 93, *Centuries of Meditations*, ed. Bertram Dobell (Bertram Dobell, 1908), 71.

22 Saint Makarios of Egypt, "The Raising of the Intellect," in *The Philokalia, Vol. 3: The Complete Text; Compiled by St. Nikodimos of the Holy Mountain and St. Makarios of Corinth*, trans. and ed. G. E. H. Palmer, Philip Sherrard, and Kallistos Ware (Faber and Faber, 1995), 314.

23 Chāndogya Upanishad 8:7–12, *The Upanishads*, trans. Juan Mascaró (Penguin Books, 1965), 125.

24 Meister Eckhart, "Sermons and Collations, 29: The Angel Gabriel was sent," in *Meister Eckhart*, trans. C. De B. Evans, ed. Franz Pfeiffer (John M. Watkins, 1924), 80.

25 Titus Burckhardt, "Modern Psychology," in *Mirror of the Intellect: Essays on Traditional Science and Sacred Art*, trans. and ed. William Stoddart (State University of New York Press, 1987), 50.

26 Śrī Ramana Maharshi, "Talk 238—July 20th, 1936," in *Talks with Sri Ramana Maharshi* (Sri Ramanasramam, 1996), 191.

27 Clement of Alexandria, quoted in Eric Osborn, *Clement of Alexandria* (Cambridge University Press, 2005), 144.

28 Bhagavad Gītā 10:20, *The Bhagavad-Gītā with the Commentary of Śrī Śankarachārya,* trans. Alladi Mahadeva Sastri (V. Ramaswamy Sastrulu & Sons, 1961), 241.

29 Meister Eckhart, "Sermon 1," in *Meister Eckhart: Teacher and Preacher,* ed. Bernard McGinn (Paulist Press, 1986), 241.

30 Aśvaghoṣa, "The Cause and Conditions of Man's Being in Samsara—Consciousness," in *The Awakening of Faith: Attributed to Aśvaghosha*, trans. Yoshito S. Hakeda (Columbia University Press, 1967), 50.

31 Huang Po, "The Chün Chou Record," in *The Zen Teaching of Huang Po: On the Transmission of Mind*, trans. John Blofeld (Grove Press, 1958), 29–30.

32 See Sigmund Freud, "Chapter 1," in *Civilization and Its Discontents*, trans. and ed. James Strachey (W. W. Norton & Company, 1989), 10–21.

33 See Samuel Bendeck Sotillos, "The Deification of the Psyche: Carl Jung and the Spiritual Crisis of the Modern World," *Sacred Web: A Journal of Tradition and Modernity*, vol. 51 (2025).

34 Whitall N. Perry, "Drug-Induced Mysticism: The Mescalin Hypothesis," in *Challenges to a Secular Society* (The Foundation for Traditional Studies, 1996), 10.

35 René Guénon, "The Confusion of the Psychic and the Spiritual," in *The Reign of Quantity and the Signs of the Times*, trans. Lord Northbourne (Sophia Perennis, 2001), 239–240. See also Rama P. Coomaraswamy, "The Problems that Result from Locating Spirituality in the Psyche," *Sacred Web: A Journal of Tradition and Modernity*, vol. 9 (Summer 2002), 101–124.

Chapter 2 — The Inner and Outer Human Being

1 Śrī Nisargadatta Maharaj, "In the Supreme the Witness Appears," in *I Am That: Talks with Sri Nisargadatta Maharaj*, trans. Maurice Frydman, ed. Sudhakar S. Dikshit (Acorn Press, 1999), 294.

2 Zhūangzi, "Autumn Floods," in *Chuang Tzu: Basic Writings*, trans. Burton Watson (Columbia University Press, 1996), 104.

3 Ibn 'Arabī, "The Wisdom of Exaltation in the Word of Noah," in *The Bezels of Wisdom*, trans. R. W. J. Austin (Paulist Press, 1980), 73.

4 Sagāthakam, Verse 235, *The Laṅkāvatāra Sūtra: A Mahāyāna Text*, trans. D. T. Suzuki (Prajñā Press, 1978), 245.

5 Abū Bakr Sirāj ad-Dīn, "The Lore of Certainty," in *The Book of Certainty: The Sufi Doctrines of Faith, Vision and Gnosis* (Islamic Texts Society, 1996), 21.

6 Johannes Scotus Erigena, De Divisione Naturae, quoted in Henry Bett, *Johanes Scotus Erigena: A Study in Mediaeval Philosophy* (Cambridge University Press, 1925), 55–56.

7 Jāmī, quoted in Reynold A. Nicholson, *The Mystics of Islam* (Routledge & Kegan Paul, 1975), 82.

8 Sabine Hossenfelder, "A Warning," in *Existential Physics: A Scientist's Guide to Life's Biggest Questions* (Viking, 2022), xvii.

9 Theodore Roszak, "Afterword: The Idols of the Bedchamber," in *The Gendered Atom: Reflections on the Sexual Psychology of Science* (Conari Press, 1999), 154.

10 James Hillman, "A Psyche the Size of the Earth: A Psychological Foreword," in *Ecopsychology: Restoring the Earth, Healing the Mind*, eds. Theodore Roszak, Mary E. Gomes, and Allen D. Kanner (Sierra Club Book, 1995), xvii.

11 See Samuel Bendeck Sotillos, "Recovering the Eye of the Heart," *The Mountain Path*, vol. 59, no. 3 (July/September 2022), 29–45.

12 Whitall N. Perry, quoted in Gray Henry, "Ways of Knowing: An Interview with Whitall N. Perry," *Sophia: A Journal of Traditional Studies*, vol. 3, no. 2 (Winter 1997), 97–98.

13 R. D. Laing, "The Embodied and Unembodied Self," in *The Divided Self: An Existential Study in Sanity and Madness* (Penguin Books, 1976), 65.

14 René Guénon, "*Spiritus, Anima, Corpus*," in *The Great Triad*, trans. Henry D. Fohr, ed. Samuel D. Fohr (Sophia Perennis, 2004), 68; "Cartesian bifurcation created a dualism between mind and matter which has dominated Western thought since the seventeenth century, a dualism which has led many to choose the primacy of matter over mind and to establish the view that in the beginning was matter and not consciousness." [Seyyed Hossein Nasr, "In the Beginning was Consciousness," in *The Essential Seyyed Hossein Nasr*, ed. William C. Chittick (World Wisdom, 2007), 224.]

15 Ludwig Binswanger, quoted in *Existence: A New Dimension in Psychiatry and Psychology*, eds. Rollo May, Ernest Angel, and Henri F. Ellenberger (Basic Books, 1958), 11.

16 Sigmund Freud, "Chapter 1," in *Civilization and Its Discontents*, trans. and ed. James Strachey (W. W. Norton & Company, 1989), 12.

17 Sigmund Freud, "Chapter 1," in *Civilization and Its Discontents*, trans. and ed. James Strachey (W. W. Norton & Company, 1989), 13.

18 John B. Watson, "What is Behaviorism? The Old and New Psychology Contrasted," in *Behaviorism* (W. W. Norton & Company, 1970), 3.

19 B. F. Skinner, "What Is Man?," in *Beyond Freedom and Dignity* (Bantam, 1972), 205.

20 B. F. Skinner, "What Is Man?," in *Beyond Freedom and Dignity* (Bantam, 1972), 190–191.

21 Victor Danner, "The Inner and Outer Man," in *Traditional Modes of Contemplation and Action: A Colloquium held at Rothko Chapel Houston Texas*, eds. Yusuf Ibish and Peter Lamborn Wilson (Imperial Iranian Academy of Philosophy, 1977), 411.

22 Maurice Merleau-Ponty, preface to *Phenomenology of Perception* (Routledge, 1962), xi.

23 Rūmī, quoted in William C. Chittick, *The Sufi Path of Love: The Spiritual Teachings of Rumi* (State University of New York Press, 1983), 161.

24 Rūmī, quoted in William C. Chittick, *The Sufi Path of Love: The Spiritual Teachings of Rumi* (State University of New York Press, 1983), 41.

25 Saint Thomas Aquinas, Question 26, Fourth Article, *Summa Theologica, Part II (Second Part), First Number, QQ. I–XLVI*, trans. Fathers of the English Dominican Province (R. & T. Washbourne, 1917), 336.

26 Plato, Republic 10.604b, *The Collected Dialogues of Plato,* eds. Edith Hamilton and Huntington Cairns (Princeton University Press, 1980), 829.

27 Kurt Almqvist, "Every Branch in Me," *Studies in Comparative Religion,* vol. 15, nos. 3 & 4 (Summer/Autumn 1983), 194.

28 Rūmī, quoted in William C. Chittick, *The Sufi Path of Love: The Spiritual Teachings of Rumi* (State University of New York Press, 1983), 276.

29 Bhagavad Gītā 10:20, *The Bhagavad-Gītā with the Commentary of Śrī Śankarachāryā*, trans. Alladi Mahadeva Sastri (V. Ramaswamy Sastrulu & Sons, 1961), 241.

30 Isaac the Syrian, "The Six Treatises on the Behaviour of Excellence," in *Mystic Treatises by Isaac of Nineveh*, trans. A. J. Wensinck (Koninklijke Akademie van Wettenschappen, 1923), 8.

31 *The Cloud of Unknowing and Other Works*, trans. Clifton Wolters (Penguin Books, 1978), 72.

32 Ananda K. Coomaraswamy, "On the Indian and Traditional Psychology, or Rather Pneumatology," in *Coomaraswamy, Vol. 2, Selected Papers: Metaphysics*, ed. Roger Lipsey (Princeton University Press, 1978), 371.

33 Frithjof Schuon, "The Argument Founded on Substance," in *Logic and Transcendence*, trans. Peter N. Townsend (Perennial Books, 1984), 82.

34 Marco Pallis, "Do Clothes Make the Man?," in *The Way and the Mountain: Tibet, Buddhism, and Tradition*, ed. Joseph A. Fitzgerald (World Wisdom, 2008), 153.

35 Martin Lings, "The Heart," in *What is Sufism?* (University of California Press, 1975), 54.

36 M. Ali Lakhani, "The Black Mole on the Cheek of the Beloved: The Problem of Metaphysical Ambiguity," *Sacred Web: A Journal of Tradition and Modernity*, vol. 26 (Winter 2010), 12.

37 Muṇḍaka Upanishad 3:1:1; Shvetāshvatara Upanishad 4:6, quoted in René Guénon, *Man and His Becoming According to the Vedanta*, trans. Richard C. Nicholson (Sophia Perennis, 2004), 46.

38 Muṇḍaka Upanishad 3:1:1; Shvetāshvatara Upanishad 4:6, quoted in René Guénon, *Man and His Becoming According to the Vedanta*, trans. Richard C. Nicholson (Sophia Perennis, 2004), 34.

39 Maitrī Upanishad 6:34, *The Thirteen Principal Upanishads*, trans. Robert Ernest Hume (Oxford University Press, 1921), 447.

40 Meister Eckhart, "Tractates 18: Commentary on the Gospel of St. John," in *Meister Eckhart,* trans. C. De B. Evans, ed. Franz Pfeiffer (John M. Watkins, 1924), 403.

41 Meister Eckhart, "On Detachment," in *The Essential Sermons, Commentaries, Treatises, and Defense*, trans. Edmund Colledge and Bernard McGinn (Paulist Press, 1981), 290.

42 Origen, Part 1—The Commentary: Prologue, *The Song of Songs: Commentary and Homilies*, trans. R. P. Lawson (Newman Press, 1956), 25.

43 Angelus Silesius, quoted in Jeffrey L. Sammons, *Angelus Silesius* (Twayne Publishers, 1967), 54.

44 Manṣūr al-Ḥallāj, quoted in Reynold A. Nicholson, *The Mystics of Islam* (Routledge & Kegan Paul, 1975), 151.

45 Ḥāfiẓ, quoted in Margaret Smith, *Readings from the Mystics of Islam* (Luzac and Company, 1950), 115.

46 Plotinus, Ennead 5.8.2, *The Enneads*, trans. Stephen MacKenna (Penguin Books, 1991), 412.

47 Johannes Tauler, "From the Second Sermon for the Twelfth Sunday after Trinity," in *Selections from the Life and Sermons of the Reverend Doctor John Tauler*, trans. Susanna Winkworth (Roberts Brothers, 1878), 142.

48 Zhūangzi, "On Declining Power," in *Chuang Tzu: Mystic, Moralist, and Social Reformer*, trans. Herbert A. Giles (Bernard Quaritch, 1889), 381.

49 Jakob Böhme, quoted in Franz Hartmann, *The Life and Doctrines of Jacob Boehme: The God–Taught Philosopher* (Occult Publishing Company, 1891), 280.

50 Paracelsus, "Arts, a Gift of God," in *Paracelsus: Selected Writings*, trans. Norbert Guterman, ed. Jolande Jacobi (Princeton University Press, 1988), 133.

51 Chapter 68, *The Cloud of Unknowing and Other Works*, trans. Clifton Wolters (Penguin Books, 1978), 143.

52 Sarrāj, quoted in *Knowledge of God in Classical Sufism: Foundations of Islamic Mystical Theology*, trans. John Renard (Paulist Press, 2004), 83.

53 Zhūangzi, "Mastering Life," in *Chuang Tzu: Basic Writings*, trans. Burton Watson (Columbia University Press, 1996), 122.

54 Philip Sherrard, introduction to *Human Image, World Image: The Death and Resurrection of Sacred Cosmology* (Denise Harvey, 2004), 8.

55 Mulla Sadra, "Principle (concerning the soul as 'spiritual body')," in *The Wisdom of the Throne: An Introduction to the Philosophy of Mulla Sadra*, trans. James Winston Morris (Princeton University Press, 1981), 148.

56 Paracelsus, "Inner and Outer Worlds," in *Paracelsus: Selected Writings*, trans. Norbert Guterman, ed. Jolande Jacobi (Princeton University Press, 1988), 121.

57 Heart Sūtra, quoted in *Buddhist Scriptures*, trans. Edward Conze (Penguin Books, 1959), 162.

58 Joseph Epes Brown, "Contemplation Through Action," in *The Spiritual Legacy of the American Indian: Commemorative Edition with Letters While Living with Black Elk*, eds. Marina Brown Weatherly, Elenita Brown and Michael Oren Fitzgerald (World Wisdom, 2007), 62.

59 Paracelsus, "Man and His Body," in *Paracelsus: Selected Writings*, trans. Norbert Guterman, ed. Jolande Jacobi (Princeton University Press, 1988), 21.

60 Logion 22, *The Gospel According to Thomas: Coptic Text Established and Translated*, trans. Antoine Guillaumont, Henri-Charles Puech, Gilles Quispel, Walter C. Till, and Yassah 'Abd al-Masīḥ (E. J. Brill, 1976), 17, 19.

61 Śrī Rāmakrishna, "Bankim Chandra," in *The Gospel of Ramakrishna: Originally recorded in Bengali by M., a disciple of the Master*, trans. Swāmi Nikhilānanda (New York, NY: Ramakrishna-Vivekananda Center, 1977), p. 667.

62 'Ayn al-Quḍāt, quoted in Mohammed Rustom, *Inrushes of the Heart: The Sufi Philosophy of 'Ayn al-Quḍāt* (State University of New York Press, 2023), 124.

63 Nikitas Stithatos, "On the Practice of the Virtues: One Hundred Texts," in *The Philokalia, Vol. 4: The Complete Text; Compiled by St. Nikodimos of the Holy Mountain and St. Makarios of Corinth*, trans. and ed. G. E. H. Palmer, Philip Sherrard, and Kallistos Ware (Faber and Faber, 1998), 92.

64 Śrī Ramana Maharshi, "Talk 398—April 14th, 1937," in *Talks with Sri Ramana Maharshi* (Sri Ramanasramam, 1996), 370.

65 See Seyyed Hossein Nasr, "The Wisdom of the Body," in *Religion and the Order of Nature* (Oxford University Press, 1996), 235–269.

66 Paracelsus, "Nature of Disease," in *Paracelsus: Selected Writings*, trans. Norbert Guterman, ed. Jolande Jacobi (Princeton University Press, 1988), 76.

67 Rūmī, Discourse 11, *Discourses of Rumi*, trans. A. J. Arberry (Routledge-Curzon, 2004), 61.

68 Saint John Cassian, "On the Eight Vices," in *The Philokalia, Vol. 1: The Complete Text; Compiled by St. Nikodimos of the Holy Mountain and St. Makarios of Corinth*, trans. and ed. G. E. H. Palmer, Philip Sherrard, and Kallistos Ware (Faber and Faber, 1983), 76.

69 'Alī ibn Abī Ṭālib, quoted in William C. Chittick, *Sufism: A Beginner's Guide* (Oneworld Publications, 2008), 104.

70 Philip Sherrard, "The Roman Background," in *The Greek East and the Latin West: A Study in The Christian Tradition* (Denise Harvey, 1995), 20.

71 Seyyed Hossein Nasr, "Self-Awareness and Ultimate Selfhood: The Role of the Sacred Science of the Soul," in *The Need for a Sacred Science* (State University of New York Press, 1993), 15–16.

72 Frithjof Schuon, "Being Conscious of the Real," in *The Play of Masks* (World Wisdom Books, 1992), 82.

73 Meister Eckhart, "Sayings—67," in *Meister Eckhart*, trans. C. De B. Evans, ed. Franz Pfeiffer (John M. Watkins, 1924), 438.

74 Socrates, quoted in Phaedrus 279b, *The Dialogues of Plato, Vol. I*, trans. Benjamin Jowett (Oxford University Press, 1892), 420.

Chapter 3 — Realms of Consciousness and the Real

1 Jakob Böhme, quoted in Franz Hartmann, *The Life and Doctrines of Jacob Boehme: The God–Taught Philosopher* (Occult Publishing Company, 1891), 292.

2 Maitrī Upanishad 6:24, *The Upanishads*, trans. Juan Mascaró (Penguin Books, 1965), 103.

3 Milarepa, "Story 9: The Gray Rock Vajra Enclosure," in *The Hundred Thousand Songs of Milarepa*, trans. Garma C. C. Chang (Shambhala Publications, 1977), 97.

4 Ibn 'Arabī, quoted in Toshihiko Izutsu, *Sufism and Taoism: A Comparative Study of Key Philosophical Concepts* (University of California Press, 1984), 7.

5 Edward F. Kelly, Emily Williams Kelly, Adam Crabtree, Alan Gauld, Michael Grosso, and Bruce Greyson, preface and acknowledgments in *Irreducible Mind: Toward a Psychology for the 21st Century* (Rowman & Littlefield Publishers, 2010), xiii, xiv.

6 George Trumbull Ladd, "Nature of Physiological Psychology," in *Outlines of Physiological Psychology: A Text–Book of Mental Science for Academies and Colleges* (Charles Scribner's Sons, 1908), 3.

7 William James, "Epilogue: Psychology and Philosophy," in *Psychology: Briefer Course* (Henry Holt and Company, 1923), 468.

8 See John B. Watson, "Psychology as the Behaviorist Views It," *Psychological Review*, vol. 20, no. 2 (March 1913), 158–177.

9 John B. Watson, "Psychology as the Behaviorist Views It," *Psychological Review*, vol. 20, no. 2 (March 1913), 163, 177.

10 Sigmund Freud, "Distortion in Dreams," in *The Interpretation of Dreams*, trans. and ed. James Strachey (John Wiley & Sons, 1963), 144.

11 See Samuel Bendeck Sotillos, "The Deification of the Psyche: Carl Jung and the Spiritual Crisis of the Modern World," *Sacred Web: A Journal of Tradition and Modernity*, vol. 51 (2025).

12 C. G. Jung, "Definitions," in *Psychological Types or The Psychology of Individuation*, trans. H. Godwyn Baynes (Harcourt, Brace & Company, 1923), 536.

13 C. G. Jung, "Psychological Aspects of the Mother Archetype" (1938/1954), in *The Archetypes and the Collective Unconscious*, trans. R. F. C. Hull (Princeton University Press, 1980), 96.

14 Cyril Burt, "The Concept of Consciousness," *British Journal of Psychology*, vol. 53, no. 3 (August 1962), 229.

15 Sufi adage, quoted in Ibn 'Arabī, *The Wisdom of the Prophets (Fusus al-Hikam)*, trans. Titus Burckhardt and Angela Culme-Seymour (Beshara Publications, 1975), 11.

16 Ḥadīth, quoted in Gai Eaton, *Islam and the Destiny of Man* (State University of New York Press, 1985), 110.

17 Maitrī Upanishad 6:24, *The Upanishads*, trans. Juan Mascaró (Penguin Books, 1965), 104.

18 George Trumbull Ladd, "Method, Sources, and Division of Psychology," in *Psychology, Descriptive and Explanatory: A Treatise of the Phenomena, Laws, and Development of Human Mental Life* (Charles Scribner's Sons, 1895), 17.

19 Carl R. Rogers, "Do We Need 'A' Reality?," in *A Way of Being* (Houghton Mifflin Company, 1995), 102.

20 Sigmund Freud, "The Question of a *Weltanschauung*" (1933 [1932]), in *New Introductory Lectures on Psycho-Analysis*, trans. and ed. James Strachey (W. W. Norton & Company, 1989), 217.

21 Susan M. Watkins, "Togetherness in Space: Class Dreams and Co-Creations," in *Conversations with Seth: Book Two* (Moment Point Press, 2006), 41.

22 René Guénon, "The Illusion of 'Ordinary Life,'" in *The Reign of Quantity and the Signs of the Times*, trans. Lord Northbourne (Sophia Perennis, 2004), 101.

23 Māṇḍūkya Upanishad 1:1:4, *The Upanishads, Vol. 1*, trans. Swāmi Nikhilānanda (Harper & Brothers Publishers, 1949), 262.

24 William Law, *The Works of the Reverend William Law, Vol. VI* (G. Moreton, 1893), 116.

25 John Milton, 1.254–255, *Paradise Lost, Book 1*, ed. Frederick Gorse (Blackie and Son, 1895), 33.

26 C. G. Jung, "The Practical Use of Dream-Analysis" (1934), in *The Collected Works of C.G. Jung, Vol. 16: The Practice of Psychotherapy*, trans. R. F. C. Hull (Princeton University Press, 1985), 153.

27 Mircea Eliade, "The Doctrines of Yoga," in *Yoga: Immortality and Freedom*, trans. Willard R. Trask (Princeton University Press, 1973), 23.

28 Shankara, Brahmasūtrabhāṣya I.1.5, *The Vedānta Sutras of Bādarāyana with a Commentary by Śaṅkara, Part 1*, trans. George Thibaut (Dover Publications, 1962), 51.

29 Marco Pallis, "The Round of Existence," in *Peaks and Lamas* (Alfred A. Knopf, 1949), 127.

30 William James, "Mysticism," in *The Varieties of Religious Experience: A Study in Human Nature* (Penguin Books, 1985), 388.

31 Frithjof Schuon, "Some Observations on a Problem of the Afterlife," in *Dimensions of Islam*, trans. Peter N. Townsend (George Allen and Unwin, 1970), 139.

32 Toshihiko Izutsu, "The Basic Structure of Metaphysical Thinking in Islam," in *Creation and the Timeless Order of Things: Essays in Islamic Mystical Philosophy* (White Cloud Press, 1994), 6–7.

33 Ashtāvakra Gītā 1:11, *The Heart of Awareness: A Translation of the Ashtavakra Gita*, trans. Thomas Byrom (Shambhala Publications, 1990), 3.

34 Dhammapada 1:1, *The Dhammapada*, trans. Irving Babbitt (New Directions, 1965), 3.

35 Rūmī, quoted in William C. Chittick, *The Sufi Path of Love: The Spiritual Teachings of Rumi* (State University of New York Press, 1983), 96.

36 William James, "The Sentiment of Rationality," in *The Will to Believe, and Other Essays in Popular Philosophy* (Longmans, Green, and Company, 1907), 103.

37 Bhagavad Gītā 2:16, *The Bhagavad Gita*, trans. Juan Mascaró (Penguin Books, 1962), 11.

38 Swāmi Nikhilānanda, quoted in *The Māṇḍūkya Upaniṣad with Gauḍapāda's Kārikā and Śaṅkara's Commentary*, trans. Swāmi Nikhilānanda (Sri Ramakrishna Ashrama, 1949), 71.

39 Śrī Ramana Maharshi, "Life in the World," in *The Teachings of Ramana Maharshi in His Own Words*, ed. Arthur Osborne (Samuel Weiser, 1978), 91.

40 Buddha Shakyamuni, Verse 1, *The Dhammapada: The Path of Perfection*, trans. Juan Mascaró (Penguin Books, 1973), 35.

41 Saraha, quoted in *Buddhist Scriptures*, ed. Donald S. Lopez Jr. (Penguin Books, 2004), 482.

42 Śrī Ramana Maharshi, "Talk 39—September 22nd, 1936," in *Talks with Sri Ramana Maharshi* (Sri Ramanasramam, 1996), 46.

43 John Smith, "Chapter 6—A Third Deduction," in *Selected Discourses* (Cambridge University Press, 1859), 151.

44 Boethius, "Book 2," in *The Consolation of Philosophy*, trans. Richard H. Green (Dover Publications, 2002), 24.

45 Berakhot 55b, quoted in *The Babylonian Talmud: Berakhot*, trans. Simon Maurice, ed. Isadore Epstein (Soncino Press, 1948), 341–342.

46 Sanā'ī, quoted in *Islamic Spirituality: Foundations*, ed. Seyyed Hossein Nasr (Crossroad, 1987), 397.

47 Ralph Waldo Emerson, "Journal Entry—December 20th, 1822," in *The Journals and Miscellaneous Notebooks of Ralph Waldo Emerson, Vol. II: 1822–1826*, eds. William H. Gilman, Alfred R. Ferguson, and Merrell R. Davis (Belknap Press, 1961), 71.

48 Rabbi Israel of Ruzhin, quoted in *The Hasidic Anthology: Tales and Teachings of the Hasidim*, trans. Louis I. Newman (Schocken Books, 1963), 91.

49 Manu 1:14, *The Laws of Manu,* trans. Georg Bühler (Clarendon Press, 1886), 6.

50 Śrī Rāmakrishna, "Advice to Ishan—Saturday, October 11, 1884," in *The Gospel of Ramakrishna: Originally recorded in Bengali by M., a disciple of the Master*, trans. Swāmi Nikhilānanda (Ramakrishna-Vivekananda Center, 1977), 615.

51 Chāndogya Upanishad 7:3:1, *The Principal Upanishads*, trans. and ed. Swāmi Nikhilānanda (Dover Publications, 2003), 338.

52 Fu-Ta-shih, quoted in Masao Abe, *Zen and Comparative Studies: Part Two of a Two-Volume Sequel to Zen and Western Thought*, ed. Steven Heine (University of Hawai'i Press, 1997), 71.

53 Saint Nikitas Stithatos, "On Spiritual Knowledge, Love and the Perfection of Living: One Hundred Texts," in *The Philokalia, Vol. 4: The Complete Text; Compiled by St. Nikodimos of the Holy Mountain and St. Makarios of Corinth*, trans. and ed. G. E. H. Palmer, Philip Sherrard, and Kallistos Ware (Faber and Faber, 1998), 139.

54 Moses Maimonides, "On the Terms: The Intellectus, the Intelligens and the Intelligibile," in *The Guide for the Perplexed*, trans. Michael Friedländer (Dover, 1956), 100.

55 Taittirīya Upanishad 3:4:1, *The Upanishads*, trans. Juan Mascaró (Penguin Books, 1965), 111.

56 Śrī Śaṅkarācārya, 521, *Vivekachudamani of Sri Sankaracharya: Text with English Translation, Notes and an Index,* trans. Swāmi Mādhavānanda (Advaita Ashrama, 1921), 226.

57 Parmenides of Elea, Fragment 3, *Fragments: A Text and Translation with an Introduction*, trans. David Gallop (University of Toronto Press, 2000), 57.

58 Rabbi Nachman, quoted in Martin Buber, *The Tales of Rabbi Nachman*, trans. Maurice Friedman (Indiana University Press, 1962), 13.

59 Toshihiko Izutsu, "The Basic Structure of Metaphysical Thinking in Islam," in *Creation and the Timeless Order of Things: Essays in Islamic Mystical Philosophy* (White Cloud Press, 1994), 7.

60 Shinran, *The Essential Shinran: A Buddhist Path of True Entrusting*, ed. Alfred Bloom (World Wisdom, 2007), 47.

61 William Blake, "A Memorable Fancy," in *The Marriage of Heaven and Hell* (John W. Luce and Company, 1906), 26.

62 Māṇḍūkya Upanishad 3:1, *The Upanishads*, trans. Juan Mascaró (Penguin Books, 1965), 80.

63 Meister Eckhart, "Commentary on Exodus," in *Meister Eckhart: Teacher and Preacher*, ed. Bernard McGinn (Paulist Press, 1986), 76.

64 Maitrī Upanishad 6:24, *The Upanishads*, trans. Juan Mascaró (Penguin Books, 1965), 103.

65 Li Qing-an, quoted in *The Taoist Classics, Vol. 2: The Collected Translations of Thomas Cleary* (Shambhala Publications, 1999), 520.

66 C. G. Jung, "The Aims of Psychotherapy," in *Modern Man in Search of a Soul*, trans. W. S. Dell and Cary F. Baynes (Harcourt, Brace & World, 1933), 72–73.

67 Saint Peter of Damaskos, "Book 1: On Building up the Soul through the Virtues," in *The Philokalia, Vol. 3: The Complete Text; Compiled by St. Nikodimos of the Holy Mountain and St. Makarios of Corinth*, trans. and ed. G. E. H. Palmer, Philip Sherrard, and Kallistos Ware (Faber and Faber, 1995), 182.

68 Theoliptos, Metropolitan of Philadelphia, "On Inner Work in Christ and the Monastic Profession," in *The Philokalia, Vol. 4: The Complete Text; Compiled by St. Nikodimos of the Holy Mountain and St. Makarios of Corinth*, trans. and ed. G. E. H. Palmer, Philip Sherrard, and Kallistos Ware (Faber and Faber, 1998), 179.

69 Aśvaghoṣa, "The Cause and Conditions of Man's Being in Samsara—Consciousness," in *The Awakening of Faith: Attributed to Aśvaghosha*, trans. Yoshito S. Hakeda (Columbia University Press, 1967), 50.

70 Tennō Dōgo, quoted in D. T. Suzuki, *Zen and Japanese Culture* (Princeton University Press, 2019), 13.

71 Zhūangzi, "How to Govern," in *Chuang Tzu: Mystic, Moralist, and Social Reformer*, trans. Herbert A. Giles (Bernard Quaritch, 1889), 97.

72 Frithjof Schuon, "Knowledge and Love," in *Spiritual Perspectives and Human Facts: A New Translation with Selected Letters*, trans. Mark Perry, Jean-Pierre Lafouge and James S. Cutsinger, ed. James S. Cutsinger (World Wisdom, 2007), 162.

73 Padmasambhāva, quoted in *The Tibetan Book of the Great Liberation,* ed. W. Y. Evans-Wentz (Oxford University Press, 1954), 211.

74 Saint Francis de Sales, "Letter 97—To Madame de Chantal," in *A Selection from the Spiritual Letters of S. Francis de Sales* (Rivingtons, 1871), 228.

75 Julian of Norwich, "Long Text, The Thirteenth Revelation," in S*howings*, trans. Edmund Colledge and James Walsh (Paulist Press, 1978), 225.

76 William Shakespeare, Hamlet 2.2, *A New Variorum Edition of Shakespeare, Vol. 3: Hamlet*, ed. Horace Howard Furness (J. B. Lippincott Company, 1877), 154.

77 René Guénon, "Communication with the Dead," in *The Spiritist Fallacy*, trans. Alvin Moore, Jr. and Rama P. Coomaraswamy (Sophia Perennis, 2001), 163.

78 William James, "Mysticism," in *The Varieties of Religious Experience: A Study in Human Nature* (Penguin Books, 1985), 388.

Chapter 4 — The Enneagram's Science of the Soul

1 Shaykh 'Abd Allāh al-Fā'iz ad-Dāghestanī, quoted in Shaykh Muhammad Hisham Kabbani, *Classical Islam and the Naqshbandi Sufi Tradition* (Islamic Supreme Council of America, 2004), 404.

2 René Guénon, "Individualism," in *The Crisis of the Modern World,* trans. Arthur Osborne, Marco Pallis and Richard C. Nicholson (Sophia Perennis, 2004), 56–57.

3 James Moore, "The Enneagram: A Developmental Study," *Religion Today: A Journal of Contemporary Religions*, vol. 5, no. 3 (October 1986/January 1987), 1.

4 Helen Palmer, quoted in "Special Forum: The Enneagram in Contention," *Gnosis*, no. 42 (Winter 1997), 14.

5 J. G. Bennett, "The Great Laws," in *Gurdjieff: Making a New World* (Harper & Row, 1973), 293.

6 Ken Wilber, "The Enneagram and the Basic Skeleton," in *A Brief History of Everything* (Shambhala Publications, 1996), 210.

7 Barbara Metz and John Burchill, *The Enneagram and Prayer: Discovering Our True Selves Before God* (Dimension Books, 1987), 11.

8 See Laleh Bakhtiar, *Traditional Psychoethics and Personality Paradigm* (Institute of Traditional Psychoethics and Guidance, 1993); Laleh Bakhtiar, *Moral Healer's Handbook: Psychology of Spiritual Chivalry* (Institute of Traditional Psychoethics and Guidance, 1994); Laleh Bakhtiar, *Moral Healing Through the Most Beautiful Names: The Practice of Spiritual Chivalry* (Institute of Traditional Psychoethics and Guidance, 1994). Laleh Bakhtiar, *The Sufi Enneagram: The Secrets of the Symbol Unveiled* (Institute of Traditional Psychology, 2013); Laleh Bakhtiar, *Rumi's Original Sufi Enneagram* (Institute of Traditional Psychology, 2013).

9 René Guénon, "The Directions of Space," in *The Symbolism of the Cross,* trans. Angus Macnab (Sophia Perennis, 2004), 22.

10 René Guénon, "Word and Symbol," in *Symbols of Sacred Science,* trans. Henry D. Fohr, ed. Samuel D. Fohr (Sophia Perennis, 2004), 10.

11 Frithjof Schuon, "Traces of Being, Proofs of God," in *Roots of the Human Condition* (World Wisdom, 2002), 57.

12 Frithjof Schuon, "Traces of Being, Proofs of God," in *Roots of the Human Condition* (World Wisdom, 2002), 57.

13 Clement of Alexandria, "The Instructor, Book 3, Chapter 1," in *The Writings of Clement of Alexandria*, trans. William Wilson (T. & T. Clark, 1867), 273.

14 Henry Corbin, "The Question of Comparative Philosophy: Convergences in Iranian and European Thought," *Spring: An Annual of Archetypal Psychology and Jungian Thought* (1980), p. 3.

15 "Corbin . . . used to translate phenomenology . . . to the Persian-speaking students as *kashf al-maḥjūb*, literally 'rending asunder of the veil to reveal the hidden essence,' and considered his method . . . to be spiritual hermeneutics *(al-ta'wīl)* as understood in classical Sufi and Shi'ite thought." [Seyyed Hossein Nasr, "Religion and Religions," in Religion and the Order of Nature (Oxford University Press, 1996), 26.]

16 Oscar Ichazo, quoted in Andrea Isaacs and Jack Labanauskas, "Interview with Oscar Ichazo," *Enneagram Monthly*, vol. 2, no. 11 (November 1996), 18.

17 René Guénon, "Word and Symbol," in *Symbols of Sacred Science*, trans. Henry D. Fohr, ed. Samuel D. Fohr (Sophia Perennis, 2004), 9.

18 Titus Burckhardt, "The Traditional Sciences in Fez," in *Mirror of the Intellect: Essays on Traditional Science and Sacred Art*, trans. and ed. William Stoddart (State University of New York Press, 1987), 173.

19 René Guénon, "The Great Parody: or Spirituality Inverted," in *The Reign of Quantity and the Signs of the Times*, trans. Lord Northbourne (Sophia Perennis, 2001), 267.

20 Shaykh Muhammad Hisham Kabbani, "A Meeting with Gurdjieff," in *Classical Islam and the Naqshbandi Sufi Tradition* (Islamic Supreme Council of America, 2004), 403–405.

21 James Moore, "The Enneagram: A Developmental Study," *Religion Today: A Journal of Contemporary Religions*, vol. 5, no. 3 (October 1986/January

1987), 1; An updated version of this article was made available in March 2004.

22 Gurdjieff, quoted in P. D. Ouspensky, *In Search of the Miraculous: Fragments of an Unknown Teaching* (Harcourt, Brace and World, 1949), 294.

23 James Webb, "The Sources of the System," in *The Harmonious Circle: The Lives and Work of G. I. Gurdjieff, P. D. Ouspensky, and Their Followers* (G. P. Putnam's Sons, 1987), 505; "Gurdjieff's favorite symbol was the Enneagram." [Whitall N. Perry, "The Teaching," in *Gurdjieff in the Light of Tradition* (Sophia Perennis, 2001), 49.]

24 See Sam Keen, "A Conversation about Ego Destruction with Oscar Ichazo," *Psychology Today*, vol. 7, no. 2 (July 1973), 64–72; Katinka Matson, "Arica/Oscar Ichazo," in *The Psychology Today Omnibook of Personal Development* (William Morrow and Company, 1977), 52–55; Andrew Rawlinson, "Oscar Ichazo," in *The Book of Enlightened Masters: Western Teachers in Eastern Traditions* (Open Court, 1997), 331–333.

25 Oscar Ichazo, "Letter to the Transpersonal Community," *The Arican: International Journal of Arica Institute*, no. 5 (Autumn 1991), 108.

26 Oscar Ichazo, quoted in Sam Keen, "A Conversation about Ego Destruction with Oscar Ichazo," *Psychology Today*, vol. 7, no. 2 (July 1973), 64, 67.

27 Amy Wallace, "I Meet the World's Most Elusive Man," in *Sorcerer's Apprentice: My Life with Carlos Castaneda* (Frog, 2003), 16. See also Richard de Mille, *Castaneda's Journey: The Power and the Allegory* (Capra Press, 1976); Richard de Mille, ed., *The Don Juan Papers: Further Castaneda Controversies* (Ross-Erikson Publishers, 1980).

28 See John C. Lilly, *The Deep Self: Profound Relaxation and the Tank Isolation Technique* (Simon & Schuster, 1977), 220–221.

29 Oscar Ichazo, quoted in Sam Keen, "A Conversation about Ego Destruction with Oscar Ichazo," *Psychology Today*, vol. 7, no. 2 (July 1973), 64.

30 David S. Flattery and Reza Leah Landman, eds., *Catalyst of Miracles: The Unknown Claudio Naranjo* (Gateways Books and Tapes, 2012).

31 Frederick S. Perls, *In and Out the Garbage Pail* (Bantam Books, 1979), 35.

32 Jeffrey J. Kripal, "Oscar Ichazo and Arica," in *Esalen: America and the Religion of No Religion* (University of Chicago Press, 2007), 177–180.

33 Claudio Naranjo, "A Report to the 'First International Enneagram Conference,'" *Enneagram Monthly*, vol. 2, no. 2 (February 1996), 16; See also OM C. Parkin and Boris Fittkau, "The Distorted Enneagram: The Gnosis Interview with Claudio Naranjo," *Gnosis*, no. 41 (Fall 1996), 20–24.

34 See Rama P. Coomaraswamy, *The Destruction of the Christian Tradition: Updated and Revised* (World Wisdom, 2006); Mark Perry, *Uprooting the Vineyard: The Fate of the Catholic Church After Vatican II* (World Wisdom, 2025).

35 See Richard Rohr and Andreas Ebert, *The Enneagram: A Christian Perspective* (Crossroad, 2001).

36 See Mitch Pacwa, *Catholics and the New Age: How Good People Are Being Drawn into Jungian Psychology, the Enneagram, and the Age of Aquarius* (Servant Publications, 1992).

37 Oscar Ichazo, "Letter to the Transpersonal Community," *The Arican: International Journal of Arica Institute*, no. 5 (Autumn 1991), 112.

38 Helen Palmer, quoted in "Special Forum: The Enneagram in Contention," *Gnosis*, no. 42 (Winter 1997), 13.

39 Helen Palmer, quoted in Richard Smoley, "Why the Enneagram? An Interview with Helen Palmer," *Gnosis*, no. 32 (Summer 1994), 19.

40 Claudio Naranjo, "A Report to the 'First International Enneagram Conference,'" *Enneagram Monthly*, vol. 2, no. 2 (February 1996), 16; See also OM C. Parkin and Boris Fittkau, "The Distorted Enneagram: The Gnosis Interview with Claudio Naranjo," *Gnosis*, no. 41 (Fall 1996), 20–24.

41 Oscar Ichazo, quoted in Andrea Isaacs and Jack Labanauskas, "Interview with Oscar Ichazo," *Enneagram Monthly*, vol. 2, no. 11 (November 1996), 18.

42 Gurdjieff, quoted in P. D. Ouspensky, *In Search of the Miraculous: Fragments of an Unknown Teaching* (Harcourt, Brace and World, 1949), 294.

43 J. Walter Driscoll, *Gurdjieff: An Annotated Bibliography* (Garland, 1985), 89.

44 Helen Palmer, quoted in Oscar Ichazo, "Letter to the Transpersonal Community," *The Arican: International Journal of Arica Institute*, no. 5 (Autumn 1991), 111.

45 John C. Lilly and Joseph E. Hart, "The Arica Training," in *Transpersonal Psychologies*, ed. Charles T. Tart (Harper & Row, 1975), 333; See also John C. Lilly, "My First Trip to Chile: Oscar Ichazo" and "Second Trip to Chile: States of Consciousness Defined," in *The Center of the Cyclone* (Bantam Books, 1973), 148–154, 155–165.

46 Oscar Ichazo, "Letter to the Transpersonal Community," *The Arican: International Journal of Arica Institute*, no. 5 (Autumn 1991), 93.

47 Oscar Ichazo, quoted in Sam Keen, "A Conversation about Ego Destruction with Oscar Ichazo," *Psychology Today*, vol. 7, no. 2 (July 1973), 64.

48 Oscar Ichazo, quoted in John Bleibtreu (ed.), *Interviews with Oscar Ichazo* (Arica Institute Press, 1982), 176.

49 Oscar Ichazo, "Letter to the Transpersonal Community," *The Arican: International Journal of Arica Institute*, no. 5 (Autumn 1991), 104; See also Dorothy De Christopher, "I am the Root of a New Tradition," in *Interviews with Oscar Ichazo*, ed. John Bleibtreu (Arica Institute Press, 1982), 129–150; Paradoxically, Ichazo appears to be affirming the same position as Gurdjieff, yet now divorced from the Fourth Way system: "The teaching whose theory is here being set out is completely self-supporting and independent of other lines and it has been completely unknown up to the present time." [Gurdjieff, quoted in P. D. Ouspensky, *In Search of the Miraculous: Fragments of an Unknown Teaching* (Harcourt, Brace and World, 1949), 286.]

50 Claudio Naranjo, quoted in OM C. Parkin and Boris Fittkau, "The Distorted Enneagram: The Gnosis Interview with Claudio Naranjo," *Gnosis*, no. 41 (Fall 1996), 22.

51 John C. Lilly and Joseph E. Hart, "The Arica Training," in *Transpersonal Psychologies*, ed. Charles T. Tart (Harper & Row, 1975), 341.

52 John C. Lilly and Joseph E. Hart, "The Arica Training," in *Transpersonal Psychologies*, ed. Charles T. Tart (Harper & Row, 1975), 341.

53 Oscar Ichazo, "Letter to the Transpersonal Community," *The Arican: International Journal of Arica Institute*, no. 5 (Autumn 1991), 106.

54 OM C. Parkin and Boris Fittkau, "The Distorted Enneagram: The Gnosis Interview with Claudio Naranjo," *Gnosis*, no. 41 (Fall 1996), 22.

55 OM C. Parkin and Boris Fittkau, "The Distorted Enneagram: The Gnosis Interview with Claudio Naranjo," *Gnosis*, no. 41 (Fall 1996), 22.

56 Claudio Naranjo, "A Report to the 'First International Enneagram Conference,'" *Enneagram Monthly*, vol. 2, no. 2 (February 1996), 16.

57 OM C. Parkin and Boris Fittkau, "The Distorted Enneagram: The Gnosis Interview with Claudio Naranjo," *Gnosis*, no. 41 (Fall 1996), 22.

58 James Moore, "The Long Search," in *Gurdjieff: The Anatomy of a Myth* (Element, 1991), 31.

59 Claudio Naranjo, "Acknowledgement," to *Ennea-Type Structures: Self-Analysis for the Seeker* (Gateways/IDHHB, 1990), viii.

60 Helen Palmer, "Contributors to the System," in *The Enneagram* (HarperCollins, 1991), 46.

61 Claudio Naranjo, "A Report to the 'First International Enneagram Conference,'" *Enneagram Monthly*, vol. 2, no. 2 (February 1996), 16.

62 See an interview with Naranjo conducted by E. J. Gold, "The Origin of the Enneagram: Claudio Naranjo Speaks," uploaded on June 18, 2010, http://www.youtube.com/watch?v=wlO3KJWnNd8; See also "Claudio Naranjo—Seeker After Truth—Interview by Iain McNay," uploaded on December 21, 2010, http://www.youtube.com/watch?v=s7MSZfVZzJ0.

63 Eli Jaxon-Bear, quoted in "Special Forum: The Enneagram in Contention," *Gnosis*, no. 42 (Winter 1997), 15.

64 Claudio Naranjo, foreword to *Character and Neurosis: An Integrative View* (Gateways/IDHHB, 2003), xxx.

65 Helen Palmer, "Contributors to the System," in *The Enneagram* (HarperCollins, 1991), 47.

66 Claudio Naranjo, foreword to *Character and Neurosis: An Integrative View* (Gateways/IDHHB, 2003), xxx.

67 See Claudio Naranjo, *Ennea-Type Structures: Self-Analysis for the Seeker* (Gateways/IDHHB, 1990).

68 Claudio Naranjo, foreword to *Character and Neurosis: An Integrative View* (Gateways/IDHHB, 2003), xxviii.

69 Idries Shah, "Symbols, especially the Enneagon," in *The Commanding Self* (Octagon Press, 1997), 286–287.

70 Here are some works influenced by or containing Idries Shah's ideas within modern psychology: Idries Shah, "The Value of the Past," *Journal of Humanistic Psychology*, vol. 16, no. 3 (July 1976), 92; Claudio Naranjo and Robert E. Ornstein, *On the Psychology of Meditation* (Viking Press, 1971); Arthur J. Deikman, "Sufism and Psychiatry," in *Transpersonal Psychotherapy, Second Edition*, ed. Seymour Boorstein (State University of New York Press, 1996), 241–260; Robert E. Ornstein, *The Psychology of Consciousness* (Viking Press, 1972); Robert E. Ornstein, "Contemporary Sufism," in *Transpersonal Psychologies*, ed. Charles T. Tart (Harper & Row, 1975), 353–388; Robert E. Ornstein, ed., *The Nature of Human Consciousness: A Book of Readings* (Viking Press, 1974), 271–309; Charles T. Tart, *Waking Up: Overcoming the Obstacles to Human Potential* (New Science Library, 1986); Charles T. Tart, *Open Mind, Discriminating Mind: Reflections on Human Possibilities* (Harper & Row, 1989); Robert Frager and James Fadiman, "Sufism," in *Personality and Personal Growth* (HarperCollins, 1984), 478–513.

71 Annemarie Schimmel provides her appraisal of Idries Shah: "He has no scholarly background, and his ramblings combine things which can really not be brought together; historical interest is nil, and accuracy very limited . . . I am willing to accept a genuine Sufi, who is not a scholar but has a deep experience, if his words radiate truth and honesty, even though he may be unable to express himself in an 'academic' style; that is not the problem; but I cannot accept Idries Shah's claims which are mere pretensions." [Quoted

from a letter dated May 25, 1985, in Peter Lamborn Wilson, "The Strange Fate of Sufism in the New Age," in *New Trends and Developments in the World of Islam*, ed. Peter B. Clarke (Luzac Oriental Press, 1997), 193–194]; "Idries Shah, *The Sufis* [1964], as well as his other books, should be avoided by serious students." [Annemarie Schimmel, "What is Sufism?," in *Mystical Dimensions of Islam* (University of North Carolina Press, 1975), 9]; See also L. P. Elwell-Sutton, "Sufism and Pseudo-Sufism," *Encounter*, vol. 44, no. 5 (May 1975), 9–17; Martin Lings, "Book Review—The Sufis," *Tomorrow*, vol. 3, no. 1 (Winter 1965), 56–57; R. N. J. A., "Book Reviews—The Book of the Book by Idries Shah," *Studies in Comparative Religion*, vol. 4, no. 3 (Summer 1970), 188–190; James Moore, "Neo-Sufism: The Case of Idries Shah," *Religion Today: A Journal of Contemporary Religions*, vol. 3, no. 3 (1986), 4–8.

72 Don Richard Riso, "Enneagram Interpretations and Contributions," in *Discovering Your Personality Type: The Enneagram Questionnaire* (Houghton Mifflin, 1992), 117.

73 Kathleen Riordan Speeth, "Who Was Gurdjieff?," in *The Gurdjieff Work* (Jeremy P. Tarcher/Putnam, 1989), 9.

74 Helen Palmer, "Background of the System and an Introduction to Type," in *The Enneagram* (HarperCollins, 1991), 3. For more information on Palmer and Gurdjieff's Fourth Way teaching, see William Patrick Patterson, *Talking with the Left Hand: Enneagram Craze, People of the Bookmark, & The Mouravieff "Phenomenon"* (Arete Communications, 1998).

75 Oscar Ichazo, quoted in Michael J. Goldberg, "Inside the Enneagram Wars," *LA Weekly* (October 15–21, 1993), 24.

76 A. H. Almaas, "A Brief History of the Enneagram," in *Facets of Unity: The Enneagram of Holy Ideas* (Diamond Books, 1998), 3; See also Oscar Ichazo, foreword to A. H. Almaas, *Facets of Unity: The Enneagram of Holy Ideas* (Diamond Books, 1998), v–viii.

77 OM C. Parkin and Boris Fittkau, "The Distorted Enneagram: The Gnosis Interview with Claudio Naranjo," *Gnosis*, no. 41 (Fall 1996), 23.

78 Claudio Naranjo, "A Report to the 'First International Enneagram Conference,'" *Enneagram Monthly*, vol. 2, no. 2 (February 1996), 17.

79 Shaykh Muhammad Hisham Kabbani, "A Meeting with John Bennett," in *Classical Islam and the Naqshbandi Sufi Tradition* (Islamic Supreme Council of America, 2004), 449–451.

80 Shaykh 'Abd Allāh al-Fā'iz ad-Dāghestanī, quoted in Shaykh Muhammad Hisham Kabbani, *Classical Islam and the Naqshbandi Sufi Tradition* (Islamic Supreme Council of America, 2004), 404.

81 James Webb, "The Sources of the System," in *The Harmonious Circle: The Lives and Work of G. I. Gurdjieff, P. D. Ouspensky, and Their Followers* (G. P. Putnam's Sons, 1987), 499–542; We might make note of Kircher's warning about unqualified individuals pursuing the esoteric knowledge of the nine-pointed symbol of the Enneagram: "And I have exposed to the curious reader things which are told to few. Farewell, and guard your tongue." [Quoted in James Webb, "The Sources of the System," in *The Harmonious Circle: The Lives and Work of G. I. Gurdjieff, P. D. Ouspensky, and Their Followers* (G. P. Putnam's Sons, 1987), 508.]

82 Gurdjieff, quoted in P. D. Ouspensky, *In Search of the Miraculous: Fragments of an Unknown Teaching* (Harcourt, Brace and World, 1949), 102.

83 Oscar Ichazo, "Letter to the Transpersonal Community," *The Arican: International Journal of Arica Institute*, no. 5 (Autumn 1991), 101.

84 See Seyyed Hossein Nasr, foreword to Laleh Bakhtiar, *Moral Healer's Handbook: Psychology of Spiritual Chivalry* (Institute of Traditional Psychoethics and Guidance, 1994), vii–viii.

85 Helen Palmer, "Background of the System and an Introduction to Type," in *The Enneagram* (HarperCollins, 1991), 9.

86 Helen Palmer, "Background of the System and an Introduction to Type," in *The Enneagram* (HarperCollins, 1991), 9.

87 Oscar Ichazo, quoted in Andrea Isaacs and Jack Labanauskas, "Interview with Oscar Ichazo, Part 3," *Enneagram Monthly*, vol. 3, no. 1 (January 1997), 21.

88 Robert E. Ornstein, "Toward a Complete Psychology," in *The Psychology of Consciousness* (Viking Press, 1972), 11.

89 Oscar Ichazo, quoted in Andrea Isaacs and Jack Labanauskas, "Interview with Oscar Ichazo, Part 3," *Enneagram Monthly,* vol. 3, no. 1 (January 1997), 21.

90 Helen Palmer, "Contributors to the System," in *The Enneagram* (HarperCollins, 1991), 52.

91 Chögyam Trungpa, quoted in Daniel Goleman, foreword to *The Sanity We Are Born With: A Buddhist Approach to Psychology,* ed. Carolyn Rose Gimian (Shambhala Publications, 2005), vii; "Many modern psychologists have found that the discoveries and explanations of the abhidharma coincide with their own recent discoveries and new ideas; as though the abhidharma, which was taught 2,500 years ago, had been redeveloped in the modern idiom." [Chögyam Trungpa, introduction to *Glimpses of Abhidharma: From a Seminar on Buddhist Psychology* (Shambhala Publications, 2001), 2.]

92 Robert E. Ornstein, introduction to Claudio Naranjo and Robert E. Ornstein, *On the Psychology of Meditation* (Viking Press, 1971), 139.

93 P. D. Ouspensky, "First Lecture," in *The Psychology of Man's Possible Evolution* (Vintage Books, 1981), 4.

94 P. D. Ouspensky, "First Lecture," in *The Psychology of Man's Possible Evolution* (Vintage Books, 1981), 3.

95 P. D. Ouspensky, "First Lecture," in *The Psychology of Man's Possible Evolution* (Vintage Books, 1981), 3.

96 Frithjof Schuon, "The Psychological Imposture," *Tomorrow*, vol. 14, no. 2 (Spring 1966), 98–101.

97 Richard of Saint Victor, Benjamin Minor, Capitulum 75, quoted in *The Cell of Self-knowledge: Seven Early English Mystical Treatises printed by Henry Pepwell in 1521*, ed. Edmund G. Gardner (Chatto & Windus, 1925), xv.

98 Helen Palmer, "Background of the System and an Introduction to Type," in *The Enneagram* (HarperCollins, 1991), 3.

99 Hameed Ali, quoted in Tony Schwartz, "Personality and Essence: Helen Palmer, the Enneagram, and Hameed Ali," in *What Really Matters: Searching for Wisdom in America* (Bantam Books, 1996), 406.

100 'Alī B. 'Uthmān al-Jullābī al-Hujwīrī, *The Kashf al-Maḥjub: The Oldest Persian Treatise on Sufism*, trans. Reynold A. Nicholson (Luzac and Company, 1911), 14.

101 See Samuel Bendeck Sotillos, "The Deification of the Psyche: Carl Jung and the Spiritual Crisis of the Modern World," *Sacred Web: A Journal of Tradition and Modernity*, vol. 51 (2025).

102 Robert E. Ornstein, "The Traditional Esoteric Psychologies," in *The Psychology of Consciousness* (Viking Press, 1972), 95–179.

103 See Peter Lamborn Wilson, "The Strange Fate of Sufism in the New Age," in *New Trends and Developments in the World of Islam*, ed. Peter B. Clarke (Luzac Oriental Press, 1997), 179–209.

104 C. G. Jung, "Schiller's Ideas on the Type Problem" (1921), in *The Collected Works of C. G. Jung, Vol. 6: Psychological Types*, trans. R. F. C. Hull (Princeton University Press, 1976), 131.

105 Frithjof Schuon, "Gnosis, Language of the Self," in *Gnosis: Divine Wisdom*, trans. G. E. H. Palmer (Perennial Books, 1990), 67.

106 American Psychiatric Association, *Diagnostic and Statistical Manual of Mental Disorders, Fifth Edition, Text Revision* (American Psychiatric Association, 2022), 735.

107 Lao Tzu, Chapter 16, *The Way of Lao Tzu (Tao-te ching)*, trans. Wing-Tsit Chan (Bobbs-Merrill Company, 1963), 128.

108 Frithjof Schuon, "The Ancient Worlds in Perspective," in *Light on the Ancient Worlds*, trans. Lord Northbourne (World Wisdom Books, 1984), 7.

109 Frithjof Schuon, "First Collection," in *Primordial Meditation: Contemplating the Real*, trans. Gillian Harris and Angela Schwartz (Matheson Trust, 2015), 23.

110 Frithjof Schuon, "The Spiritual Virtues," in *Spiritual Perspectives and Human Facts: A New Translation with Selected Letters*, trans. James S. Cutsinger (World Wisdom, 2007), 196.

111 Rūmī, quoted in William C. Chittick, *The Sufi Path of Love: The Spiritual Teachings of Rumi* (State University of New York Press, 1983), 177.

112 Gurdjieff, quoted in P. D. Ouspensky, *In Search of the Miraculous: Fragments of an Unknown Teaching* (Harcourt, Brace and World, 1949), 294.

113 Plotinus, Ennead 5.1.11, *The Enneads*, trans. Stephen MacKenna (Penguin Books, 1991), 360.

114 Alan of Lille, quoted in *Bonaventure: The Soul's Journey into God, The Tree of Life, The Life of St. Francis*, trans. Ewert Cousins (Paulist Press, 1978), 100.

115 Private correspondence with Laleh Bakhtiar.

116 C. G. Jung, "The Apollonian and the Dionysian" (1921), in *The Collected Works of C. G. Jung, Vol. 6: Psychological Types*, trans. R. F. C. Hull and H. G. Baynes, eds. Gerhard Adler and R. F. C. Hull (Princeton University Press, 1976), 143.

117 René Guénon, "Relationships of Unity and Multiplicity," in *The Multiple States of the Being*, trans. Henry D. Fohr, ed. Samuel D. Fohr (Sophia Perennis, 2001), 32.

118 René Guénon, "The Metaphysical Notion of Freedom," in *The Multiple States of the Being*, trans. Henry D. Fohr, ed. Samuel D. Fohr (Sophia Perennis, 2001), 90.

119 Lao Tzu, "Chapter 19," in *The Wisdom of Laotse*, trans. and ed. Lin Yutang (Michael Joseph, 1948), 119–120.

120 René Guénon, "The Resolution of Opposites," in *The Symbolism of the Cross*, trans. Angus Macnab (Sophia Perennis, 2004), 45.

121 Buddha Shakyamuni, 8:103–106, *The Dhammapada: The Path of Perfection*, trans. Juan Mascaró (Penguin Books, 1973), 50.

122 Martin Lings, "The Degrees," in *Muhammad: His Life Based on the Earliest Sources* (Inner Traditions, 1983), 327–328.

123 Thomas Yellowtail, quoted in Michael Oren Fitzgerald, *Yellowtail, Crow Medicine Man and Sun Dance Chief: An Autobiography* (University of Oklahoma Press, 1994), 139–140.

124 Shaykh ad-Darqāwī, *Letters of a Sufi Master*, trans. Titus Burckhardt (Fons Vitae, 1998), 76–77.

125 Richard Leviton, "Trademarking the New Age: Can Spiritual and Intellectual Ideas be Copyrighted?," *East West Journal*, vol. 21, no. 3 (March 1991), 36.

126 Lord Northbourne, "The Beauty of Flowers," in *Looking Back on Progress*, ed. Christopher James, 5th Lord Northbourne (Sophia Perennis, 2001), 46.

127 Rūmī, quoted in William C. Chittick, *The Sufi Path of Love: The Spiritual Teachings of Rumi* (State University of New York Press, 1983), 173.

Chapter 5 — Entheogens and Sacred Psychology

1 Śrī Rāmakrishna, "Pundit Shashadhar," in *The Gospel of Ramakrishna: Originally recorded in Bengali by M., a disciple of the Master,* trans. Swāmi Nikhilānanda (Ramakrishna-Vivekananda Center, 1977), 464.

2 Saint Peter of Damaskos, "Book 1: The Great Value of Love and of Advice given with Humility," in *The Philokalia, Vol. 3: The Complete Text; Compiled by St. Nikodimos of the Holy Mountain and St. Makarios of Corinth*, trans. and ed. G. E. H. Palmer, Philip Sherrard, and Kallistos Ware (Faber and Faber, 1995), 185.

3 Seung Sahn, "Special Medicine and Big Business," in *Dropping Ashes on the Buddha: The Teaching of Zen Master Seung Sahn*, ed. Stephen Mitchell (Grove Press, 1976), 97.

4 Paracelsus, "Preparation of Remedies," in *Paracelsus: Selected Writings*, trans. Norbert Guterman, ed. Jolande Jacobi (Princeton University Press, 1988), 95.

5 Albert Hofmann, "Can Insight into the Truths of Natural Science Be Therapeutically Effective in Psychology?," in *LSD and the Divine Scientist: The*

Final Thoughts and Reflections of Albert Hofmann, trans. Annabel Moynihan (Park Street Press, 2013), 45.

6 Antonin Artaud, "The Peyote Rite among the Tarahumara," in *The Peyote Dance*, trans. Helen Weaver (Farrar, Straus and Giroux, 1976), 22.

7 Here are a few citations that come from within the psychedelic movement challenging the notion that entheogens can produce religious-mystical experiences equal to those of the saints and sages of the spiritual traditions: "[H]ighly improbable that a true spiritual experience could follow from ingesting a particular chemical." [Alan Watts, "The Soul-Searchers," in *In My Own Way: An Autobiography, 1915–1965* (Pantheon Books, 1972), 342]; "I am not so foolish as to equate what happens under the influence of mescalin or of any other drug, prepared or in the future preparable, with the realization of the end and ultimate purpose of human life: Enlightenment, the Beatific Vision." [Aldous Huxley, *The Doors of Perception and Heaven and Hell* (Harper and Row, 1990), 73]; After many decades of discussion and debate, even psychedelic pioneers openly admit their uncertainty, admitting that the "question whether ... psychedelics can induce genuine spiritual experience is still open." [Stanislav Grof, "Non-Therapeutic Uses of LSD," in *LSD Psychotherapy* (Hunter House, 1980), 264]; We recall the well-known words of Neem Karoli Baba, who was given a psychedelic to see what he thought of it in terms of Spiritual Realization: "[I]t's useful, [but] not the true *samadhi*." [Neem Karoli Baba, quoted in Ram Dass, *The Only Dance There Is* (Anchor Books, 1974), 112]; See R. C. Zaehner, *Mysticism, Sacred and Profane: An Inquiry into some Varieties of Praeternatural Experience* (Oxford University Press, 1967); Laurent Weichberger with Laura Smith, eds., *A Mirage Will Never Quench Your Thirst: A Source of Wisdom about Drugs* (Sheriar Foundation, 2003).

8 See Samuel Bendeck Sotillos, "Book Review—The Immortality Key: The Secret History of the Religion with No Name," *Transcendent Philosophy: An International Journal for Comparative Philosophy and Mysticism*, vol. 24 (December 2023), 165–173.

9 See Whitall N. Perry, "Drug-Induced Mysticism: The Mescalin Hypothesis," in *Challenges to a Secular Society* (Foundation for Traditional Studies, 1996), 7–16; Mark Perry, "The Forbidden Door," in *The Mystery of*

Individuality: Grandeur and Delusion of the Human Condition (World Wisdom, 2012), 245–271.

10 James F. T. Bugental, "Living Is Only in the Now," in *Psychotherapy Isn't What You Think: Bringing the Psychotherapeutic Engagement Into the Living Moment* (Zeig, Tucker & Company, 1999), 61.

11 Stanislav Grof, "Critical Variables in LSD Therapy," in *LSD Psychotherapy* (Hunter House, 1980), 109.

12 Robert E. L. Masters and Jean Houston, "Toward an Individual Psychedelic Psychotherapy," in *Psychedelics: The Uses and Implications of Hallucinogenic Drugs*, eds. Bernard Aaronson and Humphry Osmond (Anchor Books, 1970), 342.

13 See, for example, "The theoretical basis of psychedelic therapy is rather underdeveloped." [Lester Grinspoon and James B. Bakalar, "Therapeutic Uses," in *Psychedelic Drugs Reconsidered* (Basic Books, 1981), 194.]

14 William V. Caldwell, "Appendix: Indications for the Use of Psychedelic Agents in Therapy," in *LSD Psychotherapy: An Exploration of Psychedelic and Psycholytic Therapy* (Grove Press, 1969), 285.

15 See Thomas Insel, *Healing: Our Path from Mental Illness to Mental Health* (Penguin Books, 2022).

16 Osmond coined the term "psychedelic" in his correspondence with Huxley. In responding to a letter that Osmond received from Huxley, he wrote in poetic reflection: "To fathom Hell or soar angelic, / Just take a pinch of psychedelic." [quoted in Aldous Huxley, "Letter to Humphry Osmond—March 30, 1956," in *Letters of Aldous Huxley*, ed. Grover Smith (Chatto and Windus, 1969), 795.]

17 See Carl A. P. Ruck, Jeremy Bigwood, Danny Staples, Jonathan Ott, and R. Gordon Wasson, "Entheogens," in *The Road to Eleusis: Unveiling the Secret of the Mysteries*, eds. R. Gordon Wasson, Albert Hofmann, and Carl A. P. Ruck (Hermes Press, 1998), 137–139.

18 Gerald Moore and Larry Schiller, "LSD: The Exploding Threat of the Mind Drug That Got Out of Control," *Life*, vol. 60, no. 12 (March 25, 1966).

19 "LSD—A Dangerous Drug," *New England Journal of Medicine*, vol. 273, no. 23 (December 2, 1965), 1280.

20 Sidney Cohen, quoted in *Organization and Coordination of Federal Drug Research and Regulatory Programs: LSD* (U.S. Government Printing Office, 1966), 152.

21 See Martin A. Lee and Bruce Shlain, *Acid Dreams: The Complete History of LSD: The CIA, The Sixties, and Beyond* (Grove Press, 1992); H. P. Albarelli Jr., *A Terrible Mistake: The Murder of Frank Olson, and the CIA's Secret Cold War Experiments* (Trine Day, 2009); Dana Strauss, Sara de la Salle, Jordan Sloshower, and Monica T. Williams, "Research Abuses Against People of Colour and Other Vulnerable Groups in Early Psychedelic Research," *Journal of Medical Ethics*, vol. 48, no. 10 (2022), 728–737.

22 See Tom O'Neill with Dan Piepenbring, *Chaos: Charles Manson, the CIA, and the Secret History of the Sixties* (Little, Brown and Company, 2019).

23 Jonathan Ott, preface to Albert Hofmann, *LSD: My Problem Child*, trans. Jonathan Ott (McGraw-Hill Book Company, 1980), vii.

24 See Samuel Bendeck Sotillos, "A Wisdom That Transcends All Times and Places: An Introduction to the Perennial Philosophy," *The Mountain Path*, vol. 59, no. 1 (January/March 2022), 29–46.

25 Louis Lewin, preface to *Phantastica: A Classic Survey on the Use and Abuse of Mind-Altering Plants* (Park Street Press, 1998), xv.

26 Richard Evans Schultes, *A Contribution to Our Knowledge of Rivea corymbosa: the Narcotic Ololiuqui of the Aztecs* (Botanical Museum of Harvard University, 1941).

27 Albert Hofmann, "The Active Principles of the Seeds of Rivea corymbosa and Ipomoea violacea," *Botanical Museum Leaflets*, vol. 20, no. 6 (November 1963), 194–212.

28 R. Gordon Wasson, "Seeking the Magic Mushroom," *Life*, vol. 42, no. 19 (May 13, 1957), 100–120.

29 Valentina P. Wasson, "I Ate the Sacred Mushrooms," *This Week* (May 19, 1957), 8–10, 36.

30 Jan Irving, "R. Gordon Wasson: The Man, the Legend, the Myth: Beginning a New History of Magic Mushrooms, Ethnomycology, and the Psychedelic Revolution," in *Entheogens and the Development of Culture: The Anthropology and Neurobiology of Ecstatic Experience*, ed. John A. Rush (North Atlantic Books, 2013), 565–619.

31 John Marks, *The Search for the "Manchurian Candidate": The CIA and Mind Control: The Secret History of the Behavioral Sciences* (W. W. Norton and Company, 1991); Stephen Kinzer, *Poisoner in Chief: Sidney Gottlieb and the CIA Search for Mind Control* (St. Martin's Griffin, 2020).

32 Richard Evans Schultes, "Plantae Mexicanae II: The Identification of Teonanacatl, a Narcotic Basidiomycete of the Aztecs," *Botanical Museum Leaflets*, vol. 7, no. 3 (February 1939), 37–54; Richard Evans Schultes, "Teonanacatl: The Narcotic Mushroom of the Aztecs," *American Anthropologist*, vol. 42, no. 3 (July/September 1940), 429–443.

33 "I was whirled through an experience which could be described in many extravagant metaphors but which was above all and without question the deepest religious experience of my life." [Timothy Leary, "The Religious Experience: Its Production and Interpretation," *Psychedelic Review*, vol. 1, no. 3 (1964), 324.]

34 Timothy Leary, "Sacred Mushrooms of Mexico," in *Flashbacks: A Personal and Cultural History of an Era* (Jeremy P. Tarcher/Putnam Book, 1990), 33.

35 See Richard de Mille, *Castaneda's Journey: The Power and the Allegory* (Capra Press, 1976); Richard de Mille, ed., *The Don Juan Papers: Further Castaneda Controversies* (Ross-Erikson Publishers, 1980).

36 See Lisa Aldred, "Plastic Shamans and Astroturf Sun Dances: New Age Commercialization of Native American Spirituality," *American Indian Quarterly*, vol. 24, no. 3 (Summer 2000), 329–352; Christopher Partridge, "Modern Psychedelic Gnosis," in *The Gnostic World,* eds. Garry W. Trompf, Gunner B. Mikkelsen, and Jay Johnston (Routledge, 2019), 652–662.

37 Huston Smith, preface to R. Gordon Wasson, Albert Hofmann, and Carl A. P. Ruck, *The Road to Eleusis: Unveiling the Secret of the Mysteries* (Hermes Press, 1998), 10.

38 Laura Huxley, "Disregarded in the Darkness" (1955), in *Moksha: Aldous Huxley's Classic Writings on Psychedelics and the Visionary Experience*, eds. Michael Horowitz and Cynthia Palmer (Park Street Press, 1999), 74.

39 Huston Smith, "Psychedelic Theophanies and the Religious Life," *Christianity and Crisis*, vol. 27, no. 11 (June 1967), 146.

40 See Aleister Crowley, *Diary of a Drug Fiend* (Samuel Weiser, 1997).

41 Aleister Crowley, "The Law of Thelema," in *The Book of the Law* (Red Wheel/Weiser Books, 1976), 9.

42 Saint Augustine, Homily 7 on the First Epistle of John, *A Select Library of the Nicene and Post-Nicene Fathers of the Christian Church*, ed. Philip Schaff (Christian Literature Company, 1888), 504.

43 See Timothy Leary, *High Priest* (Ronin Publishing, 1995).

44 See Timothy Leary, *Start Your Own Religion* (Kriya Press, 1967).

45 See Chögyam Trungpa, *Cutting through Spiritual Materialism*, edited by John Baker and Marvin Casper (Shambhala Publications, 2002).

46 See Frederic Spiegelberg, *The Religion of No-Religion* (James Ladd Delkin, 1953).

47 Albert Hofmann, "LSD Experience and Reality," in *LSD: My Problem Child*, trans. Jonathan Ott (McGraw-Hill Book Company, 1980), 208.

48 William Shakespeare, 2.1.12–14, *As You Like It*, eds. Barbara A. Mowat and Paul Werstine (Washington Square Press, 2004), 49.

49 Alan Watts, prologue to *The Joyous Cosmology: Adventures in the Chemistry of Consciousness* (Vintage, 1965), 26.

50 Zhūangzi, "External Things," in *Chuang Tzu: Basic Writings*, trans. Burton Watson (Columbia University Press, 1996), 140.

51 Huston Smith, "Psychedelic Theophanies and the Religious Life," in *Cleansing the Doors of Perception: The Religious Significance of Entheogenic Plants and Chemicals* (Jeremy P. Tarcher/Putnam, 2000), 41, 42.

52 Rick Strassman, "Stepping on Holy Toes," in *DMT: The Spirit Molecule: A Doctor's Revolutionary Research into the Biology of Near-Death and Mystical Experiences* (Park Street Press, 2000), 306.

53 See Samuel Bendeck Sotillos, "The Eclipse of the Soul and the Rise of the Ecological Crisis," *Spirituality Studies*, vol. 8, no. 2 (Fall 2022), 34–55.

54 See Samuel Bendeck Sotillos, "The Metaphysics of Trauma," *Transcendent Philosophy: An International Journal for Comparative Philosophy and Mysticism*, vol. 23 (December 2022), 23–53.

55 María Sabina, quoted in Álvaro Estrada, *María Sabina: Her Life and Chants*, trans. Henry Munn (Ross-Erikson, 1981), 73.

56 María Sabina, quoted in Álvaro Estrada, *María Sabina: Her Life and Chants*, trans. Henry Munn (Ross-Erikson, 1981), 91, 90.

57 R. Gordon Wasson, "A Retrospective Essay," in Álvaro Estrada, *María Sabina: Her Life and Chants*, trans. Henry Munn (Ross-Erikson, 1981), 20.

58 R. Gordon Wasson, quoted in Robert Forte, "A Conversation with R. Gordon Wasson (1898–1986)," *ReVision: The Journal of Consciousness and Change*, vol. 10, no. 4 (Spring 1988), 17.

59 R. Gordon Wasson, "The Shaman and the Mushroom: New Perspectives," in *The Wonderous Mushroom: Mycholatry in Mesoamerica* (McGraw-Hill Book Company, 1980), 223.

60 Humphry Osmond, "A Review of the Clinical Effects of Psychotomimetic Agents," in *LSD: The Consciousness-Expanding Drug*, ed. David Solomon (G. P. Putnam's Sons, 1964), 143.

61 Ben Sessa, "Why Psychiatry Needs 3,4-Methylenedioxymethamphetamine: A Child Psychiatrist's Perspective," *Neurotherapeutics*, vol. 14, no. 3 (July 2017), 742.

62 See Samuel Bendeck Sotillos, "The Decolonization of Psychology or the Science of the Soul," *Spirituality Studies*, vol. 7, no. 1 (Spring 2021), 18–37.

63 Ludwig Binswanger, quoted in Rollo May, "The Origins and Significance of the Existential Movement in Psychology," in *Existence: A New Dimension*

in Psychiatry and Psychology, eds. Rollo May, Ernest Angel, and Henri F. Ellenberger (Basic Books, 1958), 11.

64 R. D. Laing, "Differences Between Social and Medical Diagnosis," in *The Politics of the Family and Other Essays* (Routledge, 2001), 39.

65 See David N. Elkins, "The Medical Model in Psychotherapy: Its Limitations and Failures," *Journal of Humanistic Psychology*, vol. 49, no. 1 (January 2009), 66–84.

66 Stanislav Grof, "The Nature of Reality: Dawning of a New Paradigm," in *Beyond the Brain: Birth, Death, and Transcendence in Psychotherapy* (State University of New York Press, 1985), 51.

67 George L. Engel, "The Need for a New Medical Model: A Challenge for Biomedicine," *Science*, vol. 196, no. 4286 (April 1977), 129.

68 George L. Engel, "The Need for a New Medical Model: A Challenge for Biomedicine," *Science*, vol. 196, no. 4286 (April 1977), 133.

69 See S. Nassir Ghaemi, "The Rise and Fall of the Biopsychosocial Model," *British Journal of Psychiatry*, vol. 195, no. 1 (July 2009), 3–4; S. Nassir Ghaemi, *The Rise and Fall of the Biopsychosocial Model: Reconciling Art and Science in Psychiatry* (Johns Hopkins University Press, 2009).

70 Humphry Osmond, "A Review of the Clinical Effects of Psychotomimetic Agents," in *LSD: The Consciousness-Expanding Drug*, ed. David Solomon (G. P. Putnam's Sons, 1964), 141.

71 Charles Savage, quoted in *The Use of LSD in Psychotherapy: Transactions of a Conference on D-Lysergic Acid Diethylamide (LSD-25) April 22, 23, and 24, 1959, Princeton, N.J.*, ed. Harold A. Abramson (Josiah Macy Jr. Foundation, 1960), 193.

72 Whitall N. Perry, "Drug-Induced Mysticism: The Mescalin Hypothesis," in *Challenges to a Secular Society* (The Foundation for Traditional Studies, 1996), 10.

73 René Guénon, "The Confusion of the Psychic and the Spiritual," in *The Reign of Quantity and the Signs of the Times*, trans. Lord Northbourne (Sophia Perennis, 2001), 239–240.

74 Lama Anagarika Govinda, "Consciousness Expansion and Disintegration versus Concentration and Spiritual Regeneration," *The Mountain Path*, vol. 9, no. 1 (January 1972), 27.

75 Lama Anagarika Govinda, "Consciousness Expansion and Disintegration versus Concentration and Spiritual Regeneration," *The Mountain Path*, vol. 9, no. 1 (January 1972), 30.

76 Chögyam Trungpa, quoted in Rick Fields, *How the Swans Came to the Lake: A Narrative History of Buddhism in America* (Shambhala Publications, 1986), 309.

77 Mircea Eliade, "General Considerations. Recruiting Methods. Shamanism and Mystical Vocation," in *Shamanism: Archaic Techniques of Ecstasy*, trans. Willard R. Trask (Princeton University Press, 1974), 5.

78 Gerardo Reichel-Dolmatoff, "The Cultural Context of an Aboriginal Hallucinogen: *Banisteriopsis Caapi,*" in *Flesh of the Gods: The Ritual Use of Hallucinogens*, ed. Peter T. Furst (Praeger Publications, 1974), 102.

79 Quoted in James W. Fernandez, *Bwiti: An Ethnography of the Religious Imagination in Africa* (Princeton University Press, 1982), 488–489.

80 Ṛgveda 8:48:3, *The Hymns of the Ṛgveda*, trans. Ralph T. H. Griffith, ed. J. L. Shastri (Motilal Banarsidass Publishers, 1999), 198.

81 Patañjali 4:1, *How to Know God: The Yoga Aphorisms of Patanjali,* trans. Swami Prabhavananda and Christopher Isherwood (Signet Books, 1969), 141.

82 See Samuel Bendeck Sotillos, "Realms of Consciousness and the Real," *Spirituality Studies*, vol. 9, no. 1 (Spring 2023), 12–21.

83 Charles T. Tart, introduction to *States of Consciousness* (E. P. Dutton, 1975), vii.

84 Stanislav Grof, preface to *When the Impossible Happens: Adventures in Non-Ordinary Realities* (Sounds True, 2006), xx.

85 Andrew Weil, "Why People Take Drugs," in *The Natural Mind: An Investigation of Drugs and the Higher Consciousness* (Houghton Mifflin Company, 1986), 19.

86 Timothy Leary, "Harvard Drug Research," in *Flashbacks: A Personal and Cultural History of an Era* (Jeremy P. Tarcher/Putnam Book, 1990), 42.

87 Albert Hofmann, "Can Insight into the Truths of Natural Science Be Therapeutically Effective in Psychology?," in *LSD and the Divine Scientist: The Final Thoughts and Reflections of Albert Hofmann*, trans. Annabel Moynihan (Park Street Press, 2013), 57.

88 Douglas R. Hofstadter and Daniel C. Dennett, introduction to *The Mind's I: Fantasies and Reflections on Self and Soul*, eds. Douglas R. Hofstadter and Daniel C. Dennett (Bantam Books, 1982), 8.

89 Marco Pallis, "The Round of Existence," in *Peaks and Lamas* (Alfred A. Knopf, 1949), 127.

90 William James, "Mysticism," in *The Varieties of Religious Experience: A Study in Human Nature* (Penguin Books, 1985), 388.

91 "[P]erceiving in an unhabitual way." [William James, "The Perception of 'Things,'" in *The Principles of Psychology, Vol. 2* (Henry Holt & Company, 1918), 110.]

92 See Samuel Bendeck Sotillos, "The Inner and Outer Human Being," *The Mountain Path*, vol. 60, no. 2 (April/June 2023), 9–26.

93 Quoted in César Calvo, *The Three Halves of Ino Moxo: Teachings of the Wizard of the Upper Amazon*, trans. Kenneth A. Symington (Inner Traditions International, 1995), 139.

94 Nikitas Stithatos, "On the Practice of the Virtues: One Hundred Texts," in *The Philokalia, Vol. 4: The Complete Text; Compiled by St. Nikodimos of the Holy Mountain and St. Makarios of Corinth*, trans. and ed. G. E. H. Palmer, Philip Sherrard, and Kallistos Ware (Faber and Faber, 1998), 92.

95 Śrī Ramana Maharshi, "Talk 398—April 14th, 1937," in *Talks with Sri Ramana Maharshi* (Sri Ramanasramam, 1996), 370.

96 See Seyyed Hossein Nasr, "The Wisdom of the Body," in *Religion and the Order of Nature* (Oxford University Press, 1996), 235–269.

97 Paracelsus, "Nature of Disease," in *Paracelsus: Selected Writings,* trans. Norbert Guterman, ed. Jolande Jacobi (Princeton University Press, 1988), 76.

98 Rūmī, Discourse 11, *Discourses of Rumi*, trans. A. J. Arberry (Routledge-Curzon, 2004), 61.

99 Saint John Cassian, "On the Eight Vices," in *The Philokalia, Vol. 1: The Complete Text; Compiled by St. Nikodimos of the Holy Mountain and St. Makarios of Corinth*, trans. and ed. G. E. H. Palmer, Philip Sherrard, and Kallistos Ware (Faber and Faber, 1983), 76.

100 'Alī ibn Abī Ṭālib, quoted in William C. Chittick, *Sufism: A Beginner's Guide* (Oneworld Publications, 2008), 104.

101 Marlene Dobkin de Rios, "Traditional Amazonian Healing Practices: Tribe and Town," in *Amazon Healer: The Life and Times of an Urban Shaman* (Prism Press, 1992), 53.

102 René Guénon, "Against Mixing Traditional Forms," in *Perspectives on Initiation*, trans. Henry D. Fohr, ed. Samuel D. Fohr (Sophia Perennis, 2001), 46.

103 Stanislav Grof, "New Perspectives in Psychotherapy and Self-Exploration," in *Psychology of the Future: Lessons from Modern Consciousness Research* (State University of New York Press, 2000), 182.

104 C. G. Jung, "Dream-Analysis in Its Practical Application," in *Modern Man in Search of a Soul*, trans. W. S. Dell and Cary F. Baynes (Harcourt, Brace & World, 1933), 17.

105 Timothy Leary, Ralph Metzner, and Richard Alpert, "General Introduction," to *The Psychedelic Experience: A Manual Based on the Tibetan Book of the Dead* (Citadel Press, 1990), 11.

106 Sidney Cohen, "Debriefings," in *The Beyond Within: The LSD Story* (Atheneum, 1972), 104–105.

107 Stanislav Grof, "Critical Variables in LSD Therapy," in *LSD Psychotherapy* (Hunter House, 1980), 47.

108 Stanislav Grof, "Appendix A: Principles of LSD Psychotherapy," in *The Adventure of Self-Discovery: Dimensions of Consciousness and New Perspectives in Psychotherapy and Inner Exploration* (State University of New York Press, 1988), 289.

109 Sidney Cohen, "The Worst That Can Happen," in *The Beyond Within: The LSD Story* (Atheneum, 1972), 267.

110 Anthony K. Busch and Warren C. Johnson, "L.S.D. 25 as an Aid in Psychotherapy: Preliminary Report of a New Drug," *Diseases of the Nervous System*, vol. 11, no. 8 (August 1950), 243.

111 Robert Masters and Jean Houston, "Some Varieties of the Psychedelic Experience," in *The Varieties of Psychedelic Experience: The Classic Guide to the Effects of LSD on the Human Psyche* (Park Street Press, 2000), 3.

112 Stanislav Grof, "Epilogue: The Future of LSD Psychotherapy," in *LSD Psychotherapy* (Hunter House, 1980), 297.

113 Sidney Cohen, "Postview," in *The Beyond Within: The LSD Story* (Atheneum, 1972), 240.

114 Abram Hoffer, "Treatment of Alcoholism with Psychedelic Therapy," in *Psychedelics: The Uses and Implications of Hallucinogenic Drugs*, eds. Bernard Aaronson and Humphry Osmond (Anchor Books, 1970), 366.

115 Aldous Huxley, *The Doors of Perception and Heaven and Hell* (Harper and Row, 1990), 23.

116 See Henri Bergson, *Matter and Memory*, trans. Nancy Margaret Paul and W. Scott Palmer (George Allen & Unwin, 1929).

117 Charlie D. Broad, "The Relevance of Psychical Research to Philosophy," in *Religion, Philosophy and Psychical Research: Selected Essays* (Harcourt, Brace & Company, 1953), 23.

118 Myron J. Stolaroff, "Introduction to the Second Edition," in *The Secret Chief Revealed: Conversations with Leo Zeff, a Pioneer in the Underground*

Psychedelic Therapy Movement (Multidisciplinary Association for Psychedelic Studies, 2022), xiii.

119 Aldous Huxley, *The Doors of Perception and Heaven and Hell* (Harper and Row, 1990), 53.

120 George Greer, "Using MDMA in Psychotherapy," *Advances*, vol. 2, no. 2 (Spring 1985), 58.

121 Myron J. Stolaroff, "Selection and Preparation: Selecting the Client," in *The Secret Chief Revealed: Conversations with Leo Zeff, a Pioneer in the Underground Psychedelic Therapy Movement* (Multidisciplinary Association for Psychedelic Studies, 2022), 25.

122 Sophie Adamson and Ralph Metzner, "The Nature of the MDMA Experience and Its Role in Healing, Psychotherapy, and Spiritual Practice," *Re-Vision: The Journal of Consciousness and Change*, vol. 10, no. 4 (Spring 1988), 59.

123 Henry Munn, "The Mushrooms of Language," in *Hallucinogens and Shamanism*, ed. Michael J. Harner (Oxford University Press, 1973), 105.

124 Aldous Huxley, "Letter to Humphry Osmond—February 3, 1955," in *Letters of Aldous Huxley*, ed. Grover Smith (Chatto and Windus, 1969), 729.

125 Humphry Osmond, "On Being Mad," in *Psychedelics: The Uses and Implications of Hallucinogenic Drugs*, eds. Bernard Aaronson and Humphry Osmond (Anchor Books, 1970), 22.

126 Sidney Cohen, "LSD and the Anguish of Dying," *Harper's Magazine,* vol. 231, no. 1384 (September 1965), 71.

127 John N. Sherwood, Myron J. Stolaroff, and Willis W. Harman, "The Psychedelic Experience—A New Concept in Psychotherapy," *Journal of Neuropsychiatry*, vol. 4, no. 2 (November-December 1962), 77.

128 Sigmund Freud, "The Ego and the Id" (1923), in *The Ego and the Id,* trans. Joan Riviere, ed. James Strachey (W. W. Norton & Company, 1989), 19.

129 Sigmund Freud, "Chapter 1," in *Civilization and Its Discontents*, trans. and ed. James Strachey (W. W. Norton & Company, 1989), 12.

130 Sigmund Freud, "A Difficulty in the Path of Psycho-Analysis" (1917), in *The Standard Edition of the Complete Psychological Works of Sigmund Freud, Vol. 17*, trans. and ed. James Strachey (Hogarth Press and the Institute of Psycho-Analysis, 1955), 143.

131 Sophie Adamson and Ralph Metzner, "The Nature of the MDMA Experience and Its Role in Healing, Psychotherapy, and Spiritual Practice," *Re-Vision: The Journal of Consciousness and Change*, vol. 10, no. 4 (Spring 1988), 61.

132 Stanislav Grof, "Critical Variables in LSD Therapy," in *LSD Psychotherapy* (Hunter House, 1980), 52.

133 Seng-ts'an, "On Believing in Mind," quoted in *Buddhist Scriptures,* trans. Edward Conze (Penguin Books, 1959), 171.

134 Aldous Huxley, *The Doors of Perception and Heaven and Hell* (Harper and Row, 1990), 86.

135 Stanislav Grof, "General Introduction," in *Realms of the Human Unconscious: Observations from LSD Research* (E. P. Dutton, 1976), 6.

136 Stanislav Grof, "Critical Variables in LSD Therapy," in *LSD Psychotherapy* (Hunter House, 1980), 89.

137 Myron J. Stolaroff, "Selection and Preparation: Selecting the Client," in *The Secret Chief Revealed: Conversations with Leo Zeff, a Pioneer in the Underground Psychedelic Therapy Movement* (Multidisciplinary Association for Psychedelic Studies, 2022), 14.

138 Sidney Cohen, "Psychotherapy with LSD: Pro and Con," in *The Beyond Within: The LSD Story* (Atheneum, 1972), 205.

139 Rūmī, Book 1, Verse 3224, *The Mathnawī of Jalālu'ddīn Rūmī, Vol. 2*, trans. Reynold A. Nicholson (Luzac and Company, 1926), 175.

140 Rūmī, Book 1, Verse 3227, *The Mathnawī of Jalālu'ddīn Rūmī, Vol. 2*, trans. Reynold A. Nicholson (Luzac and Company, 1926), 175.

141 William V. Caldwell, "Divisions of the Mind," in *LSD Psychotherapy: An Exploration of Psychedelic and Psycholytic Therapy* (Grove Press, 1969), 190.

142 Stanislav Grof, "Principles of LSD Psychotherapy," in *LSD Psychotherapy* (Hunter House, 1980), 156.

143 Octavio Paz, "Henri Michaux," in *Alternating Current*, trans. Helen Lane (Arcade Publishing, 1990), 84.

144 Antonin Artaud, "The Peyote Rite among the Tarahumara," in *The Peyote Dance*, trans. Helen Weaver (Farrar, Straus and Giroux, 1976), 38.

145 Timothy Leary, quoted in "Playboy Interview: Timothy Leary," *Playboy*, vol. 13, no. 9 (September 1966), 96.

146 Gerardo Reichel-Dolmatoff, "Man and the Supernatural," in *Amazon Cosmos: The Sexual and Religious Symbolism of the Tukano Indians* (Chicago University Press, 1974), 127.

147 Timothy Leary, "Ecstasy Attacked—Ecstasy Defended," in *The Politics of Ecstasy* (Ronin Publishing, 1990), 85–86.

148 Betty Eisner, "Set, Setting, and Matrix," *Journal of Psychoactive Drugs*, vol. 29, no. 2 (June 1997), 215.

149 Lao Tzu, Chapter 56, *Tao Teh Ching*, trans. John C. H. Wu (Shambhala Publications, 2017), 63.

150 Shunryū Suzuki, prologue to *Zen Mind, Beginner's Mind*, ed. Trudy Dixon (Weatherhill, 1995), 21.

151 Sengcan (Seng-ts'an), *Hsin-hsin Ming: Verses on the Faith-Mind,* trans. Richard B. Clarke (White Pine Press, 1984), unpaginated.

152 Marlene Dobkin de Rios, "The Transducer Effect," in *Amazon Healer: The Life and Times of an Urban Shaman* (Prism Press, 1992), 25.

153 Marlene Dobkin de Rios, "Traditional Amazonian Healing Practices: Tribe and Town," in *Amazon Healer: The Life and Times of an Urban Shaman* (Prism Press, 1992), 58.

154 Stanislav Grof, "Principles of LSD Psychotherapy," in *LSD Psychotherapy* (Hunter House, 1980), 150.

155 Marlene Dobkin de Rios, "Don Hilde's Clients," in *Amazon Healer: The Life and Times of an Urban Shaman* (Prism Press, 1992), 94.

156 R. Gordon Wasson, "The Divine Mushroom of Immortality," in *Flesh of the Gods: The Ritual Use of Hallucinogens*, ed. Peter T. Furst (Praeger Publications, 1974), 197.

157 "If the doors of perception were cleansed everything would appear to man as it is, infinite." [William Blake, "A Memorable Fancy," in *The Marriage of Heaven and Hell* (John W. Luce and Company, 1906), 26.]

158 Meister Eckhart, "Sermon 69," in *Meister Eckhart: Teacher and Preacher*, ed. Bernard McGinn (Paulist Press, 1986), 311.

159 Meister Eckhart, "German Works, Selected Sermons," in *Meister Eckhart: The Essential Sermons, Commentaries, Treatises, and Defense*, trans. Edmund Colledge, O. S. A. and Bernard McGinn (Paulist Press, 1981), 180.

160 See Samuel Bendeck Sotillos, "Recovering the Eye of the Heart," *The Mountain Path*, vol. 59, no. 3 (July/September 2022), 29–45.

161 René Guénon, "Ontology of the Burning Bush," in *The Symbolism of the Cross,* trans. Angus Macnab (Sophia Perennis, 2001), 92.

162 Quoted in E. F. Schumacher, *A Guide for the Perplexed* (Harper & Row, 1977), 39.

163 Parmenides, quoted in Ananda K. Coomaraswamy, *What is Civilization?* (Golgonooza Press, 1989), 35.

164 Ingmar Gorman, Elizabeth M. Nielson, Aja Molinar, Ksenia Cassidy, and Jonathan Sabbagh, "Psychedelic Harm Reduction and Integration: A Transtheoretical Model for Clinical Practice," *Frontiers in Psychology*, vol. 12 (March 2021), unpaginated.

165 Betty Eisner and Sidney Cohen, "Psychotherapy with Lysergic Acid Diethylamide," *Journal of Nervous and Mental Disease*, vol. 127, no. 6 (December 1958), 533.

166 Anja Loizaga-Velder and Armando Loizaga Pazzi, "Therapist and Patient Perspectives on Ayahuasca-Assisted Treatment for Substance Dependence," in *The Therapeutic Use of Ayahuasca*, eds. Beatriz Caiuby Labate and Clancy Cavnar (Springer, 2014), 148.

167 Françoise Bourzat with Kristina Hunter, "Returning Home: The Art of Integration," in *Consciousness Medicine: Indigenous Wisdom, Entheogens, and Expanded States of Consciousness for Healing and Growth* (North Atlantic Books, 2019), 179.

168 Betty Eisner and Sidney Cohen, "Psychotherapy with Lysergic Acid Diethylamide," *Journal of Nervous and Mental Disease*, vol. 127, no. 6 (December 1958), 533.

169 Geoff J. Bathje, Eric Majeski, and Mesphina Kudowor, "Psychedelic Integration: An Analysis of the Concept and its Practice," *Frontiers in Psychology,* vol. 13 (August 2022), unpaginated.

170 Betty Eisner, "Set, Setting, and Matrix," *Journal of Psychoactive Drugs*, vol. 29, no. 2 (June 1997), 215.

171 Stanislav Grof, "Principles of LSD Psychotherapy," in *LSD Psychotherapy* (Hunter House, 1980), 152.

172 Joseph Epes Brown, "The Spiritual Legacy," in *The Spiritual Legacy of the American Indian: Commemorative Edition with Letters While Living with Black Elk*, eds. Marina Brown Weatherly, Elenita Brown, and Michael Oren Fitzgerald (World Wisdom, 2007), 34.

173 Seyyed Hossein Nasr, "Knowledge of the Sacred as Deliverance," in *Knowledge and the Sacred* (State University of New York Press, 1989), 330.

174 Meister Eckhart, "German Works," in *Meister Eckhart: The Essential Sermons, Commentaries, Treatises, and Defense*, trans. Edmund Colledge and Bernard McGinn (Paulist Press, 1981), 216.

175 Quoted in Leo Schaya, *Universal Aspects of the Kabbalah and Judaism*, ed. Roger Gaetani (World Wisdom, 2014), 134.

176 Mircea Eliade, "Initiatory Sickness and Dreams," in *Shamanism: Archaic Techniques of Ecstasy*, trans. Willard R. Trask (Princeton University Press, 1974), 43.

177 Albert Hofmann, "Meditation and Sensory Perception: The Search for Happiness and Meaning," in *LSD and the Divine Scientist: The Final Thoughts and Reflections of Albert Hofmann*, trans. Annabel Moynihan (Park Street Press, 2013), 78.

178 Sidney Cohen, "Psychotherapy with LSD: Pro and Con," in *The Beyond Within: The LSD Story* (Atheneum, 1972), 202.

179 Michael Murphy, quoted in Allan Hunt Badiner, "A Buddhist-Psychedelic History of Esalen Institute: An Interview with Founder Michael Murphy and President George Leonard," in *Zig Zag Zen: Buddhism and Psychedelics*, ed. Allan Hunt Badiner (Chronicle Books, 2002), 82.

180 Huston Smith, "Encountering God," in *The Way Things Are: Conversations with Huston Smith on the Spiritual Life*, ed. Phil Cousineau (University of California Press, 2003), 97.

181 William A. Richards, "Psychedelic Frontiers in Medicine," in *Sacred Knowledge: Psychedelics and Religious Experiences* (Columbia University Press, 2018), 143.

182 Betty Eisner and Sidney Cohen, "Psychotherapy with Lysergic Acid Diethylamide," *Journal of Nervous and Mental Disease*, vol. 127, no. 6 (December 1958), 531.

183 Betty Eisner and Sidney Cohen, "Psychotherapy with Lysergic Acid Diethylamide," *Journal of Nervous and Mental Disease*, vol. 127, no. 6 (December 1958), 532.

184 Aldous Huxley, quoted in Laura Archera Huxley, *This Timeless Moment: A Personal View of Aldous Huxley* (Ballantine Books, 1971), 147.

185 Rick Strassman, "Preparation for the Journey," in Rick Strassman, Slawek Wojtowicz, Luis Eduardo Luna, and Ede Frecska, *Inner Paths to Outer Space: Journeys to Alien Worlds through Psychedelics and Other Spiritual Technologies* (Park Street Press, 2008), 293.

186 Timothy Leary, "Trip 8—February 1961," in *High Priest* (Ronin Publishing, 1995), 170.

187 Aldous Huxley, *The Doors of Perception and Heaven and Hell* (Harper and Row, 1990), 22.

188 Aldous Huxley, *The Doors of Perception and Heaven and Hell* (Harper and Row, 1990), 18.

189 James Terrill, Charles Savage, and Donald D. Jackson, "LSD, Transcendence, and the New Beginning," in *LSD: The Consciousness-Expanding Drug*, ed. David Solomon (G. P. Putnam's Sons, 1964), 192.

190 James Terrill, Charles Savage, and Donald D. Jackson, "LSD, Transcendence, and the New Beginning," in *LSD: The Consciousness-Expanding Drug*, ed. David Solomon (G. P. Putnam's Sons, 1964), 198.

191 Adelle Davis (Jane Dunlap, pseudonym), "The Golden Light," in *Exploring Inner Space: Personal Experiences Under LSD-25* (Harcourt, Brace and World, 1961), 73.

192 Eric Voegelin, "The End of Modernity," in *The New Science of Politics: An Introduction* (University of Chicago, 1952), 163.

193 Titus Burckhardt, "Sufi Interpretation of the Qur'ān," in *Introduction to Sufi Doctrine*, trans. D. M. Matheson (World Wisdom, 2008), 38.

194 Aldous Huxley, "Wanted, a New Pleasure," in *Music at Night and Other Essays* (Doubleday Doran and Company, 1931), 227.

195 See Aldous Huxley, "Writers and Readers," in *The Olive Tree: And Other Essays* (Chatto and Windus, 1947), 1–45.

196 See Gorman Beauchamp, "Island: Aldous Huxley's Psychedelic Utopia," *Utopian Studies*, vol. 1, no. 1 (1990), 59–72.

197 Aldous Huxley, "Chapter 9," in *Island* (Flamingo, 1994), 153.

198 Aldous Huxley, "Chapter 10," in *Island* (Flamingo, 1994), 192–193.

199 Aldous Huxley, "Chapter 10," in *Island* (Flamingo, 1994), 193.

200 Albert Hofmann, "Introduction to Fourth Edition," in Stanislav Grof, *LSD Psychotherapy: The Healing Potential of Psychedelic Medicine* (Multidisciplinary Association for Psychedelic Studies, 2008), 8.

201 Stanislav Grof, "Critical Variables in LSD Therapy," in *LSD Psychotherapy* (Hunter House, 1980), 74.

202 Walter N. Pahnke and William A. Richards, "Implications of LSD and Experimental Mysticism," *Journal of Religion and Health*, vol. 5, no. 3 (July 1966), 175.

203 See John Markoff, *What the Dormouse Said: How the Sixties Counterculture Shaped the Personal Computer Industry* (Penguin Books, 2005).

204 See Ray Kurzweil, *The Age of Spiritual Machines: When Computers Exceed Human Intelligence* (Penguin Books, 1999).

205 Ḥadīth, quoted in Cyril Glassé, *The New Encyclopedia of Islam* (AltaMira Press, 2002), 129.

206 Thomas Traherne, 1.29, *Centuries of Meditations*, ed. Bertram Dobell (Bertram Dobell, 1908), 20.

207 Monsignor J. Edward Brown, letter dated December 8, 1957, quoted in Brad Holden, *Seattle Mystic Alfred M. Hubbard: Inventor, Bootlegger, and Psychedelic Pioneer* (History Press, 2021), 83.

208 Huston Smith, "A Final Examination," in *The World's Religions: Our Great Wisdom Traditions* (HarperCollins Publishers, 1991), 389.

209 Myron J. Stolaroff, "Introduction to the Second Edition," in *The Secret Chief Revealed: Conversations with Leo Zeff, a Pioneer in the Underground Psychedelic Therapy Movement* (Multidisciplinary Association for Psychedelic Studies, 2022), xii.

210 Saint Teresa of Ávila, "The Second Dwelling Places," in *Teresa of Avila: The Interior Castle* (Paulist Press, 1979), 51.

211 Mou-Tzu, quoted in *The Buddhist Tradition in India, China and Japan*, ed. William Theodore de Bary (Vintage Book, 1972), 132.

212 Frithjof Schuon, Poem 20, *World Wheel, Volumes I–III: Poems by Frithjof Schuon* (World Wisdom, 2006), 66.

213 William Blake, "Chorus," in *The Marriage of Heaven and Hell* (John W. Luce and Company, 1906), 47.

214 Goethe, "Lines Written upon the Contemplation of Schiller's Skull" (1826), in Paul Carus, *Goethe, with Special Consideration of His Philosophy* (Open Court Publishing Company, 1915), 50.

215 William Shakespeare, Hamlet 1.5, *A New Variorum Edition of Shakespeare, Vol. 3: Hamlet*, ed. Horace Howard Furness (J. B. Lippincott Company, 1877), 116.

Chapter 6 — The Nature of True Well-Being

1 Virginia Satir, foreword to Yetta Bernhard, *Self Care* (Celestial Arts, 1975), v.

2 See Steve Salerno, *SHAM: How the Self-Help Movement Made America Helpless* (Three Rivers Press, 2005).

3 Huston Smith, "Flakes of Fire, Handfuls of Light," in *Beyond the Post-Modern Mind* (Crossroad, 1982), 95.

4 Yetta Bernhard, "About Bernhard," in *Self Care* (Celestial Arts, 1975), 8.

5 Yetta Bernhard, "About Bernhard," in *Self Care* (Celestial Arts, 1975), 8.

6 Bhagavad Gītā 10:20, *The Bhagavad-Gītā with the Commentary of Śrī Śankarachāryā*, trans. Alladi Mahadeva Sastri (V. Ramaswamy Sastrulu & Sons, 1961), 241.

7 Rūmī, quoted in William C. Chittick, *The Sufi Path of Love: The Spiritual Teachings of Rumi* (State University of New York Press, 1983), 213.

8 Chögyam Trungpa, "Spiritual Materialism," in *Cutting Through Spiritual Materialism*, eds. John Baker and Marvin Casper (Shambhala Publications, 2002), 13.

9 John Welwood, "Embodying Your Realization: Psychological Work in the Service of Spiritual Development," in *Toward a Psychology of Awakening: Buddhism, Psychotherapy, and the Path of Personal and Spiritual Transformation* (Shambhala Publications, 2000), 207.

10 John Donne, "Meditation 17," in *Devotions Upon Emergent Occasions,* ed. John Sparrow (Cambridge University Press, 1923), 98.

11 Michel Foucault, "The Cultivation of the Self," in *The History of Sexuality, Vol. 3: The Care of the Self*, trans. Robert Hurley (Pantheon Books, 1986), 47.

12 Bhagavad Gītā 18:66, *The Bhagavad-Gītā with the Commentary of Śrī Śankarachāryā*, trans. Alladi Mahadeva Sastri (V. Ramaswamy Sastrulu & Sons, 1961), 5.

13 Christopher Lasch, "The Awareness Movement and the Social Invasion of the Self," in *The Culture of Narcissism: American Life in an Age of Diminishing Expectations* (W. W. Norton & Company, 1978), 13.

14 Jagadguru His Holiness Sri Chandrasekharendra Saraswati Swamigal, Sankaracharya of Kanchi, "Punya (Virtuous Action)," in *Introduction to Hindu Dharma: Illustrated*, ed. Michael Oren Fitzgerald (World Wisdom, 2008), 5.

15 Black Elk, forward to Joseph Epes Brown, *The Sacred Pipe: Black Elk's Account of the Seven Rites of the Oglala Sioux* (University of Oklahoma Press, 1989), xx.

16 Sigmund Freud, "The Ego and the Id" (1923), in *The Ego and the Id,* trans. Joan Riviere, ed. James Strachey (W. W. Norton & Company, 1989), 19.

17 Sigmund Freud, "Chapter 1," in *Civilization and Its Discontents*, trans. and ed. James Strachey (W. W. Norton & Company, 1989), 12.

18 Sigmund Freud, "A Difficulty in the Path of Psycho-Analysis" (1917), in *The Standard Edition of the Complete Psychological Works of Sigmund Freud, Vol. 17*, trans. and ed. James Strachey (Hogarth Press and the Institute of Psycho-Analysis, 1955), 143.

19 Bhagavad Gītā 3:2, *The Bhagavad-Gītā with the Commentary of Śrī Śankarachārya*, trans. Alladi Mahadeva Sastri (Ramaswamy Sastrulu & Sons, 1961), 95.

20 Swami Ramdas, quoted in *The Essential Swami Ramdas: Commemorative Edition*, ed. Susunaga Weeraperuma (World Wisdom, 2005), 1.

21 Saint Augustine, "Book 1," in *The Confessions of St. Augustine*, trans. F. J. Sheed (Sheed & Ward, 1959), 3.

22 Julian of Norwich, "Long Text," in *Showings*, trans. Edmund Colledge, James Walsh, and Jean Leclercq (Paulist Press, 1978), 313.

23 Dōgen Kigen, "Shōbōgenzō Genjōkōan," trans. Norman Waddell and Masao Abe, *The Eastern Buddhist*, vol. 5, no. 2 (October 1972), 134.

24 Saint Ignatius, "Second Week," in *The Spiritual Exercises of St. Ignatius*, trans. Anthony Mottola (Image Books, 1964), 87.

25 René Guénon, "The State of Deep Sleep or the Condition of *Prājña,*" in *Man and His Becoming According to the Vedanta*, trans. Richard C. Nicholson (Sophia Perennis, 2004), 96.

26 Śrī Ramana Maharshi, "Talk 321—January 7th, 1937," in *Talks with Sri Ramana Maharshi* (Sri Ramanasramam, 1996), 284.

27 Whitall N. Perry, "Realization and Identity," in *A Treasury of Traditional Wisdom*, ed. Whitall N. Perry (Simon and Schuster, 1971), 858.

28 Frithjof Schuon, "Thought: Light and Perversion," in *The Transfiguration of Man* (World Wisdom Books, 1995), 3.

29 Titus Burckhardt, introduction in *Sacred Art in East and West*, trans. Lord Northbourne (Perennial Books, 1976), 9.

30 William Shakespeare, 1.3.78, *The Tragedy of Hamlet*, ed. Edward Dowden (Methuen and Company, 1899), 33.

Sources

Chapter 1. "Modern Psychology and the Loss of Transcendence." *Journal of Comparative Literature and Aesthetics* 47, no. 4 (Winter 2024): 23–31.

Chapter 2. "The Inner and Outer Human Being." *Mountain Path* 60, no. 2 (April/June 2023): 9–26.

Chapter 3. "Realms of Consciousness and the Real." *Spirituality Studies* 9, no. 1 (Spring 2023): 12–21.

Chapter 4. "The Enneagram's Science of the Soul." *Spirituality Studies* 10, no. 2 (Fall 2024): 2–21.

Chapter 5. "Entheogens and Sacred Psychology." *Spirituality Studies* 10, no. 1 (Spring 2024): 41–68.

Chapter 6. "Why Self-Care Is Not Enough: The Nature of True Well-Being." *Spiritual Psychology and Counseling* 9, no. 2 (2024): 133–144.

Bibliography

Aaronson, Bernard, and Humphry Osmond, eds. *Psychedelics: The Uses and Implications of Hallucinogenic Drugs*. Anchor Books, 1970.

Abe, Masao. *Zen and Comparative Studies: Part Two of a Two-Volume Sequel to Zen and Western Thought*. Edited by Steven Heine. University of Hawai'i Press, 1997.

Abramson, Harold A., ed. *The Use of LSD in Psychotherapy: Transactions of a Conference on D-Lysergic Acid Diethylamide (LSD-25) April 22, 23, and 24, 1959, Princeton, N.J.* Josiah Macy Jr. Foundation, 1960.

Adamson, Sophie, and Ralph Metzner. "The Nature of the MDMA Experience and Its Role in Healing, Psychotherapy, and Spiritual Practice." *ReVision: The Journal of Consciousness and Change* 10, no. 4 (Spring 1988): 59–72.

Albarelli, H. P., Jr. *A Terrible Mistake: The Murder of Frank Olson, and the CIA's Secret Cold War Experiments*. Trine Day, 2009.

Aldred, Lisa. "Plastic Shamans and Astroturf Sun Dances: New Age Commercialization of Native American Spirituality." *American Indian Quarterly* 24, no. 3 (Summer 2000): 329–52.

Almaas, A. H. (A. Hameed Ali). *Facets of Unity: The Enneagram of Holy Ideas*. Diamond Books, 1998.

Almqvist, Kurt. "Every Branch in Me." *Studies in Comparative Religion* 15, nos. 3–4 (Summer/Autumn 1983): 194–96.

Alpert, Richard (Ram Dass). *The Only Dance There Is*. Anchor Books, 1974.

American Psychiatric Association. *Diagnostic and Statistical Manual of Mental Disorders, Fifth Edition, Text Revision*. American Psychiatric Association, 2022.

Aquinas, Thomas. *Summa Theologica, Part I, Third Number, QQ. LXXV–CXIX*. Translated by Fathers of the English Dominican Province. R. & T. Washbourne, 1912.

Aquinas, Thomas. *Summa Theologica, Part II (Second Part), First Number, QQ. I–XLVI*. Translated by Fathers of the English Dominican Province. R. & T. Washbourne, 1917.

Artaud, Antonin. *The Peyote Dance*. Translated by Helen Weaver. Farrar, Straus and Giroux, 1976.

Augustine, Aurelius. *The Confessions of St. Augustine*. Translated by F. J. Sheed. Sheed & Ward, 1959.

Augustine, Aurelius. "Homily 7 on the First Epistle of John." In *A Select Library of the Nicene and Post-Nicene Fathers of the Christian Church*. Edited by Philip Schaff, 501–5. Christian Literature Company, 1888.

Awakening of Faith: Attributed to Aśvaghosha, The. Translated by Yoshito S. Hakeda. Columbia University Press, 1967.

Awakening of Faith: The Classic Exposition of Mahayana Buddhism, The. Translated by Teitaro Suzuki. Dover Publications, 2003.

Babylonian Talmud: Berakhot, The. Translated by Simon Maurice, edited by Isadore Epstein. Soncino Press, 1948.

Badiner, Allan Hunt, ed. *Zig Zag Zen: Buddhism and Psychedelics*. Chronicle Books, 2002.

Bakhtiar, Laleh. *Moral Healer's Handbook: Psychology of Spiritual Chivalry*. Institute of Traditional Psychoethics and Guidance, 1994.

Bakhtiar, Laleh. *Moral Healing through the Most Beautiful Names: The Practice of Spiritual Chivalry*. Institute of Traditional Psychoethics and Guidance, 1994.

Bakhtiar, Laleh. *Rumi's Original Sufi Enneagram*. Institute of Traditional Psychology, 2013.

Bakhtiar, Laleh. *The Sufi Enneagram: The Secrets of the Symbol Unveiled*. Institute of Traditional Psychology, 2013.

Bakhtiar, Laleh. *Traditional Psychoethics and Personality Paradigm*. Institute of Traditional Psychoethics and Guidance, 1993.

Bathje, Geoff J., Eric Majeski, and Mesphina Kudowor. "Psychedelic Integration: An Analysis of the Concept and Its Practice." *Frontiers in Psychology* 13 (August 2022): 824077. DOI: https://doi.org/10.3389/fpsyg.2022.824077.

Beauchamp, Gorman. "Island: Aldous Huxley's Psychedelic Utopia." *Utopian Studies* 1, no. 1 (1990): 59–72.

Bendeck Sotillos, Samuel. "Book Review—How to Change Your Mind: What the New Science of Psychedelics Teaches Us About Consciousness, Dying, Addiction, Depression, and Transcendence." *Transcendent Philosophy: An International Journal for Comparative Philosophy and Mysticism* 23 (December 2022): 113–35.

Bendeck Sotillos, Samuel. "Book Review—The Immortality Key: The Secret History of the Religion with No Name." *Transcendent Philosophy: An International Journal for Comparative Philosophy and Mysticism* 24 (December 2023): 165–73.

Bendeck Sotillos, Samuel. "Book Review–My Altered States: A Doctor's Extraordinary Account of Trauma, Psychedelics, and Spiritual Growth." *Journal of Psychedelic Studies* 9, no. 2 (June 2025): 99–101.

Bendeck Sotillos, Samuel. "Book Review—Sacred Knowledge: Psychedelics and Religious Experiences." *Spiritual Psychology and Counseling* 8, no. 2 (2023): 195–99.

Bendeck Sotillos, Samuel. "The Decolonization of Psychology or the Science of the Soul." *Spirituality Studies* 7, no. 1 (Spring 2021): 18–37.

Bendeck Sotillos, Samuel. "The Deification of the Psyche: Carl Jung and the Spiritual Crisis of the Modern World." *Sacred Web: A Journal of Tradition and Modernity* 51 (2025).

Bendeck Sotillos, Samuel. "The Eclipse of the Soul and the Rise of the Ecological Crisis." *Spirituality Studies* 8, no. 2 (Fall 2022): 34–55.

Bendeck Sotillos, Samuel. "The Enneagram's Science of the Soul." *Spirituality Studies* 10, no. 2 (Fall 2024): 2–21.

Bendeck Sotillos, Samuel. "Entheogens and Sacred Psychology." *Spirituality Studies* 10, no. 1 (Spring 2024): 41–68.

Bendeck Sotillos, Samuel. "The Inner and Outer Human Being." *Mountain Path* 60, no. 2 (April/June 2023): 9–26.

Bendeck Sotillos, Samuel. "The Metaphysics of Trauma." *Transcendent Philosophy: An International Journal for Comparative Philosophy and Mysticism* 23 (December 2022): 23–53.

Bendeck Sotillos, Samuel. "Modern Psychology and the Loss of Transcendence." *Journal of Comparative Literature and Aesthetics* 47, no. 4 (Winter 2024): 23–31.

Bendeck Sotillos, Samuel. "On the Science of the Soul: A Conversation with Seyyed Hossein Nasr." *Journal of Transpersonal Psychology* 53, no. 2 (2021): 191–209.

Bendeck Sotillos, Samuel. "Realms of Consciousness and the Real." *Spirituality Studies* 9, no. 1 (Spring 2023): 12–21.

Bendeck Sotillos, Samuel. "Recovering the Eye of the Heart." *Mountain Path* 59, no. 3 (July/September 2022): 29–45.

Bendeck Sotillos, Samuel. "Why Self-Care Is Not Enough: The Nature of True Well-Being." *Spiritual Psychology and Counseling* 9, no. 2 (2024): 133–44.

Bendeck Sotillos, Samuel. "A Wisdom That Transcends All Times and Places: An Introduction to the Perennial Philosophy." *Mountain Path* 59, no. 1 (January/March 2022): 29–46.

Bennett, J. G. *Gurdjieff: Making a New World*. Harper & Row, 1973.

Bergson, Henri. *Matter and Memory*. Translated by Nancy Margaret Paul and W. Scott Palmer. George Allen & Unwin, 1929.

Bernhard, Yetta. *Self Care*. Celestial Arts, 1975.

Bett, Henry. *Johanes Scotus Erigena: A Study in Mediaeval Philosophy*. Cambridge University Press, 1925.

Bhagavad Gita, The. Translated by Juan Mascaró. Penguin Books, 1962.

Bhagavad-Gītā with the Commentary of Śrī Śankarachāryā, The. Translated by Alladi Mahadeva Sastri. V. Ramaswamy Sastrulu & Sons, 1961.

Black Elk. Foreword to *The Sacred Pipe: Black Elk's Account of the Seven Rites of the Oglala Sioux*, by Joseph Epes Brown, xix–xx. University of Oklahoma Press, 1989.

Blake, William. *The Marriage of Heaven and Hell*. John W. Luce and Company, 1906.

Bleibtreu, John, ed. *Interviews with Oscar Ichazo*. Arica Institute Press, 1982.

Bloom, Alfred, ed. *The Essential Shinran: A Buddhist Path of True Entrusting*. World Wisdom, 2007.

Boethius. *The Consolation of Philosophy*. Translated by Richard H. Green. Dover Publications, 2002.

Boorstein, Seymour, ed. *Transpersonal Psychotherapy, Second Edition*. State University of New York Press, 1996.

Bourzat, Françoise, with Kristina Hunter. *Consciousness Medicine: Indigenous Wisdom, Entheogens, and Expanded States of Consciousness for Healing and Growth*. North Atlantic Books, 2019.

Bṛhadāraṇyaka Upaniṣad with the Commentary of Śankarācāryā, The. Translated by Swāmi Mādhavānanda. Advaita Ashrama, 1950.

Broad, Charlie D. *Religion, Philosophy and Psychical Research: Selected Essays*. Harcourt, Brace & Company, 1953.

Brown, Joseph Epes. *The Spiritual Legacy of the American Indian: Commemorative Edition with Letters While Living with Black Elk*. Edited by Marina Brown Weatherly, Elenita Brown, and Michael Oren Fitzgerald. World Wisdom, 2007.

Buber, Martin. *The Tales of Rabbi Nachman*. Translated by Maurice Friedman. Indiana University Press, 1962.

Buddha Shakyamuni. *The Dhammapada*. Translated by Irving Babbitt. New Directions, 1965.

Buddha Shakyamuni. *The Dhammapada: The Path of Perfection*. Translated by Juan Mascaró. Penguin Books, 1973.

Buddhist Scriptures. Translated by Edward Conze. Penguin Books, 1959.

Bugental, James F. T. *Psychotherapy Isn't What You Think: Bringing the Psychotherapeutic Engagement into the Living Moment*. Zeig, Tucker & Company, 1999.

Burckhardt, Titus. *Alchemy: Science of the Cosmos, Science of the Soul*. Translated by William Stoddart. Element Books, 1986.

Burckhardt, Titus. *Chartres and the Birth of the Cathedral*. Translated by William Stoddart. Golgonooza Press, 1995.

Burckhardt, Titus. *Introduction to Sufi Doctrine*. Translated by D. M. Matheson. World Wisdom, 2008.

Burckhardt, Titus. *Mirror of the Intellect: Essays on Traditional Science and Sacred Art*. Translated and edited by William Stoddart. State University of New York Press, 1987.

Burckhardt, Titus. *Sacred Art in East and West*. Translated by Lord Northbourne. Perennial Books, 1976.

Burt, Cyril. "The Concept of Consciousness." *British Journal of Psychology* 53, no. 3 (August 1962): 229–42.

Busch, Anthony K., and Warren C. Johnson. "L.S.D. 25 as an Aid in Psychotherapy: Preliminary Report of a New Drug." *Diseases of the Nervous System* 11, no. 8 (August 1950): 241–43.

Caldwell, William V. *LSD Psychotherapy: An Exploration of Psychedelic and Psycholytic Therapy*. Grove Press, 1969.

Calvo, César. *The Three Halves of Ino Moxo: Teachings of the Wizard of the Upper Amazon*. Translated by Kenneth A. Symington. Inner Traditions International, 1995.

Carus, Paul. *Goethe, with Special Consideration of His Philosophy*. Open Court Publishing Company, 1915.

Chittick, William C., ed. *The Essential Seyyed Hossein Nasr*. World Wisdom, 2007.

Chittick, William C. *Ibn 'Arabi: Heir to the Prophets*. Oneworld Publications, 2005.

Chittick, William C. *The Sufi Path of Love: The Spiritual Teachings of Rumi*. State University of New York Press, 1983.

Chittick, William C. *Sufism: A Beginner's Guide*. Oneworld Publications, 2008.

Clarke, Peter B., ed. *New Trends and Developments in the World of Islam*. Luzac Oriental Press.

Cleary, Thomas. *The Taoist Classics, Vol. 2: The Collected Translations of Thomas Cleary*. Shambhala Publications, 1999.

Clement of Alexandria. *The Writings of Clement of Alexandria*. Translated by William Wilson. T. & T. Clark, 1867.

Cloud of Unknowing and Other Works, The. Translated by Clifton Wolters. Penguin Books, 1978.

Cohen, Sidney. *The Beyond Within: The LSD Story*. Atheneum, 1972.

Cohen, Sidney. "LSD and the Anguish of Dying." *Harper's Magazine* 231, no. 1384 (September 1965): 69–78.

Coomaraswamy, Ananda K. *Coomaraswamy, Vol. 2, Selected Papers: Metaphysics*. Edited by Roger Lipsey. Princeton University Press, 1978.

Coomaraswamy, Ananda K. *What is Civilization?* Golgonooza Press, 1989.

Coomaraswamy, Rama P. *The Destruction of the Christian Tradition: Updated and Revised*. World Wisdom, 2006.

Coomaraswamy, Rama P. "The Problems that Result from Locating Spirituality in the Psyche." *Sacred Web: A Journal of Tradition and Modernity* 9 (Summer 2002), pp. 101–24.

Corbin, Henry. "The Question of Comparative Philosophy: Convergences in Iranian and European Thought." Translated by Jane A. Pratt. *Spring: An Annual of Archetypal Psychology and Jungian Thought* (1980): 1–20.

Crowley, Aleister. *The Book of the Law*. Red Wheel/Weiser Books, 1976.

Crowley, Aleister. *Diary of a Drug Fiend*. Samuel Weiser, 1997.

Danner, Victor. "The Inner and Outer Man." In *Traditional Modes of Contemplation and Action: A Colloquium held at Rothko Chapel Houston Texas*, edited by Yusuf Ibish and Peter Lamborn Wilson, 407–12. Imperial Iranian Academy of Philosophy, 1977.

Darqāwī, al-'Arabī, ad-. *Letters of a Sufi Master*. Translated by Titus Burckhardt. Fons Vitae, 1998.

Davis, Adelle (Jane Dunlap, pseudonym). *Exploring Inner Space: Personal Experiences Under LSD-25*. Harcourt, Brace, and World, 1961.

de Bary, William Theodore, ed. *The Buddhist Tradition in India, China, and Japan*. Vintage Book, 1972.

de Mille, Richard. *Castaneda's Journey: The Power and the Allegory*. Capra Press, 1976.

de Mille, Richard, ed. *The Don Juan Papers: Further Castaneda Controversies*. Ross-Erikson Publishers, 1980.

Deutsch, Eliot, and Rohit Dalvi, eds. *The Essential Vedānta: A New Source Book of Advaita Vedānta*. World Wisdom, 2004.

Dikshit, Sudhakar S., ed. *I Am That: Talks with Sri Nisargadatta Maharaj*. Translated by Maurice Frydman. Acorn Press, 1999.

Dobkin de Rios, Marlene. *Amazon Healer: The Life and Times of an Urban Shaman*. Prism Press, 1992.

Dōgen. "Shōbōgenzō Genjōkōan." Translated by Norman Waddell and Masao Abe. *Eastern Buddhist* 5, no. 2 (October 1972): 129–40.

Donne, John. *Devotions upon Emergent Occasions*. Edited by John Sparrow. Cambridge University Press, 1923.

Driscoll, J. Walter. *Gurdjieff: An Annotated Bibliography*. Garland, 1985.

Eaton, Gai. *Islam and the Destiny of Man*. State University of New York Press, 1985.

Eckhart, Meister. *The Complete Mystical Works of Meister Eckhart*. Translated and edited by Maurice O'C. Walshe. Crossroad Publishing Company, 2009.

Eckhart, Meister. *Meister Eckhart*. Translated by C. De B. Evans, edited by Franz Pfeiffer. John M. Watkins, 1924.

Eckhart, Meister. *Meister Eckhart: The Essential Sermons, Commentaries, Treatises, and Defense*. Translated by Edmund Colledge and Bernard McGinn. Paulist Press, 1981.

Eckhart, Meister. *Meister Eckhart: Teacher and Preacher*. Edited by Bernard McGinn. Paulist Press, 1986.

Editors. "LSD—A Dangerous Drug." *New England Journal of Medicine* 273, no. 23 (December 2, 1965): 1280.

Eisner, Betty. "Set, Setting, and Matrix." *Journal of Psychoactive Drugs* 29, no. 2 (June 1997): 213–16. DOI: https://doi.org/10.1080/02791072.1997.10400190.

Eisner, Betty, and Sidney Cohen. "Psychotherapy with Lysergic Acid Diethylamide." *Journal of Nervous and Mental Disease* 127, no. 6 (December 1958): 528–39. DOI: https://doi.org/10.1097/00005053-195812000-00006.

Eliade, Mircea. *Shamanism: Archaic Techniques of Ecstasy*. Translated by Willard R. Trask. Princeton University Press, 1974.

Eliade, Mircea. *Yoga: Immortality and Freedom*. Translated by Willard R. Trask. Princeton University Press, 1973.

Elkins, David N. "The Medical Model in Psychotherapy: Its Limitations and Failures." *Journal of Humanistic Psychology* 49, no. 1 (January 2009): 66–84. DOI: https://doi.org/10.1177/0022167807307901.

Elwell-Sutton, L. P. "Sufism and Pseudo-Sufism." *Encounter* 44, no. 5 (May 1975): 9–17.

Emerson, Ralph Waldo. *The Journals and Miscellaneous Notebooks of Ralph Waldo Emerson, Vol. II: 1822–1826*. Edited by William H. Gilman, Alfred R. Ferguson, and Merrell R. Davis. Belknap Press, 1961.

Engel, George L. "The Need for a New Medical Model: A Challenge for Biomedicine." *Science* 196, no. 4286 (April 1977): 129–36. DOI: https://doi.org/10.1126/science.847460.

Estrada, Álvaro. *María Sabina: Her Life and Chants*. Translated by Henry Munn. Ross-Erikson, 1981.

Evans-Wentz, W. Y., ed. *The Tibetan Book of the Great Liberation*. Oxford University Press, 1954.

Fernandez, James W. *Bwiti: An Ethnography of the Religious Imagination in Africa*. Princeton University Press, 1982.

Fields, Rick. *How the Swans Came to the Lake: A Narrative History of Buddhism in America*. Shambhala Publications, 1986.

Fitzgerald, Michael Oren. *Yellowtail, Crow Medicine Man and Sun Dance Chief: An Autobiography*. University of Oklahoma Press, 1994.

Flattery, David S., and Reza Leah Landman, eds. *Catalyst of Miracles: The Unknown Claudio Naranjo*. Gateways Books and Tapes, 2012.

Forte, Robert. "A Conversation with R. Gordon Wasson (1898–1986)." *ReVision: The Journal of Consciousness and Change* 10, no. 4 (Spring 1988): 13–30.

Foucault, Michel. *The History of Sexuality, Vol. 3: The Care of the Self.* Translated by Robert Hurley. Pantheon Books, 1986.

Frager, Robert, and James Fadiman. *Personality and Personal Growth*. HarperCollins, 1984.

Francis de Sales, Saint. *A Selection from the Spiritual Letters of S. Francis de Sales*. Rivingtons, 1871.

Freud, Sigmund. *Civilization and Its Discontents*. Translated and edited by James Strachey. W. W. Norton & Company, 1989.

Freud, Sigmund. *The Ego and the Id*. Translated by Joan Riviere, edited by James Strachey. W. W. Norton & Company, 1989.

Freud, Sigmund. *The Future of an Illusion*. Translated and edited by James Strachey. W. W. Norton & Company, 1989.

Freud, Sigmund. *The Interpretation of Dreams*. Translated by James Strachey. John Wiley & Sons, 1963.

Freud, Sigmund. *New Introductory Lectures on Psycho-Analysis*. Translated and edited by James Strachey. W. W. Norton & Company, 1989.

Freud, Sigmund. *The Standard Edition of the Complete Psychological Works of Sigmund Freud, Vol. 17*. Translated and edited by James Strachey. Hogarth Press and the Institute of Psycho-Analysis, 1955.

Furst, Peter T., ed. *Flesh of the Gods: The Ritual Use of Hallucinogens*. Praeger Publications, 1974.

Gamard, William Sumner. "Interrater Reliability and Validity of Judgments of Enneagram Personality Types (Typology, Transpersonal, Protoanalysis)." PhD diss., California Institute of Integral Studies, 1986.

Gardner, Edmund G., ed. *The Cell of Self-knowledge: Seven Early English Mystical Treatises printed by Henry Pepwell in 1521*. Chatto & Windus, 1925.

Ghaemi, S. Nassir. "The Rise and Fall of the Biopsychosocial Model." *British Journal of Psychiatry* 195, no. 1 (July 2009): 3–4. DOI: https://doi.org/10.1192/bjp.bp.109.063859.

Ghaemi, S. Nassir. *The Rise and Fall of the Biopsychosocial Model: Reconciling Art and Science in Psychiatry*. Johns Hopkins University Press, 2009.

Glassé, Cyril. *The New Encyclopedia of Islam*. AltaMira Press, 2002.

Gold, E. J. "The Origin of the Enneagram: Claudio Naranjo Speaks." June 18, 2010. http://www.youtube.com/watch?v=wlO3KJWnNd8.

Goldberg, Michael J. "Inside the Enneagram Wars." *LA Weekly* (October 15–21, 1993): 16–19, 22–26.

Goleman, Daniel. Foreword to *The Sanity We Are Born With: A Buddhist Approach to Psychology*, by Chögyam Trungpa, vii–viii. Edited by Carolyn Rose Gimian. Shambhala Publications, 2005.

Gorman, Ingmar, Elizabeth M. Nielson, Aja Molinar, Ksenia Cassidy, and Jonathan Sabbagh. "Psychedelic Harm Reduction and Integration: A Transtheoretical Model for Clinical Practice." *Frontiers in Psychology* 12 (March 2021): 645246.

Gospel According to Thomas: Coptic Text Established and Translated, The. Translated by Antoine Guillaumont, Henri-Charles Puech, Gilles Quispel, Walter C. Till, and Yassah 'Abd al-Masīḥ. E. J. Brill, 1976.

Govinda, Lama Anāgārika. "Consciousness Expansion and Disintegration versus Concentration and Spiritual Regeneration." *Mountain Path* 9, no. 1 (January 1972): 27–30.

Greer, George. "Using MDMA in Psychotherapy." *Advances* 2, no. 2 (Spring 1985): 57–59.

Grinspoon, Lester, and James B. Bakalar. *Psychedelic Drugs Reconsidered*. Basic Books, 1981.

Grof, Stanislav. *The Adventure of Self-Discovery: Dimensions of Consciousness and New Perspectives in Psychotherapy and Inner Exploration*. State University of New York Press, 1988.

Grof, Stanislav. *Beyond the Brain: Birth, Death, and Transcendence in Psychotherapy*. State University of New York Press, 1985.

Grof, Stanislav. *LSD Psychotherapy*. Hunter House, 1980.

Grof, Stanislav. *Psychology of the Future: Lessons from Modern Consciousness Research*. State University of New York Press, 2000.

Grof, Stanislav. *Realms of the Human Unconscious: Observations from LSD Research*. E. P. Dutton, 1976.

Grof, Stanislav. *When the Impossible Happens: Adventures in Non-Ordinary Realities*. Sounds True, 2006.

Guénon, René. *The Crisis of the Modern World*. Translated by Arthur Osborne, Marco Pallis, and Richard C. Nicholson. Sophia Perennis, 2004.

Guénon, René. *The Great Triad*. Translated by Henry D. Fohr, edited by Samuel D. Fohr. Sophia Perennis, 2004.

Guénon, René. *Man and His Becoming According to the Vedānta*. Translated by Richard C. Nicholson. Sophia Perennis, 2004.

Guénon, René. *The Multiple States of the Being*. Translated by Henry D. Fohr, edited by Samuel D. Fohr. Sophia Perennis, 2001.

Guénon, René. *Perspectives on Initiation*. Translated by Henry D. Fohr, edited by Samuel D. Fohr. Sophia Perennis, 2001.

Guénon, René. *The Reign of Quantity and the Signs of the Times*. Translated by Lord Northbourne. Sophia Perennis, 2004.

Guénon, René. *The Spiritist Fallacy*. Translated by Alvin Moore, Jr. and Rama P. Coomaraswamy. Sophia Perennis, 2001.

Guénon, René. *The Symbolism of the Cross*. Translated by Angus Macnab. Sophia Perennis, 2004.

Guénon, René. *Symbols of Sacred Science*. Translated by Henry D. Fohr, edited by Samuel D. Fohr. Sophia Perennis, 2004.

Hamilton, Edith, and Huntington Cairns, eds. *The Collected Dialogues of Plato*. Princeton University Press, 1980.

Harner, Michael J., ed. *Hallucinogens and Shamanism*. Oxford University Press, 1973.

Hartmann, Franz. *The Life and Doctrines of Jacob Boehme: The God–Taught Philosopher*. Occult Publishing Company, 1891.

Heart of Awareness: A Translation of the Ashtavakra Gita, The. Translated by Thomas Byrom. Shambhala Publications, 1990.

Henry, Gray. "Ways of Knowing: An Interview with Whitall N. Perry." *Sophia: A Journal of Traditional Studies* 3, no. 2 (Winter 1997): 97–118.

Hofmann, Albert. "The Active Principles of the Seeds of *Rivea corymbosa* and *Ipomoea violacea*." *Botanical Museum Leaflets* 20, no. 6 (November 1963): 194–212.

Hofmann, Albert. "Introduction to Fourth Edition." In *LSD Psychotherapy: The Healing Potential of Psychedelic Medicine*, by Stanislav Grof, 7–8. Multidisciplinary Association for Psychedelic Studies, 2008.

Hofmann, Albert. *LSD and the Divine Scientist: The Final Thoughts and Reflections of Albert Hofmann*. Translated by Annabel Moynihan. Park Street Press, 2013.

Hofmann, Albert. *LSD: My Problem Child*. Translated by Jonathan Ott. McGraw-Hill Book Company, 1980.

Hofstadter, Douglas R., and Daniel C. Dennett, eds. *The Mind's I: Fantasies and Reflections on Self and Soul*. Bantam Books, 1982.

Holden, Brad. *Seattle Mystic Alfred M. Hubbard: Inventor, Bootlegger, and Psychedelic Pioneer*. History Press, 2021.

Hossenfelder, Sabine. *Existential Physics: A Scientist's Guide to Life's Biggest Questions*. Viking, 2022.

Huang Po. *The Zen Teaching of Huang Po: On the Transmission of Mind*. Translated by John Blofeld. Grove Press, 1958.

Hujwīrī, 'Alī B. 'Uthmān Al-Jullābī. *The Kashf al-Maḥjub: The Oldest Persian Treatise on Sufism*. Translated by Reynold A. Nicholson. Luzac and Company, 1911.

Huxley, Aldous. *The Doors of Perception and Heaven and Hell*. Harper and Row, 1990.

Huxley, Aldous. *Island*. Flamingo, 1994.

Huxley, Aldous. *Music at Night and Other Essays*. Doubleday Doran and Company, 1931.

Huxley, Aldous. *The Olive Tree: And Other Essays*. Chatto and Windus, 1947.

Huxley, Laura (Archera). "Disregarded in the Darkness." In *Moksha: Aldous Huxley's Classic Writings on Psychedelics and the Visionary Experience*. Edited by Michael Horowitz and Cynthia Palmer, 74–79. Park Street Press, 1999.

Huxley, Laura Archera. *This Timeless Moment: A Personal View of Aldous Huxley*. Ballantine Books, 1971.

Hymns of the Ṛgveda, The. Translated by Ralph T. H. Griffith, edited by J. L. Shastri. Motilal Banarsidass Publishers, 1999.

Ibn 'Arabī. *The Bezels of Wisdom*. Translated by R. W. J. Austin. Paulist Press, 1980.

Ibn 'Arabī. *The Wisdom of the Prophets (Fusus al-Hikam)*. Translated by Titus Burckhardt and Angela Culme-Seymour. Beshara, 1975.

Ichazo, Oscar. Foreword to *Facets of Unity: The Enneagram of Holy Ideas*, by A. H. Almaas, v–viii. Diamond Books, 1998.

Ichazo, Oscar. "Letter to the Transpersonal Community." *The Arican: International Journal of Arica Institute* 5 (Autumn 1991): 87–122.

Ignatius of Loyola, Saint. *The Spiritual Exercises of St. Ignatius*. Translated by Anthony Mottola. Image Books, 1964.

Insel, Thomas. *Healing: Our Path from Mental Illness to Mental Health*. Penguin Books, 2022.

Irving, Jan. "R. Gordon Wasson: The Man, the Legend, the Myth: Beginning a New History of Magic Mushrooms, Ethnomycology, and the Psychedelic Revolution." In *Entheogens and the Development of Culture: The Anthropology and Neurobiology of Ecstatic Experience*, edited by John A. Rush, 565–619. North Atlantic Books, 2013.

Isaac the Syrian. *Mystic Treatises by Isaac of Nineveh*. Translated by A. J. Wensinck. Koninklijke Akademie van Wettenschappen, 1923.

Isaacs, Andrea, and Jack Labanauskas. "Interview with Oscar Ichazo." *Enneagram Monthly* 2, no. 11 (November 1996): 1, 18–21.

Isaacs, Andrea, and Jack Labanauskas. "Interview with Oscar Ichazo, Part 3." *Enneagram Monthly* 3, no. 1 (January 1997): 1, 20–22.

Izutsu, Toshihiko. *Creation and the Timeless Order of Things: Essays in Islamic Mystical Philosophy*. White Cloud Press, 1994.

Izutsu, Toshihiko. *Sufism and Taoism: A Comparative Study of Key Philosophical Concepts*. University of California Press, 1984.

Jacobi, Jolande, ed. *Paracelsus: Selected Writings*. Translated by Norbert Guterman. Princeton University Press, 1988.

Jagadguru of Kanchi the 68th, H. H. *Introduction to Hindu Dharma: Illustrated*. Edited by Michael Oren Fitzgerald. World Wisdom, 2008.

James, William. *The Principles of Psychology, Vol. 2*. Henry Holt & Company, 1918.

James, William. *Psychology: Briefer Course*. Henry Holt and Company, 1923.

James, William. *The Varieties of Religious Experience: A Study in Human Nature*. Penguin Books, 1985.

James, William. *The Will to Believe, and Other Essays in Popular Philosophy*. Longmans, Green, and Company, 1907.

Julian of Norwich. *Showings*. Translated by Edmund Colledge, James Walsh, and Jean Leclercq. Paulist Press, 1978.

Jung, Carl G. *The Archetypes and the Collective Unconscious*. Translated by R. F. C. Hull. Princeton University Press, 1980.

Jung, Carl G. *The Collected Works of C. G. Jung, Vol. 6: Psychological Types*. Translated by R. F. C. Hull and H. G. Baynes, edited by Gerhard Adler and R. F. C. Hull. Princeton University Press, 1976.

Jung, Carl G. *The Collected Works of C. G. Jung, Vol. 16: The Practice of Psychotherapy*. Translated by R. F. C. Hull. Princeton University Press, 1985.

Jung, Carl G. *Modern Man in Search of a Soul*. Translated by W. S. Dell and Cary F. Baynes. Harcourt, Brace & World, 1933.

Jung, Carl G. *Psychological Types or The Psychology of Individuation*. Translated by H. Godwyn Baynes. Harcourt, Brace & Company, 1923.

Kabbani, Muhammad Hisham. *Classical Islam and the Naqshbandi Sufi Tradition*. Islamic Supreme Council of America, 2004.

Keen, Sam. "A Conversation about Ego Destruction with Oscar Ichazo." *Psychology Today* 7, no. 2 (July 1973): 64–72.

Kelly, Edward F., Emily Williams Kelly, Adam Crabtree, Alan Gauld, Michael Grosso, and Bruce Greyson. *Irreducible Mind: Toward a Psychology for the 21st Century*. Rowman & Littlefield Publishers, 2010.

Kinzer, Stephen. *Poisoner in Chief: Sidney Gottlieb and the CIA Search for Mind Control*. St. Martin's Griffin, 2020.

Knowledge of God in Classical Sufism: Foundations of Islamic Mystical Theology. Translated by John Renard. Paulist Press, 2004.

Kripal, Jeffrey J. *Esalen: America and the Religion of No Religion*. University of Chicago Press, 2007.

Kurzweil, Ray. *The Age of Spiritual Machines: When Computers Exceed Human Intelligence*. Penguin Books, 1999.

Ladd, George Trumbull. *Outlines of Physiological Psychology: A Text–Book of Mental Science for Academies and Colleges*. Charles Scribner's Sons, 1908.

Ladd, George Trumbull. *Psychology, Descriptive and Explanatory: A Treatise of the Phenomena, Laws, and Development of Human Mental Life*. Charles Scribner's Sons, 1895.

Laing, R. D. *The Divided Self: An Existential Study in Sanity and Madness*. Penguin Books, 1976.

Laing, R. D. *The Politics of the Family and Other Essays*. Routledge, 2001.

Lakhani, M. Ali. "The Black Mole on the Cheek of the Beloved: The Problem of Metaphysical Ambiguity." *Sacred Web: A Journal of Tradition and Modernity* 26 (Winter 2010): 9–15.

Laṅkāvatāra Sūtra: A Mahāyāna Text, The. Translated by D. T. Suzuki. Prajñā Press, 1978.

Lao Tzu. *Tao Teh Ching*. Translated by John C. H. Wu. Shambhala Publications, 2017.

Lao Tzu. *The Way of Lao Tzu (Tao-Te Ching)*. Translated by Wing-Tsit Chan. Bobbs-Merrill Company, 1963.

Lao Tzu. *The Wisdom of Laotse*. Translated and edited by Lin Yutang. Michael Joseph, 1948.

Lasch, Christopher. *The Culture of Narcissism: American Life in an Age of Diminishing Expectations*. W. W. Norton & Company, 1978.

Law, William. *The Works of the Reverend William Law, Vol. VI*. G. Moreton, 1893.

Laws of Manu, The. Translated by Georg Bühler. Clarendon Press, 1886.

Leary, Timothy. *Flashbacks: A Personal and Cultural History of an Era*. Jeremy P. Tarcher/Putnam Book, 1990.

Leary, Timothy. *High Priest*. Ronin Publishing, 1995.

Leary, Timothy. "Playboy Interview: Timothy Leary." *Playboy* 13, no. 9 (September 1966): 93–112, 250–51, 254–56.

Leary, Timothy. *The Politics of Ecstasy*. Ronin Publishing, 1990.

Leary, Timothy. "The Religious Experience: Its Production and Interpretation." *Psychedelic Review* 1, no. 3 (1964): 324–46.

Leary, Timothy. *Start Your Own Religion*. Kriya Press, 1967.

Leary, Timothy, Ralph Metzner, and Richard Alpert. 1990. *The Psychedelic Experience: A Manual Based on the Tibetan Book of the Dead*. Citadel Press.

Lee, Martin A., and Bruce Shlain. *Acid Dreams: The Complete History of LSD: The CIA, The Sixties, and Beyond*. Grove Press, 1992.

Leviton, Richard. "Trademarking the New Age: Can Spiritual and Intellectual Ideas be Copyrighted?" *East West Journal* 21, no. 3 (March 1991): 32–37.

Lewin, Louis. *Phantastica: A Classic Survey on the Use and Abuse of Mind-Altering Plants*. Park Street Press, 1998.

Lilly, John C. *The Center of the Cyclone*. Bantam Books, 1973.

Lilly, John C. *The Deep Self: Profound Relaxation and the Tank Isolation Technique*. Simon & Schuster, 1977.

Lings, Martin. "Book Review—The Sufis." *Tomorrow: The Journal of Parapsychology, Cosmology, and Traditional Studies* 3, no. 1 (Winter 1965): 56–57.

Lings, Martin. *Muhammad: His Life Based on the Earliest Sources*. Inner Traditions, 1983.

Lings, Martin. *Symbol and Archetype: A Study of the Meaning of Existence*. Quinta Essentia, 1991.

Lings, Martin. *What is Sufism?* University of California Press, 1975.

Loizaga-Velder, Anja, and Armando Loizaga Pazzi. "Therapist and Patient Perspectives on Ayahuasca-Assisted Treatment for Substance Dependence." In *The Therapeutic Use of Ayahuasca*, edited by Beatriz Caiuby Labate and Clancy Cavnar, 133–52. Springer, 2014.

Lopez, Donald S., Jr., ed. *Buddhist Scriptures*. Penguin Books, 2004.

Maimonides, Moses. *The Guide for the Perplexed*. Translated by Michael Friedländer. Dover, 1956.

Māṇḍūkya Upaniṣad with Gauḍapāda's Kārikā and Śaṅkara's Commentary, The. Translated by Swāmi Nikhilānanda. Sri Ramakrishna Ashrama, 1949.

Markoff, John. *What the Dormouse Said: How the Sixties Counterculture Shaped the Personal Computer Industry*. Penguin Books, 2005.

Marks, John. *The Search for the "Manchurian Candidate": The CIA and Mind Control: The Secret History of the Behavioral Sciences*. W. W. Norton and Company, 1991.

Masters, Robert, and Jean Houston. *The Varieties of Psychedelic Experience: The Classic Guide to the Effects of LSD on the Human Psyche*. Park Street Press, 2000.

Matson, Katinka. *The Psychology Today Omnibook of Personal Development*. William Morrow and Company, 1977.

May, Rollo, Ernest Angel, and Henri F. Ellenberger, eds. *Existence: A New Dimension in Psychiatry and Psychology*. Clarion Books, 1958.

McNay, Iain. "Claudio Naranjo—Seeker After Truth." December 21, 2010. http://www.youtube.com/watch?v=s7MSZfVZzJ0.

Merleau-Ponty, Maurice. *Phenomenology of Perception*. Routledge, 1962.

Metz, Barbara, and John Burchill. *The Enneagram and Prayer: Discovering Our True Selves Before God*. Dimension Books, 1987.

Milarepa, Jetsun. *The Hundred Thousand Songs of Milarepa*. Translated by Garma C. C. Chang. Shambhala Publications, 1977.

Milton, John. *Paradise Lost, Book 1*. Edited by Frederick Gorse. Blackie and Son, 1895.

Moore, Gerald, and Larry Schiller. "LSD: The Exploding Threat of the Mind Drug That Got Out of Control." *Life* 60, no. 12 (March 25, 1966).

Moore, James. "The Enneagram: A Developmental Study." *Religion Today: A Journal of Contemporary Religions* 5, no. 3 (October 1986/January 1987): 1–5.

Moore, James. *Gurdjieff: The Anatomy of a Myth*. Element, 1991.

Moore, James. "Neo-Sufism: The Case of Idries Shah." *Religion Today: A Journal of Contemporary Religions* 3, no. 3 (1986): 4–8.

Naranjo, Claudio. *Character and Neurosis: An Integrative View*. Gateways/IDHHB, 2003.

Naranjo, Claudio. *Ennea-Type Structures: Self-Analysis for the Seeker*. Gateways/IDHHB, 1990.

Naranjo, Claudio. "A Report to the 'First International Enneagram Conference.'" *Enneagram Monthly* 2, no. 2 (February 1996): 1, 16–17.

Naranjo, Claudio, and Robert E. Ornstein. *On the Psychology of Meditation*. Viking Press, 1971.

Nasr, Seyyed Hossein. Foreword to *Moral Healer's Handbook: Psychology of Spiritual Chivalry*, by Laleh Bakhtiar, vii–viii. Institute of Traditional Psychoethics and Guidance, 1994.

Nasr, Seyyed Hossein., ed. *Islamic Spirituality: Foundations*. Crossroad, 1987.

Nasr, Seyyed Hossein. *Knowledge and the Sacred*. State University of New York Press, 1989.

Nasr, Seyyed Hossein. *The Need for a Sacred Science*. State University of New York Press, 1993.

Nasr, Seyyed Hossein. *Religion and the Order of Nature*. Oxford University Press, 1996.

Newman, Louis I., ed. *The Hasidic Anthology: Tales and Teachings of the Hasidim*. Translated by Louis I. Newman. Schocken Books, 1963.

Nicene and Post-Nicene Fathers of the Christian Church, Vol. 5: Saint Augustine: Anti-Pelagian Writings. Edited by Philip Schaff. Christian Literature Company, 1887.

Nicholson, Reynold A. *The Mystics of Islam*. Routledge & Kegan Paul, 1975.

Northbourne, Lord. *Looking Back on Progress*. Edited by Christopher James, 5th Lord Northbourne. Sophia Perennis, 2001.

O'Neill, Tom, with Dan Piepenbring. *Chaos: Charles Manson, the CIA, and the Secret History of the Sixties*. Little, Brown and Company, 2019.

Origen of Alexandria. *The Song of Songs: Commentary and Homilies*. Translated by R. P. Lawson. Newman Press, 1956.

Ornstein, Robert E., ed. *The Nature of Human Consciousness: A Book of Readings*. Viking Press, 1974.

Ornstein, Robert E. *The Psychology of Consciousness*. Viking Press, 1972.

Osborn, Eric. *Clement of Alexandria*. Cambridge University Press, 2005.

Osborne, Arthur, ed. *The Teachings of Ramana Maharshi in His Own Words*. Samuel Weiser, 1978.

Ott, Jonathan. Preface to *LSD: My Problem Child*, by Albert Hofmann, vii–viii. Translated by Jonathan Ott. McGraw-Hill Book Company, 1980.

Ouspensky, P. D. *In Search of the Miraculous: Fragments of an Unknown Teaching*. Harcourt, Brace and World, 1949.

Ouspensky, P. D. *The Psychology of Man's Possible Evolution*. Vintage Books, 1981.

Pacwa, Mitch. *Catholics and the New Age: How Good People Are Being Drawn into Jungian Psychology, the Enneagram, and the Age of Aquarius*. Servant Publications, 1992.

Pahnke, Walter N. and William A. Richards, "Implications of LSD and Experimental Mysticism." *Journal of Religion and Health* 5, no. 3 (July 1966): 175–208.

Pallis, Marco. *Peaks and Lamas*. Alfred A. Knopf, 1949.

Pallis, Marco. *The Way and the Mountain: Tibet, Buddhism, and Tradition*. Edited by Joseph A. Fitzgerald. World Wisdom, 2008.

Palmer, G. E. H., Philip Sherrard, and Kallistos Ware, eds. *The Philokalia, Vol. 1: The Complete Text; Compiled by St. Nikodimos of the Holy Mountain and St. Makarios of Corinth*. Faber and Faber, 1983.

Palmer, G. E. H., Philip Sherrard, and Kallistos Ware, eds. *The Philokalia, Vol. 3: The Complete Text; Compiled by St. Nikodimos of the Holy Mountain and St. Makarios of Corinth*. Faber and Faber, 1995.

Palmer, G. E. H., Philip Sherrard, and Kallistos Ware, eds. *The Philokalia, Vol. 4: The Complete Text; Compiled by St. Nikodimos of the Holy Mountain and St. Makarios of Corinth*. Faber and Faber, 1998.

Palmer, Helen. *The Enneagram*. HarperCollins, 1991.

Parkin, OM C., and Boris Fittkau. "The Distorted Enneagram: The Gnosis Interview with Claudio Naranjo." *Gnosis* 41 (Fall 1996): 20–24.

Parmenides of Elea. *Fragments: A Text and Translation with an Introduction*. Translated by David Gallop. University of Toronto Press, 2000.

Partridge, Christopher. "Modern Psychedelic Gnosis." In *The Gnostic World*, edited by Garry W. Trompf, Gunner B. Mikkelsen, and Jay Johnston, 652–62. Routledge, 2019.

Patañjali. *How to Know God: The Yoga Aphorisms of Patanjali*. Translated by Swami Prabhavananda and Christopher Isherwood. Signet Books, 1969.

Patterson, William Patrick. *Talking with the Left Hand: Enneagram Craze, People of the Bookmark, & The Mouravieff "Phenomenon."* Arete Communications, 1998.

Paz, Octavio. *Alternating Current*. Translated by Helen Lane. Arcade Publishing, 1990.

Perls, Frederick S. (Fritz Perls). *In and Out the Garbage Pail*. Bantam Books, 1979.

Perry, Mark. *The Mystery of Individuality: Grandeur and Delusion of the Human Condition*. World Wisdom, 2012.

Perry, Mark. *Uprooting the Vineyard: The Fate of the Catholic Church After Vatican II*. World Wisdom, 2025.

Perry, Whitall N. *Challenges to a Secular Society*. Foundation for Traditional Studies, 1996.

Perry, Whitall N. *Gurdjieff in the Light of Tradition*. Sophia Perennis, 2001.

Perry, Whitall N., ed. *A Treasury of Traditional Wisdom*. Allen and Unwin, 1971.

Plato. *The Dialogues of Plato, Vol. 1*. Translated by Benjamin Jowett. Charles Scribner's Sons, 1911.

Plotinus. *The Enneads*. Translated by Stephen MacKenna. Penguin Books, 1991.

Principal Upanishads, The. Translated and edited by Swāmi Nikhilānanda. Dover Publications, 2003.

Rāmakrishna. *The Gospel of Ramakrishna: Originally Recorded in Bengali by M., a Cisciple of the Master*. Translated by Swāmi Nikhilānanda. Ramakrishna-Vivekananda Center, 1977.

Ramana Maharshi. *Talks with Sri Ramana Maharshi*. Sri Ramanasramam, 1996.

Rawlinson, Andrew. *The Book of Enlightened Masters: Western Teachers in Eastern Traditions*. Open Court, 1997.

Reichel-Dolmatoff, Gerardo. *Amazon Cosmos: The Sexual and Religious Symbolism of the Tukano Indians*. Chicago University Press, 1974.

Reichel-Dolmatoff, Gerardo. "The Cultural Context of an Aboriginal Hallucinogen: *Banisteriopsis Caapi*." In *Flesh of the Gods: The Ritual Use of Hallucinogens*, edited by Peter T. Furst, 84–113. Praeger Publications, 1974.

Richards, William A. *Sacred Knowledge: Psychedelics and Religious Experiences*. Columbia University Press, 2018.

Riso, Don Richard. *Discovering Your Personality Type: The Enneagram Questionnaire*. Houghton Mifflin, 1992.

R. N. J. A. "Book Reviews—The Book of the Book by Idries Shah." *Studies in Comparative Religion* 4, no. 3 (Summer 1970): 188–90.

Rogers, Carl R. *A Way of Being*. Houghton Mifflin Company, 1995.

Rohr, Richard, and Andreas Ebert. *The Enneagram: A Christian Perspective*. Crossroad, 2001.

Roszak, Theodore. *The Gendered Atom: Reflections on the Sexual Psychology of Science*. Conari Press, 1999.

Roszak, Theodore, Mary E. Gomes, and Allen D. Kanner, eds. *Ecopsychology: Restoring the Earth, Healing the Mind*. Sierra Club Book, 1995.

Ruck, Carl A. P., Jeremy Bigwood, Danny Staples, Jonathan Ott, and R. Gordon Wasson. "Entheogens." In *The Road to Eleusis: Unveiling the Secret of the Mysteries*, edited by R. Gordon Wasson, Albert Hofmann, and Carl A. P. Ruck, 137–39. Hermes Press, 1998.

Rūmī. *Discourses of Rumi*. Translated by A. J. Arberry. RoutledgeCurzon, 2004.

Rūmī. *The Mathnawī of Jalālu'ddīn Rūmī, Vol. 2*. Translated by Reynold A. Nicholson. Luzac and Company, 1926.

Rustom, Mohammed. *Inrushes of the Heart: The Sufi Philosophy of 'Ayn al-Quḍāt*. State University of New York Press, 2023.

Sadrā, Mullā. *The Wisdom of the Throne: An Introduction to the Philosophy of Mulla Sadra*. Translated by James Winston Morris. Princeton University Press, 1981.

Salerno, Steve. *SHAM: How the Self-Help Movement Made America Helpless*. Three Rivers Press, 2005.

Sammons, Jeffrey L. *Angelus Silesius*. Twayne Publishers, 1967.

Śaṅkarācārya. *Vivekachudamani of Sri Sankaracharya: Text with English Translation, Notes and an Index*. Translated by Swāmi Mādhavānanda. Advaita Ashrama, 1921.

Satir, Virginia. Foreword to *Self Care*, by Yetta Bernhard, v–vi. Celestial Arts, 1975.

Schaya, Leo. *Universal Aspects of the Kabbalah and Judaism*. Edited by Roger Gaetani. World Wisdom, 2014.

Schimmel, Annemarie. *Mystical Dimensions of Islam*. University of North Carolina Press, 1975.

Schultes, Richard Evans. *A Contribution to Our Knowledge of Rivea corymbosa: the Narcotic Ololiuqui of the Aztecs*. Botanical Museum of Harvard University, 1941.

Schultes, Richard Evans. "Plantae Mexicanae II: The Identification of Teonanacatl, a Narcotic Basidiomycete of the Aztecs." *Botanical Museum Leaflets* 7, no. 3 (February 1939): 37–54.

Schultes, Richard Evans. "Teonanacatl: The Narcotic Mushroom of the Aztecs." *American Anthropologist* 42, no. 3 (July/September 1940): 429–43.

Schumacher, E. F. *A Guide for the Perplexed*. Harper & Row, 1977.

Schuon, Frithjof. *Dimensions of Islam*. Translated by Peter N. Townsend. George Allen and Unwin, 1970.

Schuon, Frithjof. *Gnosis: Divine Wisdom*. Translated by G. E. H. Palmer. Perennial Books, 1990.

Schuon, Frithjof. *Light on the Ancient Worlds*. Translated by Lord Northbourne. World Wisdom Books, 1984.

Schuon, Frithjof. *Logic and Transcendence*. Translated by Peter N. Townsend. Perennial Books, 1984.

Schuon, Frithjof. *The Play of Masks*. World Wisdom Books, 1992.

Schuon, Frithjof. *Primordial Meditation: Contemplating the Real*. Translated by Gillian Harris and Angela Schwartz. Matheson Trust, 2015.

Schuon, Frithjof. "The Psychological Imposture." *Tomorrow: The Journal of Parapsychology, Cosmology, and Traditional Studies* 14, no. 2 (Spring 1966): 98–101.

Schuon, Frithjof. *Roots of the Human Condition*. World Wisdom, 2002.

Schuon, Frithjof. *Spiritual Perspectives and Human Facts: A New Translation with Selected Letters*. Translated by Mark Perry, Jean-Pierre Lafouge, and James S. Cutsinger, edited by James S. Cutsinger. World Wisdom, 2007.

Schuon, Frithjof. *The Transfiguration of Man*. World Wisdom Books, 1995.

Schuon, Frithjof. *World Wheel, Volumes I–III: Poems by Frithjof Schuon*. World Wisdom, 2006.

Schwartz, Tony. *What Really Matters: Searching for Wisdom in America*. Bantam Books, 1996.

Seneca. *Ad Lucilium Epistulae Morales, Vol. 1*. Translated by Richard M. Gummere. G. P. Putnam's Sons, 1917.

Sengcan (Seng-ts'an). *Hsin-Hsin Ming: Verses on the Faith-Mind*. Translated by Richard B. Clarke. White Pine Press, 1984.

Sessa, Ben. "Why Psychiatry Needs 3,4-Methylenedioxymethamphetamine: A Child Psychiatrist's Perspective." *Neurotherapeutics* 14, no. 3 (July 2017): 741–49. DOI: https://doi.org/10.1007/s13311-017-0531-1.

Seung Sahn. *Dropping Ashes on the Buddha: The Teaching of Zen Master Seung Sahn*. Edited by Stephen Mitchell. Grove Press, 1976.

Shah, Idries. *The Commanding Self*. Octagon Press, 1997.

Shah, Idries. "The Value of the Past." *Journal of Humanistic Psychology* 16, no. 3 (July 1976): 92.

Shakespeare, William. *As You Like It*. Edited by Barbara A. Mowat and Paul Werstine. Washington Square Press, 2004.

Shakespeare, William. *A New Variorum Edition of Shakespeare, Vol. 3: Hamlet*. Edited by Horace Howard Furness. J. B. Lippincott Company, 1877.

Shakespeare, William. *The Tragedy of Hamlet*. Edited by Edward Dowden. Methuen and Company, 1899.

Sherrard, Philip. *The Greek East and the Latin West: A Study in The Christian Tradition*. Denise Harvey, 1995.

Sherrard, Philip. *Human Image, World Image: The Death and Resurrection of Sacred Cosmology*. Denise Harvey, 2004.

Sherwood, John N., Myron J. Stolaroff, and Willis W. Harman. "The Psychedelic Experience—A New Concept in Psychotherapy." *Journal of Neuropsychiatry* 4, no. 2 (November/December 1962): 69–80.

Sirāj ad-Dīn, Abū Bakr. *The Book of Certainty: The Sufi Doctrines of Faith, Vision and Gnosis*. Islamic Texts Society, 1996.

Skinner, B. F. *Beyond Freedom and Dignity*. Bantam, 1972.

Smith, Grover, ed. *Letters of Aldous Huxley*. Chatto and Windus, 1969.

Smith, Huston. *Beyond the Post-Modern Mind*. Crossroad, 1982.

Smith, Huston. *Cleansing the Doors of Perception: The Religious Significance of Entheogenic Plants and Chemicals*. Jeremy P. Tarcher/Putnam, 2000.

Smith, Huston. Preface to *The Road to Eleusis: Unveiling the Secret of the Mysteries*, by R. Gordon Wasson, Albert Hofmann, and Carl A. P. Ruck, 9–10. Hermes Press, 1998.

Smith, Huston. "Psychedelic Theophanies and the Religious Life." *Christianity and Crisis* 27, no. 11 (June 1967): 144–48.

Smith, Huston. *The Way Things Are: Conversations with Huston Smith on the Spiritual Life*. Edited by Phil Cousineau. University of California Press, 2003.

Smith, Huston. *The World's Religions: Our Great Wisdom Traditions*. HarperCollins Publishers, 1991.

Smith, John. *Selected Discourses*. Cambridge University Press, 1859.

Smith, Margaret. *Readings from the Mystics of Islam*. Luzac and Company, 1950.

Smoley, Richard. "Why the Enneagram? An Interview with Helen Palmer." *Gnosis* 32 (Summer 1994): 18–24.

Solomon, David, ed. *LSD: The Consciousness-Expanding Drug*. G. P. Putnam's Sons, 1964.

"Special Forum: The Enneagram in Contention." *Gnosis* 42 (Winter 1997): 12–17.

Speeth, Kathleen Riordan. *The Gurdjieff Work*. Jeremy P. Tarcher/Putnam, 1989.

Spiegelberg, Frederic. *The Religion of No-Religion*. James Ladd Delkin, 1953.

Strassman, Rick. *DMT: The Spirit Molecule: A Doctor's Revolutionary Research into the Biology of Near-Death and Mystical Experiences*. Park Street Press, 2000.

Strassman, Rick, Slawek Wojtowicz, Luis Eduardo Luna, and Ede Frecska. *Inner Paths to Outer Space: Journeys to Alien Worlds through Psychedelics and Other Spiritual Technologies*. Park Street Press, 2008.

Strauss, Dana, Sara de la Salle, Jordan Sloshower, and Monica T. Williams. "Research Abuses against People of Colour and Other Vulnerable Groups in Early Psychedelic Research." *Journal of Medical Ethics* 48, no. 10 (2022): 728–37. DOI: https://doi.org/10.1136/medethics-2021-107262.

Stolaroff, Myron J. *The Secret Chief Revealed: Conversations with Leo Zeff, a Pioneer in the Underground Psychedelic Therapy Movement*. Multidisciplinary Association for Psychedelic Studies, 2022.

Study Quran, The: A New Translation and Commentary. Edited by Seyyed Hossein Nasr, Caner K. Dagli, Maria Massi Dakake, Joseph E. B. Lumbard, and Mohammed Rustom. HarperOne, 2015.

Subcommittee on Executive Reorganization of the Committee on Government Operations. *Organization and Coordination of Federal Drug Research and Regulatory Programs: LSD*. U.S. Government Printing Office, 1966.

Suzuki, D. T. *Zen and Japanese Culture*. Princeton University Press, 2019.

Suzuki, Shunryū. *Zen Mind, Beginner's Mind*. Edited by Trudy Dixon. Weatherhill, 1995.

Tart, Charles T. *Open Mind, Discriminating Mind: Reflections on Human Possibilities*. Harper & Row, 1989.

Tart, Charles T. *States of Consciousness*. E. P. Dutton, 1975.

Tart, Charles T., ed. *Transpersonal Psychologies*. Harper & Row, 1975.

Tart, Charles T. *Waking Up: Overcoming the Obstacles to Human Potential*. New Science Library, 1986.

Tauler, Johannes. *Selections from the Life and Sermons of the Reverend Doctor John Tauler*. Translated by Susanna Winkworth. Roberts Brothers, 1878.

Teresa of Ávila, Saint. *The Interior Castle*. Translated by Kieran Kavanaugh and Otilio Rodriguez. Paulist Press, 1979.

Thirteen Principal Upanishads, The. Translated by Robert Ernest Hume. Oxford University Press, 1921.

Traherne, Thomas. *Centuries of Meditations*. Edited by Bertram Dobell. Bertram Dobell, 1908.

Trungpa, Chögyam. *Cutting through Spiritual Materialism*. Shambhala Publications, 2002.

Trungpa, Chögyam. *Glimpses of Abhidharma: From a Seminar on Buddhist Psychology*. Shambhala Publications, 2001.

Upanishads, The. Translated by Juan Mascaró. Penguin Books, 1965.

Upanishads, The, Vol. 1. Translated by Swāmi Nikhilānanda. Harper & Brothers Publishers, 1949.

Vedānta Sutras of Bādarāyana, The, with a Commentary by Śaṅkara, Part 1. Translated by George Thibaut. Dover Publications, 1962.

Voegelin, Eric. *The New Science of Politics: An Introduction*. University of Chicago, 1952.

Wallace, Amy. *Sorcerer's Apprentice: My Life with Carlos Castaneda*. Frog, 2003.

Wasson, R. Gordon. "Seeking the Magic Mushroom." *Life* 42, no. 19 (May 13, 1957): 100–20.

Wasson, R. Gordon. *The Wonderous Mushroom: Mycholatry in Mesoamerica*. McGraw-Hill Book Company, 1980.

Wasson, Valentina P. "I Ate the Sacred Mushrooms." *This Week* (May 19, 1957): 8–10, 36.

Watkins, Susan M. *Conversations with Seth: Book Two*. Moment Point Press, 2006.

Watson, John B. *Behaviorism*. W. W. Norton & Company, 1970.

Watson, John B. "Psychology as the Behaviorist Views It." *Psychological Review* 20, no. 2 (March 1913), pp. 158–77.

Watts, Alan. *In My Own Way: An Autobiography, 1915–1965*. Pantheon Books, 1972.

Watts, Alan. *The Joyous Cosmology: Adventures in the Chemistry of Consciousness*. Vintage Books, 1965.

Webb, James. *The Harmonious Circle: The Lives and Work of G. I. Gurdjieff, P. D. Ouspensky, and Their Followers*. G. P. Putnam's Sons, 1987.

Weeraperuma, Susunaga, ed. *The Essential Swami Ramdas*. World Wisdom, 2005.

Weichberger, Laurent with Laura Smith, eds. *A Mirage Will Never Quench Your Thirst: A Source of Wisdom about Drugs*. Sheriar Foundation, 2003.

Weil, Andrew. *The Natural Mind: An Investigation of Drugs and the Higher Consciousness*. Houghton Mifflin Company, 1986.

Welwood, John. *Toward a Psychology of Awakening: Buddhism, Psychotherapy, and the Path of Personal and Spiritual Transformation*. Shambhala Publications, 2000.

Wilber, Ken. *A Brief History of Everything*. Shambhala Publications, 1996.

Zaehner, R. C. *Mysticism, Sacred and Profane: An Inquiry into some Varieties of Praeternatural Experience*. Oxford University Press, 1967.

Zhūangzi (Chuang Tzu). *Chuang Tzu: Basic Writings*. Translated by Burton Watson. Columbia University Press, 1996.

Zhūangzi (Chuang Tzu). *Chuang Tzu: Mystic, Moralist, and Social Reformer*. Translated by Herbert A. Giles. Bernard Quaritch, 1889.